THE KANJI ABC

ANDREW DYKSTRA

Associate Director
Kansai University of Foreign Studies
Honolulu Campus

William Kaufmann, Inc.
One First Street
Los Altos, CA 94022

Library of Congress Catalog Card Number: 76-58964

ISBN 0-913232-37-8

CONTENTS

THE KANJI ABC

VOLUME ONE: JME 1-100..1

VOLUME TWO: JME 101-200...51

VOLUME THREE: JME 201-300..101

VOLUME FOUR: JME 300-338..151

KATAKANA AND HIRAGANA...170

214 RADICALS WITH MEANINGS..171

STROKE INDEX FOR JME NUMBERS..175

ALPHABETICAL JAPANESE WORD INDEX FOR JME NUMBERS.....177

ALPHABETICAL CHINESE WORD INDEX FOR JME NUMBERS......183

ABOUT THE AUTHOR 187

KANJINN KOBOLD IST GEKOMMEN

The shadowed Yin and crimsoned Yang,
Vermilion Ch'in and yellowed Shang
Cry out, cry out with fearful shout!
"Who's here? Who's here to hear? Thou lout!

Dost keen the warf my skein doth make?
The mien of whose forgotten line
To thee doth mean and signify
That hath the single piercing eye;

In lines together gather take,
In scene to thee alone is seen
Where warp, where weft, where east, where west
Doth intersecting meeting lie."

"If I shall rake and slash thy mesh,
Thy mask no more shall faces hold;
Thy spaces without lines are won
And I am free, a spirit bold!"

CH'IN

SHANG

YIN

YANG

DYKSTRA

(TO FATHER)

ABOUT THE AUTHOR

DR. ANDREW DYKSTRA has always been most
fascinated by the Japanese KANJI or the
Chinese characters used in reading and
writing and even thinking by nearly one
billion of the earth's peoples. These
volumes of THE KANJI ABC are his first
publications on that subject.

The KANJI have usually been the difficult
part of an Oriental language course. Dr.
Dykstra hopes to make the KANJI a subject
of intense interest to everyone.

As pictographs, the KANJI are an international language intelligible to all of
us human beings. Many scientists and
humanists have assumed that ancient minds
are primitive, lacking the ability to
associate and reason logically. But Dr.
Dykstra believes that the ancient minds are in no way
inferior to our own, and that we have not had the acumen
to understand what they are telling us.

Dr. Dykstra was born in the historic Lushan (mountains)
of Kiangsi Province and spent his youth in China where
he graduated from the Shanghai American School. During
World War II, he received his commission from Columbia
Midshipman School, and his diploma from the Navy Oriental
Languages PostGraduate School at Colorado University and
Oklahoma State University. He was later promoted with a
speciality in Psychology in the Medical Service Corps.

After the war, Dr. Dykstra was employed by the State of
California and also taught courses for Lassen College in
Psychology, Humanities, History, Political Science, and
German. He was awarded fellowships in Law at Boalt Hall,
in Interpersonal Relations at Immaculate Heart College in
Los Angeles, in Chinese at Claremont Graduate School and
San Francisco State University, and in Japanese at UCLA.

Another of Dr. Dykstra's interests, Oriental humor, has
produced SEXY LAUGHING STORIES OF OLD JAPAN, printed by
Japan Publications, Inc., 1255 Howard Street, S.F. CA 94103
"Laughing stories" are literally what the Japanese call
the sexy and humorous tales that for centuries have been
retold by travelling story tellers who accompanied words
with vivid facial expressions, gestures, and sounds.

Dr. Dykstra hopes to transmit his pleasure in the KANJI
by his writings. His purpose is to promote understanding
between American and Oriental peoples through enjoyment
of the KANJI. Strangely enough, even the Japanese and
Chinese often have done little more than to memorize the
meanings of the KANJI, practice their writing, and enjoy
their beauty. The KANJI deserve far more than this.

THE KANJI ABC

The KANJI or characters of Japan and China, invented by the Yellow Emperor in the legendary dawn of China's history, are found in primitive form on the oracle "dragon bones" of the Shang Dynasty. They are on the bright-colored signs of San Francisco's Chinatown and in the flashing neon lights of the Tokyo Ginza District.

THE KANJI ABC explains the origin of these three-thousand-year-old pictographs to make them easy for you to learn and understand. At the same time you will discover how the users of the KANJI thought and lived.

The KANJI are an international language of symbols. Korea, Okinawa, Vietnam, and Japan, although speaking languages very different from Chinese, all accepted the KANJI with the culture of China. Thus the different peoples of the "World of Chopsticks" could communicate by writing KANJI.

Japan's Ministry of Education has helped all students of the KANJI by numbering in order of importance the KANJI which are necessary in reading Japanese. THE KANJI ABC gives you the Japanese Ministry of Education (JME) number, the radical (RAD) number for finding KANJI in the dictionary, and the number of strokes in the KANJI, also for dictionary use. The little numbers with each KANJI tell you the direction and order of the strokes. The Japanese words in large capital letters are of Chinese origin; those in small capital letters are of native origin.

The "ABC" in the title of these volumes stands for the order, simplicity, and explanation in learning to read, write, and understand. It also emphasizes the international quality of the KANJI which can also be used to write English or Swahili.

The purpose of THE KANJI ABC is to help you learn. To be scholarly is not the purpose. Some of the explanations of the KANJI can be found in other books. Many are original with us, but seem obviously correct. We have studied the KANJI or characters for many years with famous authorities like Professor Ch'en Shou-yi of the Claremont University Center, and in books like the Shuo Wen. You will notice that explanations are usually easy and consistent.

We hope that by learning the KANJI in this way, you will come to enjoy and love the KANJI. The ancient style of the KANJI or pictographic writing is often far superior to the alphabet writing of the Western world. Nowadays, for impact and retention as in international road signs and in many advertisements, the Western world turns to the earlier picture writing, the symbolism that unites and belongs to all of us as human beings.

VOLUME ONE : KANJI 001-100

means
FOOT, LEG
in Japanese kanji
+ Chinese characters

ICHI; HITOTSU, HITO, ONE, THE FIRST.

RAD	STROKE	JME
1	1	1

THE KANJI ONE ▬, THE KANJI TWO ▬, AND THE KANJI THREE ☰ ARE WRITTEN HORIZONTALLY AS STRAIGHT LINES.

THE KANJI ONE ▬ TURNED NINETY DEGREES FORMS THE ARABIC 1.

THE LINE FOR ONE ▬ REPRESENTS THE UNITY, THE ONENESS OF THE EARTH AND SKY OR THE OCEAN AND SKY MEETING AT THE HORIZON.

NI, JI; FUTATSU, FUTA, FU, TWO, THE SECOND.

RAD	STROKE	JME
7	2	2

THE TWO HORIZONTAL STROKES OF THE KANJI TWO ▬ BECOME THE ARABIC 2 WHEN A CURVED LINE IS DRAWN TO JOIN THE SEGMENTS.

COMMON AMONG MANY ANCIENT PEOPLES IS THE BELIEF IN THE SKY-FATHER ABOVE WHO IMPREGNATES WITH SEED AND FERTILIZES WITH RAIN THE EARTH-MOTHER BELOW. AN EARLY MALE CHAUVINISM, PERHAPS.

SKY-FATHER

EARTH-MOTHER

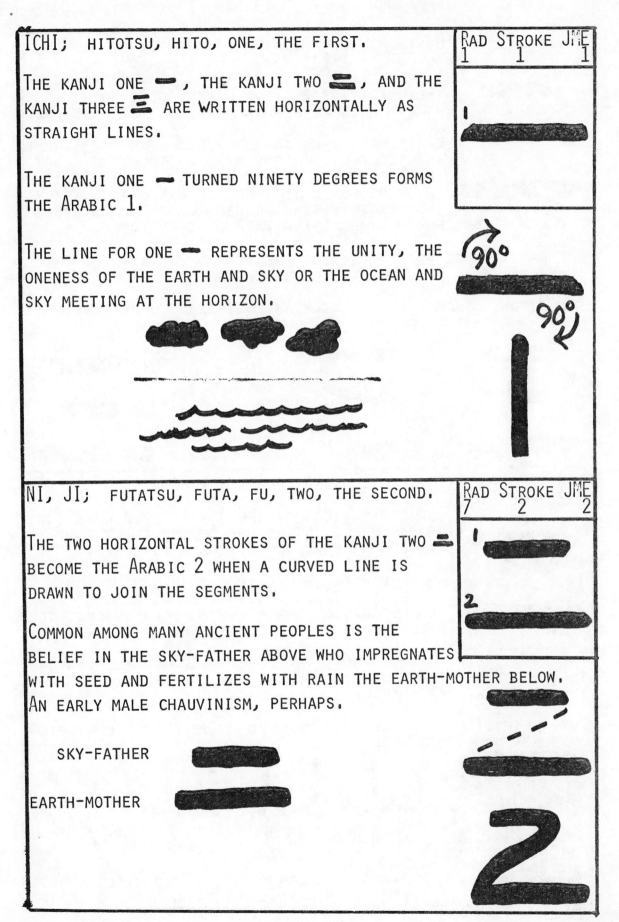

JME	Stroke	Rad
3	3	1

SAN; MITTSU, MI, THREE, THE THIRD.

A STROKE ADDED TO THE KANJI TWO 二 PRODUCES THE KANJI THREE 三. LINES ADDED TO THE KANJI THREE 三 READILY PRODUCE THE ARABIC 3.

USUALLY IN THE KANJI THREE 三 THE TOP STROKE IS MIDDLE-SIZED, THE MIDDLE STROKE IS SHORT, AND THE BOTTOM STROKE IS LONG. THIS RATIO OR SYMMETRY IS IMITATED IN MANY KANJI WHICH INCLUDE THIS KANJI THREE 三. IN SUCH CASES THE KANJI FOR THREE MAY BE FUSED WITH OTHER STROKES.

THE KANJI THREE 三 MAY BE THE CREATION OF MANKIND BY THE PAIRED 二 UPPER HEAVENLY AND LOWER EARTHLY FORCES.

THE STROKES FROM TOP TO BOTTOM ARE SUPPOSED TO REPRESENT HEAVEN, MANKIND, AND EARTH.

HEAVEN

MANKIND

EARTH

JME	Stroke	Rad
4	5	31

SHI; YOTTSU, YO, FOUR, THE FOURTH.

THE CONVENIENCE OF THE FINGERS FOR COUNTING PROBABLY LED TO THE USE OF THE QUARTET OF FINGERS OPPOSED TO THE THUMB FOR FOUR.

THESE FINGERS HELD PARALLEL HAVE THE ROUGH SHAPE OF A QUADRANGLE WHICH CAN ALSO BE SEEN IN THE ARABIC FOUR 4 WITH AN UNFINISHED TOP LINE AND AN EXTENSION FOR THE WRIST OR ARM.

THE KANJI FOUR 四 ALSO SHOWS THE QUADRANGLE AND ALSO NOTES THE SHORTNESS OF THE OUTSIDE FINGERS BY THE STROKES 八 ENCLOSING THE UPPER ANGLES.

THE ANCIENT ORIENTAL SYMBOL FOR HAND 手 IS LIKE THE ARABIC 4 BUT HAS THE THUMB ALSO.

ARABIC 4   QUADRANGLE   OMITTED   OLD SYMBOL
                IN ARABIC 4   5TH DIGIT   FOR HAND

GO; ITSUTSU, ITSU, FIVE, THE FIFTH.

RAD	STROKE	JME
7	4	5

THE KANJI FIVE 五 CONTAINS ALL PARTS OF THE ARABIC 5 BUT INCLUDES A COMPLETE VERTICAL STROKE AND OTHER SLIGHT DIFFERENCES.

THE KANJI FIVE 五 MAY BE REGARDED AS A KANJI ONE 一 ABOVE ATTACHED TO A QUADRANGLE ▢ BELOW REPRESENTING THE KANJI FOUR 四.

WHAT IS BELOW CAN ALSO BE REGARDED AS AN INVERTED AND CLOSED ARABIC 4.

KANJI ONE OVER THE QUADRANGLE

KANJI ONE OVER INVERTED ARABIC 4

KANJI ONE ATTACHED TO ARABIC 4 INVERTED & FINISHED TO SUGGEST THE KANJI FIVE

SUPERIMPOSITION

KANJI FIVE   ARAB. 5

ROKU; MUTTSU, SIX, THE SIXTH.

RAD	STROKE	JME
12	4	6

THE KANJI SIX 六 MAY BE REGARDED AS A HUMAN FIGURE WITH FOUR LIMBS, BODY, AND HEAD. THE TOTAL IS SIX.

SINCE THE STANDARD HUMAN FIGURE IS A MALE, WE HAVE A FIGURE ANALOGOUS TO THE WESTERN PHALLIC SYMBOL SIX 6 . THE SYMBOL IS ALSO WRITTEN ♂. MALENESS IN BOTH CASES.

NOTE HOW THIS HUMAN FIGURE IS ALSO FOUND IN THE KANJI TO STAND JME149 WHERE IT STANDS ON A BASELINE.

TWO ARMS & BODY   HEAD

TWO LEGS

OLD KANJI FOR SIX, (MAN)

TWO ARMS AND BODY   HEAD

TWO LEGS

BASELINE

KANJI SIX (SIX PARTS OF A MAN)

KANJI TO STAND (SHOWS THE MAN STANDING)

JME	Stroke	Rad
7	2	1

SHICHI; NANATSU, NANA, SEVEN, THE SEVENTH.

THE KANJI SEVEN 七 ROTATED 180 DEGREES INTO AN INVERTED POSITION BECOMES A EUROPEAN SEVEN WITH A CROSSPIECE 7.

ASSOCIATE KANJI SEVEN 七 WITH THE JAWS/HEADS ヒ OF DRAGON 龍. LEVIATHAN MEANS TWISTED OR COILED LIKE A MONSTROUS SERPENT WHICH HAD SEVEN 七 HEADS ヒ IN UGARIT AND OTHER LEGENDS. VICTIMS OF DRAGON'S 龍 SEVEN 七 JAWS/HEADS ヒ WERE CUT UP, MINCED 切 JME 99 AND CHANGED 化 JME 163 IN DEATH, TO DIE 死 JME 223. CROSSBAR IN SEVEN 七 AND TO CUT, MINCE 切 DOES NOT CROSS IN TO CHANGE 化 AND DIE 死.

EUROPEAN SEVEN

KANJI SEVEN

龍 DRAGON (pre-JME)

ヒ JAWS/HEADS 七 SEVEN

切 TO CUT, MINCE JME 99

化 TO CHANGE JME 163

死 DEATH, TO DIE JME 223

All kanji above have 七 or ヒ as a component.

JME	Stroke	Rad
8	2	12

HACHI; YATTSU, YA, EIGHT, THE EIGHTH.

THE KANJI EIGHT 八 IS TWO STROKES EVENLY DIVIDED TO THE LEFT AND TO THE RIGHT.

THESE TWO STROKES MEANING DIVIDE ARE ALSO IN THE KANJI SIX 六 AS THE TWO BOTTOM STROKES 八 AND IN THE KANJI FOUR 四 AS THE TWO INTERIOR STROKES 八.

SUCH TWO STROKES OPEN AT THE TOP 八 SUGGEST OR DERIVE FROM THE HUMAN LEGS SPREAD OR DIVIDED. EIGHT IS A PARTICULARLY CONVENIENT NUMBER FOR DIVISION INTO FOUR'S, TWO'S, AND ONE'S. THE EVEN NUMBERS FOUR AND SIX ARE ALSO EASILY DIVIDED.

THE ARABIC 8 IS ALSO EVENLY DIVIDED INTO TWO CIRCLES OR SPHERES. IT MAY BE REGARDED AS A CELL DIVIDING INTO TWO NEW CELLS.

ARABIC 8

ROTATED 90° AND SUPER-IMPOSED

MITOSIS (OF CELL)

KANJI SIX

KANJI FOUR

THEIR COMPONENTS FOR DIVIDE

KU, KYŪ; KOKONOTSU, KOKONO, NINE.

RAD	STROKE	JME
5	2	9

THE KANJI NINE 九 FORMS A QUARTER (QUADRANT) OF A SWASTIKA 卐 . THE SWASTIKA 卐 IS THE TURNING ROLLING JUGGERNAUT OR FORCE WHICH MOVES AND TURNS AS A WHEEL WITH ARMS AND LEGS.

WITH THE ADDITION OF A DOT OR SMALL STROKE ‧ THE KANJI NINE 九 BECOMES THE KANJI FOR CIRCLE 丸 .

OF THE FIRST TEN DIGITS, A NINE-SIDED (IRREGULAR) POLYGON IS MOST LIKE A CIRCLE. THE ARABIC NINE 9 ALSO INCLUDES A CIRCLE O , BUT IS MORE LIKE THE SWASTIKA WITH LONG ARMS AND A REDUCED CENTER 卐 .

ARMS, LEGS   KANJI NINE   NONAGON   ARABIC 9   LONG ARMED SWASTIKA

SUPERIMPOSED   KANJI CIRCLE   CIRCLE   CIRCLE TO NINE   SUPER-IMPOSED

JŪ; TŌ, TEN.

RAD	STROKE	JME
24	2	10

THE KANJI TEN 十 IS A CROSS LIKE THE ROMAN NUMERAL X OF THE SAME MEANING.

TEN ALSO IMPLIES COMPLETENESS AS TEN OF TEN PARTS SINCE ORIENTAL COUNTING IS ALSO BASED ON THE DECIMAL SYSTEM.

TEN 十 MAY BE REGARDED AS CROSSED ONE'S WHICH ARE THE BEGINNING ONE AND THE ENDING ONE.

一   丨   十   THIS TYPE OF CROSSING IS VERY COMMON IN KEEPING TALLIES.

OCCASIONALLY THE ORIENTAL WILL WRITE TWENTY AS JOINED TEN'S 廿 AND THIRTY AS LINKED TEN'S 卅 SIDE BY SIDE.

TWENTY   THIRTY   TWENTY   THIRTY   (READING DOWN)

JME	Stroke	Rad
11	4	72

NICHI, JITSU; HI, (BI), SUN, DAY; -KA, SUFFIX FOR DATES OF THE MONTH.

SUN 日 WAS ORIGINALLY A DOTTED CIRCLE ⊙ LIKE THE EGYPTIAN HIEROGLYPHIC ⊙. A MOUTH WAS A CIRCLE ○. THE ADDED DOT INDICATED WORDS OR COMMANDS.

THE SUN 日 SPEAKS THROUGH ITS WARMTH AND ITS COMMANDS ARE UNIVERSALLY OBEYED THROUGHOUT EARTH OR NATURE BY FERTILITY AND GROWTH.

THE CURVED KANJI WERE SQUARED WHEN THE BRUSH CAME INTO VOGUE. AS A RESULT SUN WAS ALTERED TO 日 AND MOUTH TO 口.

OLD ORIENTAL SYMBOL FOR MOUTH

KANJI MOUTH JME 27

OLD ORIENTAL & EGYPTIAN SUN SYMBOL

KANJI SUN

WORDS OR COMMANDS ISSUING FROM THE MOUTH OF THE SUN

JME	Stroke	Rad
12	4	74

GETSU, GATSU; TSUKI, (ZUKI), MOON, MONTH.

MOON, MONTH 月 ORIGINALLY HAD THE SHAPE OF A CRESCENT MOON). THE INTERIOR PAIR OF LINES MAY HAVE BEEN ADDED BECAUSE THE MOON RESEMBLED AN OBLIQUE ORIENTAL EYE ⌒ BUT NEEDED A PUPIL. BESIDES, A CHINESE CREATION LEGEND SAYS THE SUN AND THE MOON WERE FORMED FROM THE LEFT EYE AND RIGHT EYE OF THE CREATOR, P'AN KU. WE USE SUCH WORDS AS "THE MOON LOOKING DOWN ON US."

ORIENTAL EYES

"HORNED" MOON BOAT

MOON   MOON'S EYE

KANJI MOON

THE LOWER PART OF THE KANJI MOON 月 BECAME OPEN TO SHOW ITS RESEMBLANCE TO AN OPEN-ENDED ORIENTAL BOAT. MYTHS ALSO ASSOCIATE MOON AND BOAT. "THE MOON SAILING THE SKIES."

BOAT   MOON   EYE   MOON'S EYE   MOON BOAT

KA; HI, (BI), FIRE.

Rad	Stroke	JME
86	4	13

THE NEXT FIVE KANJI RELATE TO THE SUBSTANCES FIRE 火, WATER 水, WOOD 木, METAL 金, AND EARTH 土. THE ANCIENT ORIENTAL PHILOSOPHER LIKE HIS GREEK COUNTERPART SPECULATED ON THE COMPOSITION OF OUR WORLD AND HAD SOME SIMILAR ANSWERS. THUS THESE FIVE "ELEMENTS."

IN THE KANJI FIRE 火 YOU SEE THE PILE OF COMBUSTIBLES WITH SMOKE OR FLAMES RISING AND A SMALL STROKE TO EACH SIDE FOR THE FLAMES FLICKERING OR THE CONVECTION CURRENTS.

AS A KANJI COMPONENT FIRE MAY ALSO BE WRITTEN 灬. THIS COMPONENT REPRESENTS FOUR FLAMES AND MAY BE CONFUSED WITH A SIMILAR COMPONENT DEPICTING THE FOUR LEGS OF AN ANIMAL, ETC.

COMPONENT FOR FIRE AS USED IN A KANJI

COMPONENT FOR FIRE

SUI; MIZU, WATER.

Rad	Stroke	JME
85	4	14

IN THE KANJI WATER 水 THE MIDDLE VERTICAL | STROKE IS THE MAIN CURRENT AS YOU LOOK DOWN ON THE STREAM OR RIVER. THE SIDE STROKES TO THE LEFT フ AND TO THE RIGHT く ARE THE EDDIES STRIKING THE BANKS AND SWIRLING ABOUT.

THERE IS A COMPONENT FORM FOR WATER WRITTEN AS THREE FALLING SPLASHING DROPS.

COMPONENT FOR WATER (THREE FALLING AND SPLASHING DROPS) AS USED IN A KANJI

COMPONENT FOR WATER

THE KANJI FOR WATER SUPERIMPOSED ON A STREAM AND SHOWING THE SWIRLING CURRENTS

JME	Stroke	Rad
15	4	75

MOKU, BOKU; KI, (GI), TREE, WOOD.

TREE IS AN EXCELLENT PICTOGRAPH. THE CENTRAL VERTICAL STROKE IS THE TRUNK AND TAP ROOT. THE HORIZONTAL LINE REPRESENTS BRANCHES. THE LOWER OBLIQUE LINES ARE THE SPREADING ROOTS.

TREE

WOODS, GROVE
JME 150

FOREST
JME 41

JME	Stroke	Rad
16	8	167

KIN, GOLD; KON, (GOLD); KANE, MONEY

GOLD 金 IS A COMPOSITE KANJI CONSISTING OF A MINE TUNNEL ROOF ∧ ABOVE, A SHIELD 干 AS A SUPPORT FOR THE ROOF, TWO SMALL OBLIQUE STROKES FOR GRAINS OR NUGGETS 丷 OF GOLD, AND EARTH 土 JME 17 BELOW TO SHOW THE BASE AND SOURCE OF THE GOLD. THE KANJI FOR THE SHIELD 干 AND THE EARTH 土 ARE FUSED 王.

THE KANJI GOLD 金 ALSO MEANS MONEY 金 . AS A LEFT COMPONENT THE KANJI GOLD USUALLY INDICATE A METAL OR SOMETHING METALIC.

MINE TUNNEL ROOF SUPPORTED BY A SHIELD OVER THE EARTH WITH NUGGETS OR GRAINS OF GOLD SHINING FROM THE EARTH'S SURFACE.

MINE TUNNEL ROOF	SHIELD	SHIELD AND EARTH FUSED	EARTH	GRAINS OR NUGGETS OF GOLD

DO, TO; TSUCHI, EARTH, SOIL.

RAD	STROKE	JME
32	3	17

EARTH 土 HAS A BASELINE ― AND A PLANT OR A STEM OF GRASS 十 GROWING VERTICALLY ∤ , ORIGINALLY Ψ , MUCH LIKE THE ANCIENT PICTOGRAPH FOR HAND Ψ .

LIKE THE KANJI TREE 木 WHICH HAS A HORIZONTAL LINE ― FOR BRANCHES, THE ENDS OF THE HORIZONTAL LINE ― OF GRASS 十 WERE ONCE CURVED UPWARDS Ψ TO INDICATE SPROUTS FROM THE MAIN STEM Ψ . THUS THERE IS A CLOSE RELATIONSHIP IN THE PAST REPRESENTATION OF GRASS Ψ AND HAND Ψ .

OLD SYMBOL FOR GRASS	GRASS	BASELINE OF EARTH	EARTH PILED UP AS A MOUND OR ALTAR (SUPERIMPOSITION)

SA; HIDARI, LEFT.

RAD	STROKE	JME
48	5	18

IN LEFT 左 THE COMPONENT エ REPRESENTS A PLUMB LINE HANGING AS FROM CEILING TO FLOOR. SUCH A PLUMB LINE IS USED BY A WORKER SUCH AS A CARPENTER OR OTHER ARTISAN AND IMPLIES SKILL OR CRAFTSMANSHIP.

THE LEFT COMPONENT 𠂇 OF THE KANJI LEFT IS A HAND 𠂇 ORIGINALLY Ψ . THE COMMON UNSKILLED LABORER IS RIGHTHANDED AND USES PRIMARILY THE RIGHT HAND. THE SKILLED WORKMAN IS AMBIDEXTROUS AND USES HIS LEFT HAND ALSO AS HE PRACTICES HIS CRAFT. THEREFORE 左 MEANS LEFT.

THINK OF THE CARPENTER WITH THE HAMMER IN HIS RIGHT HAND, THE NAIL IN HIS LEFT; OR THE MASON WITH THE TROWEL IN HIS RIGHT HAND, THE BRICK IN HIS LEFT. THE KANJI エ JME 71 IMPLIES WORKER OR CONSTRUCTION.

COMPONENT FOR HAND	OLD SYMBOL LEFT HAND	WORKER CONST.	HAND & SQUARE OR PLUMB LINE	SUPERIMPOSED

JME	STROKE	RAD
19	5	30

YŪ, U; MIGI, RIGHT.

RIGHT 右 ALSO HAS THE COMPONENT FOR HAND ナ, ORIGINALLY ㄓ. IN THE KANJI RIGHT 右, HAND ナ FORMS A COMPOSITE WITH THE KANJI MOUTH 口 JME 27 ORIGINALLY ○. THE RIGHT HAND ナ IS THE ONE GENERALLY USED TO FEED THE MOUTH. THUS THE KANJI 右 MEANS RIGHT.

COMPONENT FOR HAND

OLD SYMBOL FOR RIGHT HAND

KANJI MOUTH

RIGHT

LEFT JME 18

RIGHT

JME	STROKE	RAD
20	3	1

JŌ; UE, TOP, ON, ABOVE KAMI, UPPER; NOBORU, GO UP, TOWARD; AGERU, RAISE; AGARU, RISE.

ABOVE, ON TOP, TO RISE, UPPER 上 SHOWS A FIGURE STANDING ON A BASELINE GESTURING ABOVE. (WITH THE PASSING OF TIME, THE GESTURING ARM HAS BECOME MORE AND MORE TIRED AND NOW IS OFTEN HORIZONTAL OR NEARLY SO).

UP....ON HIS FLYING CARPET

KA, GE; SHITA, UNDER, LOWER, BOTTOM;
MOTO, UNDER; SHIMO, LOWER PART, BOTTOM;
KUDARU, COME DOWN, GO DOWN;
SAGERU, KUDASU, OROSU, TO LOWER;
SAGARU, TO HANG, TO FALL

RAD	STROKE	JME
1	3	21

IF THE KANJI UP 上 JME 20 IS LEFT ON ITS
BASELINE AND TURNED TO FALL ON ITS FACE, IT
WILL MAKE THE KANJI 下 BELOW, UNDER, BOTTOM,
DOWN, ETC.

TOP,ON   UNDER,
ABOVE   LOWER,
JME 19   BOTTOM

KANJI TOP
FLIPPED TO
KANJI BOTTOM

DAI, TAI; ŌKII, LARGE, BIG, GREAT.

RAD	STROKE	JME
37	3	22

THE KANJI GREAT, BIG, LARGE 大 IS A MAN
STANDING WITH HIS LEGS SPREAD 人 AND
EXTENDING HIS ARMS HORIZONTALLY TO SHOW
GREATNESS OR BIGNESS (AS OF THE FISH HE DID
NOT CATCH).

PERSON OR MAN   EXTENDED ARMS   LARGE, BIG
JME 30   GREAT

JME.	Stroke	Rad
23	4	2

CHŪ, JŪ;   NAKA, MIDDLE, INSIDE, WITHIN,
AMONG.

MIDDLE, INSIDE, WITHIN 中 SHOWS A TARGET OR
MOUTH 口 , ORIGINALLY A CIRCLE OR DISC ◯ ,
WITH A VERTICAL LINE REPRESENTING THE ARROW |
STRIKING OR PASSING THROUGH IT.

ARROW STRIKES
OR PASSES
THROUGH TARGET
(MOUTH OR
APERTURE)

VERTICAL LINE
REPRESENTING
THE ARROW

TARGET
(MOUTH OR
APERTURE)
ORIGINALLY
A CIRCLE
OR DISC

A DRAWING FOR
IMPROVED
VISUALIZATION
(NOT AN
ALTERNATE STYLE
OF WRITING THE
KANJI)

JME	Stroke	Rad
24	3	42

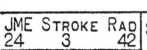

SHŌ;   CHIISAI, KO, O, LITTLE, SMALL.

LITTLE, SMALL, MINOR 小 HAS A VERTICAL LINE
FOR THE CHILD | , LITTLE 小 CONTRASTED TO
AN ADULT, WITH ITS ARMS HANGING OBLIQUELY ハ
DUE TO THE NARROWNESS OF ITS LITTLE
SHOULDERS AND DUE TO THE THICK PADDED LAYERS
OF COTTON CLOTHING IN THE COLD NORTHERN
PROVINCES.

SUPERIMPOSED

MOKU; <u>ME</u>, EYE, A LOOK.

THE KANJI EYE 目 HAS BEEN SQUARED AND TURNED VERTICALLY FROM THE NORMAL POSITION OF THE EYE ⬭. IT WAS ORIGINALLY ⊞. NOTE THE RELATIONSHIP TO THE KANJI MOON 月 JME 12, ORIGINALLY ☾, AND TO THE KANJI EAR 耳 JME 26.

THE EAR AND THE EYE ARE BOTH SENSE ORGANS WITH APERTURES. BOTH EAR AND EYE ARE COMPOSED OF CONCENTRIC CIRCULAR PATTERNS.

THE MOON 月 JME 12 WAS PREVIOUSLY LIKENED TO AN EYE 目.

RAD	STROKE	JME
109	5	25

| OLD SYMBOL FOR EYE | HORIZONTAL EYE | VERTICAL EYE | MOON MONTH JME 12 | OLD SYMBOL FOR MOON WITH EYE |

JI; MIMI, EAR.

RAD	STROKE	JME
128	6	26

THE CENTRAL PORTION OF THE KANJI EAR 耳 IS THE KANJI MOUTH 口 JME 27 FOR THE APERTURE OF THE EAR. THE KANJI MOUTH 口 IS ALSO THE CENTRAL PORTION OF THE KANJI EYE 目. THIS IS ANATOMICALLY CORRECT SINCE THE LENS IS AN APERTURE. THE MOUTH 口 ALSO SERVES TO REPRESENT THE PUPIL OR PUPIL AND IRIS.

THE IRREGULARITY OF THE EAR'S SLANTED BASE IS SHOWN BY THE BASAL OBLIQUE LINE. THE LOWER EXTREMITY OF THE LONGER VERTICAL LINE IS FOR THE LOBE OF THE EAR AND GIVES A CORRECT IMPRESSION OF IRREGULAR LENGTH, AS AN IMPRESSIONISTIC BUT NOT GRAPHIC PICTURE.

| EYE JME 25 | MOUTH JME 27 | EAR JME 26 | MOUTH OR APER- TURE OF EAR | SUPERIMPOSED |

JME	STROKE	RAD
27	3	30

KŌ, KU; KUCHI, (MOUTH), MOUTH.

MOUTH 口 IS A SQUARED CIRCLE 〇. IT HAS SUPPLEMENTARY MEANINGS SUCH AS OPENING, APERTURE.

MOUTH 口 IS VERY FREQUENT AS A KANJI COMPONENT. NOTE HOW SIZE AND PROPORTION MAY VARY AS BELOW.

FOUR JME 4   SUN JME 11   MOON,MONTH JME 12   RIGHT JME 19   MIDDLE,WITHIN INSIDE JME 23

EYE JME 25   EAR JME 26   MOUTH JME 27   FOOT,LEG JME 29   WHITE JME 37

JME	STROKE	RAD
28	4	30

SHU; TE, HAND, ARM.

HAND 手 HAS A TILTED LINE AT THE TOP FOR THE HORNLIKE THUMB ノ AND TWO HORIZONTAL LINES ニ REPRESENTING THE OTHER FOUR FINGERS LEAVING THE CENTRAL VERTICAL SHAFT OF THE HAND ｜ .

AS A COMPONENT, HAND IS WRITTEN 扌 ALSO.

AS SHOWN TO THE RIGHT, HAND IS USUALLY THE LEFT COMPONENT.

AS A COMPONENT, HAND MAY ALSO BE THE SIMPLER FORM ナ SHOWN IN LEFT JME 18 AND RIGHT JME 19. IT IS SHOWN HERE FOR REVIEW.

LEFT JME 18   RIGHT JME 19   SIMPLER FORM OF HAND   OLD FORM

SOKU, (ZOKU) MAY MEAN PAIR AS A SUFFIX;
ASHI, FOOT, LEG, PAW; TARU, BE ENOUGH,
BE SUFFICIENT.

RAD	STROKE	JME
157	7	29

FOOT, LEG 足 IS A COM-
POSITE OF A MOUTH 口
JME 27 TO REPRESENT THE
PELVIS, A VERTICAL LINE |
FOR THE LEG, A SHORT
HORIZONTAL LINE - FOR
THE KNEE AND ITS LOCA-
TION, AND TWO STROKES
BELOW 人 FORMING THE HEEL ノ AND THE
ARCHED FOOT ＼.NOTE HOW THE LAST TWO
STROKES SUGGEST THE BONES OF THE FOOT
OR OF A WOMAN'S HIGH HEELED SHOE. THE
PELVIS IS VIEWED FROM THE FRONT OR THE
BACK, THE LEG AND FOOT ARE A RIGHT
SIDE VIEW. NOTE HOW THE KANJI FAITH-
FULLY COPIES THE ENTIRE STRUCTURE.

PELVIS

← FEMUR →

←PATELLA→

TIBIA
AND
FIBULA

TARSUS ↑ PHALANGES ↗
METATARSUS

NIN, JIN; HITO, (BITO), MAN, PERSON, MANKIND.

RAD	STROKE	JME
9	2	30

MAN, PERSON 人 STANDS FACING US OR WITH HIS
BACK TO US, OR PRESENTING A SIDE VIEW AND
WALKING IN THE OLD WAY WITHOUT SWINGING HIS
ARMS.

儿

MAN AS
TWO LEGS
(COMPONENT)

THE TOP
COMPONENT
MAN

THESE TWO STROKES FOR MAN, PERSON
DRAWN SLIGHTLY DIFFERENTLY MAY BECOME
A TOP ／ OR A LEFT イ COMPONENT IN KANJI.
(THE MAN HOLDS UP ONE LEG).

MAN   LIFTS ONE LEG, LIFTS OTHER LEG

MAN
AS
LEFT
COMPONENT

JME	Stroke	Rad
31	3	39

SHI, SU; KO, (GO), CHILD, SUFFIX FOR A
FEMALE NAME.

CHILD 子 SHOWS A BABY. THE ANGLED TOP
COMPONENT IS FOR THE HEAD ⌐. THE VERTICAL
STROKE IS FOR THE BODY AND LEGS). THE
HORIZONTAL LINE IS FOR THE HANDS AND ARMS —
ON EITHER SIDE.

HEAD
ARMS
BODY
AND
LEGS

Note the tail effect as
ontogeny recaps phylogeny

JME	Stroke	Rad
32	3	38

JO, NYO; ONNA, WOMAN, GIRL, FEMALE.

THE KANJI WOMAN, GIRL, FEMALE IS BULKY IN
THE BODY FOR THE FEMALE TORSO 夂. THE
OBLIQUE LINE ABOVE IS FOR THE HEAD AND
UPSWEPT HAIRDO ノ. THE HORIZONTAL LINE
PROJECTING TO BOTH SIDES IS FOR THE ARMS —.
THE LEGS PROJECT OBLIQUELY BELOW 八.

HAIRDO
AND
HEAD
ARMS
BODY
OR TORSO

LEGS

SEN; SAKI, PREVIOUS, IN ADVANCE, AHEAD.

PREVIOUS, AHEAD 先 IS A COMPOSITE OF TWO
LEGS 儿 BELOW REPRESENTING A MAN WALKING,
AND THE KANJI FOR COW 牛 ABOVE, ABBREVIATED
TO 土 TO CONVENIENCE THE MAN'S LEGS 儿.
OX, COW 牛 IS DRAWN AS A TOP VIEW, PERHAPS
A STRETCHED HIDE.　THE OBLIQUE LINE ノ ON
THE UPPER LEFT IS THE HORN(S). THE TWO 二
HORIZONTAL LINES ARE THE FOUR LEGS
PROJECTING FROM THE VERTICAL LINE | OF THE
BODY. THE VERTICAL LINE CONTINUES BELOW AS
THE TAIL.

IN WRITING THE KANJI PREVIOUS, AHEAD 先 THE
TAIL IS REPLACED BY THE TWO LEGS 儿 OF THE
MAN AHEAD 先 LEADING THE COW.　TWO LEGS 儿
IS LEADING FOUR LEGS 牛.

THE ORIENTAL METHOD OF CONTROLING THE COW,
OX 牛 WAS TO PLACE A RING THROUGH THE
SEPTUM OF ITS SENSITIVE NOSE FOR LEADING
PURPOSES. THE LEADING PERSON 儿 WAS AHEAD
OF, PREVIOUS, OR IN ADVANCE 先. THE SAME
TECHNIQUE WAS USED IN EUROPE. RECALL "THE
OWL AND THE PUSSY CAT" GETTING THE PIG'S
NOSE RING FOR THEIR WEDDING?

RAD	STROKE	JME
10	6	33

COW

PREVIOUS,
IN ADVANCE,
AHEAD

LEGS

TAIL REPLACED
BY TWO LEGS, MAN

SEI, SHŌ, EXISTENCE, LIFE;
UMARERU, TO BE BORN; UMU, TO GIVE BIRTH;
IKIRU, TO LIVE; NAMA, RAW; KI, GENUINE,
PURE.

EXISTENCE, LIFE, TO BE BORN, TO LIVE 生
IS A GROWING STEM | COMING UP WITH LATERAL
SHOOTS 十 FROM THE EARTH 土. THE OBLIQUE
STROKE ノ IS FOR THE HEAD OF THE GRAIN, ETC.
TO SHOW THE YIELD. THUS EARTH 土 AND
THE PLANT ARE COMBINED AND HEADED 生.
ALWAYS CONSIDER THE POSSIBILITY THAT
LATERAL LINES MAY ONCE HAVE CURVED UPWARDS,
ESPECIALLY IN KANJI OF MEANINGS SUCH AS THE
ABOVE. THE ORIGINAL FORM OF 十 WAS ψ.

NOTICE THE RATIO OF THE THREE HORIZONTAL
STROKES 三.　IT IS THE SAME AS IN THE KANJI
THREE 三 JME 3.

EXISTENCE, LIFE, TO BE BORN, TO LIVE 生 IS
CLOSELY LINKED TO THE YIELD OF THE EARTH,
ESPECIALLY FOR THE NOMADIC HERDSMAN. 生 MAY
REPRESENT THE SPIKELETS, EARS, HEADS ノ OF
GRAIN, ETC. OVER PLANT LAYERS, FOLIAGE 主.

RAD	STROKE	JME
100	5	34

ノ HEAD OR
YIELD OF
THE PLANT

十　　　ψ
PLANT　PLANT
　　　(OLD
　　　SYMBOL)

生

土
EARTH JME 17

JME	STROKE	RAD
35	7	155

SEKI, SHAKU; AKAI, AKA, RED, CRIMSON, SCARLET.

RED 赤 IS A COMPOSITE OF EARTH 土 JME 17 AND FIRE 火 JME 13 WRITTEN IN A SLIGHTLY DIFFERENT FORM 小 BELOW.

IT REFERS TO THE COLOR OF LAVA OR THE VOLCANIC FIRES 小 CRATERS IN OR UNDER THE EARTH 土 .

EARTH (GRAVE-MOUND, ALTAR, ETC.) JME 17

RED CRIMSON SCARLET

EARTH,SOIL OVER FIRE COMPONENT

FIRE JME 13

FIRE COMPONENT

JME	STROKE	RAD
36	8	174

SEI, SHŌ; AOI, AO, BLUE, GREEN, UNRIPE, INEXPERIENCED.

BLUE, GREEN UNRIPE, INEXPERIENCED 青 IS A COMPOSITE OF LAYERS 主 OF PLANT LIFE ABOVE THROUGH WHICH THE MOON 月 LIGHT BELOW HAS DIFFUSED GIVING A BLUISH OR GREENISH TINGE.

JUST AS IN THE ENGLISH WORD "GREENHORN" FOR A NOVICE OR THE BLUE GRASS OF KENTUCKY, BLUE, GREEN, OR BLUISH-GREEN IS THE COLOR FOR INEXPERIENCE 青 OR UNRIPENESS SINCE NEW SHOOTS OR PLANTS ARE OF THAT COLOR BEFORE MATURATION.

LAYERS OF PLANT LIFE

MOONLIGHT CASTING BLUISH OR GREENISH SHADOWS

NOTE HOW THE UPPER COMPONENT 主 RESEMBLES JME 34 生 BUT DOES NOT HAVE THE HEAD / INDICATING RIPENESS OR YIELD. MOON WAS JME 12 月 .

"Old thujas thickly grew Casting their shades of blue.
                    Su Tung-p'o (Trans. by Dykstra)

"And smitten trees in groups and rows Beneath the tempest's tune, Stand in the mists of midnight drooping, By moss-grown rocks fantastic stooping, In the blue shadows of the yellow moon.   J. Sheridan Le Fanu (1815-73)

HAKU, BYAKU; SHIROI, SHIRO, SHIRA, WHITE.

WHITE 白 IS THE COLOR OF LIGHT WHICH COMES FROM THE SUN 日 JME 11 AS RAYS OR SHAFTS /. THE RAYS / BRING THE SUN 日 DOWN TO US.

"WAKE! For the Sun....

....strikes

The Sultan's Turret with a Shaft of Light.
(Rubáiyát)

RAD STROKE JME
106   5   37

/ RAYS WHICH BRING SUN (LIGHT) DOWN TO US.

WHITE   SUN JME 11

SAN, (ZAN); YAMA, MOUNTAIN.

MOUNTAIN 山 IS COMPOSED OF THREE VERTICAL LINES FOR PEAKS OF IRREGULAR HEIGHT RELATED TO A HORIZONTAL BASELINE.

RAD STROKE JME
46   3   38

OLD SYMBOL HAD THREE PEAKS STILL PRESENT

MOUNTAIN
WITH THREE PEAKS ABOVE AND BASELINE BELOW

JME 39	Stroke 3	Rad 47

SEN; KAWA, (GAWA), RIVER.

River 川 REPRESENTS THREE STREAMS FLOWING THROUGH SAND OR IN A DELTA.

RIVER FLOWS INTO THE SEA

JME 40	Stroke 5	Rad 102

DEN; TA, (DA), RICE FIELD.

THE RICE FIELD 田 IS SUBDIVIDED OR IRRIGATED AS FOUR SMALLER FIELDS.

IT IS ALSO A COMPOSITE OF FOUR MOUTHS. THE RICE FIELD OR RICE PADDY 田 DRINKS CONSIDERABLE QUANTITIES OF WATER.

EARTH, SOIL JME 17 AS IT MAY BE SEEN IN RICE FIELD

FOUR MOUTHS JME 27

RICE FIELD FORMED FROM FOUR MOUTHS FUSED INTO ONE KANJI

SHIN; MORI, FOREST.

FOREST 森 IS REPRESENTED BY THREE TREES
JME 15. THREE OF A KIND MAY BE USED TO
SHOW AN INCREASE IN QUANTITY, QUALITY, OR
NUMBERS. THREE OF A KIND IS COMMONLY DONE
AS IN THIS CASE BY PLACING ONE OF THE ITEM
ABOVE AND TWO BELOW.

RAD	STROKE	JME
75	12	41

TREE, WOOD JME 15

WOODS, GROVE JME 150

FOREST
JME 41

U; AME, RAIN.

RAIN 雨 IS DROPS ∴ OF WATER FALLING |
IN THE ENCLOSURE OR SPACE 冂 UNDER HEAVEN
‐
．

THE RAIN KANJI 雨 IS A TOP COMPONENT IN THE
KANJI FOR SNOW, FROST, HAIL, THUNDER, CLOUD,
ETC.

RAD	STROKE	JME
173	8	42

CLOUD JME 47

SNOW JME 100

RAIN

FROM HEAVEN

FALLS

INTO THE
ENCLOSURE
OR SPACE

THE RAIN,
RAINDROPS

"The hooded clouds, like friars,
  Tell their beads in drops of rain.
                Longfellow
"The mist and cloud will turn to rain,
  The rain to mist and cloud again,
                Longfellow

JME	Stroke	Rad
43	7	140

花

++
FUSED GRASSES
(DOUBLED)

亻 UPRIGHT
MAN

ヒ MAN IN
INVERTED
FETAL,
SITTING, OR
MUMMY POSITION

KA; HANA, FLOWER.

FLOWER 花 IS A COMPOSITE. THE TOP ++
COMPONENT MEANING GRASS OR PLANT + IS A
SINGLE GRASS OR PLANT DOUBLED AND
FUSED ++. IT IS ANOTHER INSTANCE OF
CURVED UPWARDS LINES Ψ BECOMING
HORIZONTAL FOR WRITING SPEED AND
CONVENIENCE.

THE LOWER PORTION 化 OF FLOWER 花 SHOWS A
MAN STANDING 亻 TO THE LEFT AND A MAN
SITTING ヒ WITH ARMS EXTENDED ON THE RIGHT.

THE COMBINATION 化 MEANS CHANGE OR TO
CHANGE 化 BECAUSE OF THE CHANGE IN
POSITION DESCRIBED. WHEN GRASS OR A
PLANT CHANGES, IT BECOMES A FLOWER.

SOMETIMES ヒ IS REGARDED AS THE DEATH FORM,
NOTE THE MUMMY OR FETAL POSITION ヒ, OR AS
THE INVERTED FORM WITH LEGS UP OF 人 WHICH
IS THE LIFE FORM OR NATURAL POSITION. IN
ANY CASE THE TRANSITION FROM 亻 TO ヒ IS
CHANGE. ("All flesh is grass, and all the
goodliness thereof is as the flower of the
field. Grass withereth, flower fadeth:" Is.)

JME	Stroke	Rad
44	5	112

石

CLIFFS WITH MORE
OR LESS OVERHANG

口

MOUTH JME 27
REPRESENTING A
STONE OR ROCK

SEKI, SHAKU, KOKU; ISHI, STONE.

STONE, ROCK 石 IS ANOTHER COMPOSITE.
丁 IS A CLIFF IN PROFILE WITH MORE OR LESS
OVERHANG 丁厂 AND A STONE 口 AT ITS BASE.
THE COMPOSITE 石 IS NECESSARY TO INDICATE
STONE OR ROCK SINCE MOUTH IS WRITTEN WITH
口 JME 27 ALONE. IN STONE, ROCK 石 WE
HAVE AN INSTANCE OF HOW 口 AS A KANJI
MEANS MOUTH BUT IS USED IN A COMPONENT TO
CREATE A COMPOSITE WITH A DIFFERENT MEANING.

STONES AT THE BASE OF
MESA-LIKE CLIFFS

HON, (BON), (PON), SUFFIX IN COUNTING LONG
SLENDER ARTICLES, BOOK; MOTO, ROOT, SOURCE.

RAD	STROKE	JME
75	5	45

BOOK, ROOT, SOURCE 本 CONSISTS OF TREE 木
JME 15 WITH A SHORT HORIZONTAL STROKE -
ADDED TO ALTER THE MEANING TO BOOK, ROOT,
SOURCE 本.

A BOOK 本 IS THE ROOT OR SOURCE 本 OF
KNOWLEDGE AND WOODEN (TREE) BLOCKS WERE USED
FOR EARLY PRINTING. THE SCOPE AND POWER OF
THE TREE USED AS A SOURCE OF WRITING MATERIALS AND FOR
PRINTING BLOCKS WERE ENORMOUSLY INCREASED. THE SHORT
STROKE OR DOT SIGNIFIES THIS, ANALOGOUS TO SUN 日 JME 11.

TREE, WOOD JME 15

SHORT STROKE
HAS THE EFFECT
OF A DOT AS IN
JADE JME 64 AND
DOG JME 66

BOOK, ROOT, SOURCE

SEI, SHŌ; TADASHII, CORRECT, RIGHT.

RAD	STROKE	JME
	5	46

CORRECT, RIGHT 正 IS REPRESENTED BY A HALTED
UP 上 (RIGHT) POSITION UNDER THE HORIZONTAL
LINE FOR HEAVEN 一. UPRIGHT UNDER HEAVEN
AS THE BIBLE PHRASES IT. TO STOP, TO BRING
TO A STOP 止 IS FOOT, LEG 足 JME 29 WITH THE
PELVIS REMOVED 止 AND THE FOOT FLATTENED 止
AS THOUGH SCREECHING TO A HALT. THUS RIGHT,
CORRECT 正 IS A FUSION OF UP 上, TO STOP 止,
AND HEAVEN .

FOOT, LEG
JME 29
(WITH AN
ARCHED
FOOT)

CORRECT,
RIGHT
JME 46
(WITH THE
FOOT FLAT)

HEAVEN
(AS PART
OF WORKER
AND CON-
STRUCTION)

TO STOP, TO
BRING TO A
STOP
JME 220

UPPER, ABOVE,
TOP, ON, UP,
TO GO UP
JME 20

JME 47	Stroke 12	Rad 173

UN; KUMO, (GUMO), CLOUD.

CLOUD 雲 IS A COMPOSITE WITH RAIN 雨 JME 42 AS THE TOP COMPONENT AND A COILED CLOUD ム AT THE BOTTOM UNDER LAYERS OF CLOUD = ABOVE. THE SYMBOL FOR THE COILED CLOUD ム IS GENERIC FOR CERTAIN THINGS WHICH ARE COILED, LAYERED, OR HOLDING. EXAMPLES ARE A MOUTH SPEAKING, A BASKET, A (PINE) CONE, OR AN ARM WITH THE MUSCLE CONTRACTED. THE COILED CLOUD WITH LAYERS ABOVE 云 MAY ALSO MEAN A MOUTH ム SPEAKING IN SOUND WAVES OR VIBRATIONS = AS IN WEATHER CAUSING FROSTY PUFFS OF BREATH LIKE CLOUDS. THIS MOUTH IS CONCEPTUALLY DIFFERENT THAN 口 JME 27 SINCE ム SENDS FORTH AS A GENESIS OF EXPANSION LIKE THE PINE CONE WHICH IS THE SOURCE OF SEEDLINGS, THE CLOUD WHICH CAN EXPAND AND COVER THE SKY, THE BASKET WHOSE CONTENTS CAN BE SPREAD, OR THE CONTRACTED ARM MUSCLE WHICH CAN OPEN THE ARM.

RAIN JME 42

CLOUD LAYERS

COILED CLOUD

CLOUD JME 47

JME 48	Stroke 4	Rad 31

EN; CIRCLE, YEN, JAPANESE UNIT OF CURRENCY.

CIRCLE, YEN 円 IS TWO DOORS 門 JOINED 円 WITH THEIR PANELS RAISED AS WITH A PAIR OF SWINGING DOORS. THE MOST PICTURESQUE DOORS ARE THOSE OF A "MOON-GATE" WHICH IS CIRCULAR LIKE A FULL MOON. SOME OLD ORIENTAL COINS WERE CIRCULAR AND HAD HOLES FOR STRINGING. THE KANJI HAS BEEN SQUARED FROM ITS ORIGINAL CURVED FORM.

CIRCULAR AND OPEN "MOON-GATE" AS IN A BRICK WALL

DOORS SET IN "MOON-GATE"

OLD COIN WITH SQUARE HOLE FOR STRINGING

SUPER-IMPOSITION

Ō; KING.

KING 王 IS A COMPOSITE INCLUDING THREE HORIZONTAL LINES 三. THE TOP HORIZONTAL LINE IS FOR HEAVEN, THE MIDDLE HORIZONTAL LINE IS FOR THE PEOPLE, THE BOTTOM HORIZONTAL LINE IS FOR THE EARTH. THE VERTICAL LINE REPRESENTS THE KING WHO OFFERS PRAYERS ON THE ALTARS OF EARTH FOR THE PEOPLE TO HEAVEN. THUS THE KING MEDIATES BETWEEN EARTH AND HEAVEN FOR HIS PEOPLE.

RAD	STROKE	JME
96	4	49

HEAVEN

MANKIND, MAN

EARTH   KING MEDIATES   KING JME 49

(TRIAD IN THREE JME 3)

ON, IN; NE, OTO, SOUND.

SOUND 音 IS A COMPOSITE. SOUND 音 ISSUES FROM THE MOUTH 日 OF A PERSON OR MAN 立 STANDING. 立. NOTE JME 6. A STANDING 立 POSITION IS THE BEST FOR MAKING SOUND BY SINGING, SHOUTING, ETC. TO STAND 立 IS APPROPRIATELY ABOVE SINCE SOUND WILL CARRY BETTER FROM AN ELEVATION.

RAD	STROKE	JME
180	9	50

(MAN)

STANDS (ON EARTH)

SOUNDS (AS MOUTH SPEAKS)

SOUND JME 50

MAN (SIX)

EARTH

MOUTH

WORDS

OLD SYMBOLS FOR MAN AS IN SIX JME 6 & TO STAND JME 149

JME 51	Stroke 7	Rad 9

KA; NANI, NAN, WHAT, HOW MANY.

WHAT, HOW MANY 何 ARE INTERROGATIVE QUESTIONS STRIKING LIKE NAILS 丁 FROM THE MOUTH 口 JME 27 OF THE MAN 亻(人) JME 30 WHO IS THE INTERROGATOR.

ECCLESIASTES SAYS, "THE WORDS OF THE WISE ARE AS GOADS, AND AS NAILS FASTENED BY THE MASTERS OF ASSEMBLIES."

MOUTH JME 27

MAN, PERSON JME 30 AS LEFT COMPONENT

NAIL IS AN ARCHAIC MEANING; NOW A UNIT OF LINEAR DISTANCE, "D" GRADE JME 473

WHAT? HOW MANY?

JME 52	Stroke 10	Rad 35

KA; NATSU, SUMMER.

SUMMER 夏 IS A COMPOSITE OF HEAD 百 ABOVE, THE EYE 目 SERVING TO REPRESENT A HEAD AND COVERED 冖 FOR PROTECTION FROM THE SUMMER SUN. BELOW THE HEAD 百 IS A FAN 丿 BEING WAVED BY THE HAND 又 (ORIGINAL FORM 屮) TO COOL THE HEAD 百.

COVER

EYE

HEAD

HEAD COVER

EYE JME 25

OLD SYMBOL FOR HAND

ANOTHER OLD SYMBOL

PRESENT COMPONENT FOR HAND

FAN

HAND

SUMMER

KA, KE; YA, IE, HOUSE, HOME.

RAD	STROKE	JME
40	10	53

HOUSE, HOME 家 IS A COMPOSITE OF ROOF 宀 ABOVE AND PIG, HOG 豕 COMFORTABLY AT HOME UNDERNEATH. NOTHING IS SO AT HOME AS A PIG IN ITS STY. THERE IS ALSO AN IMPLICATION OF AT-HOMENESS IN THE PIG WALLOWING IN THE DIRT OR MUD. WE ARE AT HOME WHEN WE CAN DO THIS.

THE PIG 豕 IS DRAWN IN THE VERTICAL POSITION, TUSK AND HEAD ABOVE ⼅ , TWO LEGS TO THE RIGHT ⼹ , TWO LEGS TO THE LEFT ⼻ , AND BODY WITH DANGLING TAIL DEPICTED BY THE CENTER STROKE ⼃ .

ROOF

TUSK
HEAD

RIGHT LEGS

LEFT LEGS

TAIL

PIG, HOG, BOAR
AS COMPONENT

HOUSE, HOME
(PIG UNDER ROOF)

OLD PIG SYMBOL

KAI, E, MEETING; AU, TO MEET.

RAD	STROKE	JME
9	6	54

MEETING, TO MEET 会 IS A COMPOSITE WITH A LARGE ROOF 人 ABOVE (AS IN GOLD, MONEY JME 16) AND A MOUTH BELOW ム EMANATING SOUND WAVES 二 (AS EXPLAINED IN CLOUD JME 47). AT A MEETING 会 USUALLY HELD UNDER A ROOF 人 , A MOUTH OR MOUTHS ム EMIT VIBRATIONS 二 AND VAPOR 云 .

雲　会

CLOUD   TO MEET
JME 47 MEETING

LARGE
ROOF

SOUND
VIBRATIONS
OF WORDS

MOUTH OF
SPEAKER(S)

MEETING,
TO MEET

CLOUDY VAPOR
OF SPEAKING BREATH

JME	Stroke	Rad
55	9	85

KAI; UMI, SEA, OCEAN.

SEA, OCEAN 海 HAS THREE COMPONENTS. THE THREE SMALL STROKES TO THE LEFT ⺡ REPRESENT WATER AS THREE FALLING SPLASHING DROPS. NOTE WATER 水 JME 14. THE TOP COMPONENT OF SEA, OCEAN 海 IS MAN ⼇ (人). NOTE MAN, PERSON 人 JME 30. THE RIGHT COMPONENT SHOWS A PAIR OF BREASTS WITH DOTTED NIPPLES ORIGINALLY DEPICTED 母, BUT NOW TURNED VERTICALLY FROM THEIR USUAL HUMAN POSITION. THE DOTTED NIPPLES ⁚ HAVE BEEN SIMPLIFIED TO A VERTICAL LINE | IN WRITING, BUT STILL MAY BE ENCOUNTERED AS DOTS. THE SEA, OCEAN 海 IS THE WATER ⺡ MOTHER 母 OF MAN ⼇ FROM THE STANDPOINT OF FOOD SUPPLY JUST AS HIS HUMAN MOTHER NOURISHED HIM FROM HER BREASTS.

⼇　　　⺡　　　母　　　海　　　PLANTS 主
MAN'S JME 30　WATER MOTHER (NIPPLES) IS THE SEA　DO NOT, (MILKY SAP POISON JUICES) 母

⺡　　　母　　　⼇　　　海　　　毒
WATER (BRINE) POISONOUS TO MAN IS THE SEA　POISON JME 686

JME	Stroke	Rad
56	5	36

GAI, GE; (OUTSIDE, OTHER, FOREIGN); HOKA, OTHER; SOTO, OUTSIDE.

OUTSIDE, FOREIGN, OTHER 外 IS A COMPOSITE. DIVINATION ⼘ OCCURRED IN THE EVENING 夕 AND OUTSIDE. DIVINATION ⼘ WAS DONE BY OBSERVING THE CRACKS ⼘ PRODUCED BY HEAT APPLIED TO BONE OR THE SHELL OF A TORTOISE. IN THE COMPONENT ⼘ THE VERTICAL LINE | IS A CRACK ON THE VERTICAL AXIS, THE SHORTER OBLIQUE LINE ﹨ A CRACK ON THE TRANSVERSE AXIS OF THE BONE OR TORTOISE SHELL. THE COMPONENT 夕 MEANS EVENING AND SHOWS THE MOON 月 PARTLY HIDDEN 夕 BY

月　　　夕　　　夕　　　外　　　⼘ CRACKED SHELL, BONE
MOON, MONTH JME 12　(RISING OR SINKING MOON) EVENING JME 98　OUTSIDE, OTHER, FOREIGN　DIVINATION (VENTRAL VIEW)

GAKU, LEARNING, STUDIES, SCIENCE;
MANABU, TO LEARN.

LEARNING, STUDIES, SCIENCE, TO LEARN 学 IS A
COMPOSITE OF CHILD 子 JME 31 TRAPPED OR UNDER
A COVER OR CAP ⼍ WEIGHTED WITH THE BURDEN ⺌
OF LEARNING 学.

RAD	STROKE	JME
39	8	57

BURDEN OF
LEARNING

CAP OF
LEARNING
(SOMETIMES
COVER OR TRAP)

CHILD
JME 31

LEARNING, STUDIES
SCIENCE, TO LEARN

KAN, KEN; AIDA, INTERVAL, SPACE, DISTANCE;
MA, SPACE, ROOM, INTERVAL, TIME.

SPACE, ROOM, INTERVAL, TIME, DISTANCE 間
SHOWS THE SUN 日 JME 11 SHINING INTO A SPACE
OR ROOM BETWEEN DOUBLE PANELED DOORS 門.
THIS OCCURS AT ABOUT THE SAME TIME 間 OR FOR
ABOUT THE SAME INTERVAL 間 EACH DAY. THE
WOODEN PANELS OF THE DOUBLE DOORS ARE RAISED
(AS WITH SWINGING DOORS) FOR WRITING
CONVENIENCE AND FOR THE FORMATION OF
COMPOSITES. NOTE HOW THESE PANELED DOORS RESEMBLE CIRCLE,
YEN 円 JME 48.

RAD	STROKE	JME
169	12	58

GATE JME 143
(DOUBLE DOORS)

SUN JME 11

INTERVAL, SPACE
DISTANCE, ROOM
TIME

JME	STROKE	RAD
59	6	84

KI, KE, SPIRIT, MIND, NATURE, ENERGY.

SPIRIT, MIND, NATURE, ENERGY 気 IS REPRESENTED BY GRAINS OF RICE X (PREVIOUSLY WRITTEN 米) FERMENTING AND BUBBLING IN AN ENCLOSURE TO PRODUCE VAPOR 气. NOTE JME 60. THE SEGMENTS FROM THE INTERSECTION OR CENTER CAN BE REGARDED AS GRAINS IN X OR 米. THIS FERMENTING AND VAPORIZING REPRESENTS ENERGY OR SPIRIT. RICE WINE IS THE FAVORITE ORIENTAL LIQUOR. IN ENGLISH WE SAY, "BUBBLING WITH SPIRITS," AND REFER TO "SPIRITUOUS LIQUORS" OR "SPIRITS."

(4 GRAINS OF RICE PLACED WITH ENDS TOUCHING)

VAPOR FROM FERMENTING RICE IN AN ENCLOSURE

SPIRIT, MIND NATURE, ENERGY

JME	STROKE	RAD
60	7	85

KI, (VAPOR, STEAM).

VAPOR, STEAM 气 IS REPRESENTED BY DROPS OF WATER 氵 ON THE LEFT AND RISING LAYERS OF VAPOR OR STEAM ON THE RIGHT 气. WATER PRODUCES VAPOR OR STEAM 气.

WATER COMPONENT

LAYERS OF VAPOR OR STEAM FROM ENCLOSURE

VAPOR, STEAM

KYU; YASUMI, REST, VACATION;
YASUMU, TO REST.

RAD	STROKE	JME
9	6	61

REST, VACATION 休 IS A COMPOSITE OF A MAN 亻
JME 30 TO THE LEFT OF A TREE 木 JME 15 BY
OR UNDER WHICH HE CAN REST OR VACATION.

MAN, PERSON   TREE JME 15   REST, VACATION
COMPONENT   TO REST

SUPERIMPOSED

GYŪ; USHI, CATTLE, COW, BULL, OX.

RAD	STROKE	JME
93	4	62

CATTLE, COW, BULL, OX HAS BEEN DISCUSSED AS
THE TOP COMPONENT IN PREVIOUS, IN ADVANCE,
AHEAD 先 JME 33.
THE OBLIQUE LINE IS THE HORN(S) ノ . THE
PARALLEL HORIZONTAL LINES 二 ARE THE FOUR
LEGS TWO OF WHICH ARE ATTACHED TO EACH SIDE
OF THE CENTER LINE. THE CENTER LINE IS
DIVIDED INTO THREE PARTS BY THE PARALLEL
LINES. THE UPPER PART IS THE HEAD OF THE
CATTLE, COW, BULL, OX. THE MIDDLE PART IS THE BODY. THE
LOWEST PART IS THE TAIL. THUS WE HAVE A TOP VIEW OF THE
COW OR ITS STRETCHED HIDE WITH THE HEAD UP.

HORN(S)

                                    HEAD

                                    BODY

                                    TAIL

                                              MINUS HORN(S)   COW, BULL
FOUR LEGS   HEAD, BODY, TAIL   CATTLE, OX

JME 63	Stroke 8	Rad 8

KYŌ, CAPITAL; KEI.

CAPITAL 京 IS A PICTOGRAPH OF STONE LANTERNS OR MONUMENTS FOUND IN ROWS ALONG CERTAIN HIGHWAYS IN THE CAPITAL 京 . COPIES IN VARIOUS STYLES ARE SOLD AND PLACED IN ROCK GARDENS AND PATIOS IN THE USA. THE COMPONENT 亠 INDICATES AUTHORITY OR DIRECTION OR THE BIRETTA OF THE SCHOLAR OR LEADER. THE MOUTH 口 JME 27 COMPONENT IS THE OPENING OR APERTURE THROUGH WHICH THE LIGHT WAS PLACED IN THE LANTERN. THE THREE LINES BELOW ARE THE TRIPOD LEGS OF THE LANTERN. THE CENTRAL VERTICAL LINE ↓ IS THE LEG IN THE FOREGROUND. THE OBLIQUE LINES /\ ON EITHER SIDE ARE BACKGROUND LEGS.

PICTURE OF STONE MONU-MENT IN THE CAPITAL	CAPITAL... IS A COPY OF THE MONUMENT	TRIPOD LEGS FOREGROUND CENTER LEG SIDE TO REAR	MOUTH JME 27 ADMITS LIGHT	AUTHORITY, DIRECTION... FROM THE CAPITAL

JME 64	Stroke 5	Rad 96

GYOKU, JADE; TAMA, (DAMA), BALL, SPHERE, GLOBE, BULB, BEAD, GEM, JEWEL.

JADE, BALL, GEM, JEWEL 玉 IS A COMPOSITE OF KING 王 JME 49 AND A DOT ` TO THE LOWER RIGHT. THE SEAL OF THE KING 王 WAS MADE OF JADE 玉. IT WAS USED IN LIEU OF A SIGNATURE ON HIS EDICTS OR COMMANDS. A DOT ` OFTEN REPRESENTS AN EXTENSION OF RANGE, POWER OR INFLUENCE. THE AFFIXING OF THE KING'S JADE SEAL EXTENDED HIS POWER RANGE.

KING JME 49 MEDIATES FROM EARTH TO HEAVEN FOR HIS PEOPLE	JADE, BALL, SPHERE, GEM JME 64 KING'S AUTHORITY	DOT EXTENDS POWER, RANGE INFLUENCE

KŪ; SORA, (ZORA), SKY.

RAD	STROKE	JME
116	8	65

SKY 空 IS A COMPOSITE OF THE CONSTRUCTED
HOLE ハ IN THE ROOF 宀 (AS FOR THE ESCAPE OF
SMOKE FROM THE FIRE IN PRIMITIVE DWELLINGS)
THROUGH WHICH THE SKY 空 IS VISIBLE. NOTE
HOW HOLE ハ IS RELATED TO EIGHT 八 JME 8
WHICH HAS TO DO WITH DIVIDING OR OPENING THE
LEGS, ETC.

ROOF

DIVISION
OR HOLE
(JME 8)

ACTUAL SHAPE OF
CURVED ROOF

CONSTRUCTION
JME 71

IN THE ROOF OF
HEAVEN IS AN
OPENING, HOLE
OR DIVISION
CONSTRUCTED.
IT IS THE SKY.

KEN; INU, DOG.

RAD	STROKE	JME
94	4	66

A DOG 犬 IS GREAT(NESS) 大 JME 22 EXTENDED
BY THE DOT'S ・ SYMBOLISM JUST AS JADE, BALL,
JEWEL 玉 IS AN EXTENSION OF THE AUTHORITY OR
POWER OF THE KING 王 . THE GREAT(NESS) OR
REACH, CONTROL OF THE HERDSMAN, SHEPHERD OR
HUNTER IS EXTENDED BY HIS DOG 犬 JUST AS THE
JADE 玉 SEAL EXTENDS THE CONTROL OF THE
KING 王 . IT IS AS THOUGH WHAT IS IN THE
FOREGROUND SUCH AS KING 王 OR GREAT(NESS) 大
HAS SUDDENLY REACHED PERSPECTIVE DISTANCE AS A DOT ・
SHOWING TREMENDOUS RANGE AND POWER IN TIME AND SPACE.
REVIEW JADE 玉 JME 64 TO MAKE THE ANALOGY TO DOG 犬 CLEARER.

MAN, PERSON
JME 30

GREAT, BIG
LARGE JME 22

DOT
EXTENDS
REACH OR
CONTROL

DOG

JME 67	Stroke 7	Rad 147

KEN; MIRU, TO SEE, TO LOOK.

TO SEE, TO LOOK 見 IS AN EYE 目 JME 25 (FOR THE VIEWER) MOUNTED ON A MAN'S LEGS (NOTE JME 33) SO THERE IS MOBILITY TO SEE OR TO LOOK 見 .

NOTE HOW WALKING LEGS DIFFER IN THE SIDE VIEW.

EYE JME 25

EYE

MAN WALKING

MAN JME 30
(AS TWO LEGS)

TO SEE, TO
LOOK
(MOBILE EYE)

WALKING EYE
SEES, LOOKS

JME 68	Stroke 4	Rad 8

GEN; GAN; MOTO, BEGINNING, FOUNDATION, ORIGIN.

BEGINNING, FOUNDATION, ORIGIN 元 IS A COMPOSITE OF TWO LEGS 儿 BELOW (JME 33 & 67) AND TWO HORIZONTAL LINES 二 ABOVE AS FOR BASELINE AND EARTH OR HORIZON AND HEAVEN.

THIS IS THE BEGINNING, FOUNDATION OR ORIGIN OF THINGS: A MAN WALKING, MOVING OR NOMADIC AND HIS OPERATIONAL SPACE.

HEAVEN, HORIZON

EARTH, BASELINE

MAN, PERSON
JME 30
(AS TWO LEGS)

BEGINNING
FOUNDATION
ORIGIN (MAN &
HIS SPACE)

BEGINNING
FOUNDATION
ORIGIN

KO; TO, (DO), DOOR, SUFFIX IN COUNTING HOUSES. (ENGLISH CONCEPT: "THREE DOORS DOWN THE STREET.")

THE DOOR 戸 IS A SINGLE DOOR IN CONTRAST TO THE CIRCLE 円 (OF THE MOON-GATE PAIRED DOORS) JME 48 AND THE GATE 門 (DOUBLE DOORS) JME 143 USUALLY USED FOR GATEWAYS TO ENCLOSURES AND FOR MAIN ENTRANCES. ORIENTAL DOORS WERE NOT HINGED, BUT TURNED ON PINS EXTENDING FROM THE DOOR AND SET IN SOCKETS ABOVE AND BELOW. THE TOP LINE WHICH MAY BE OBLIQUE OR HORIZONTAL REPRESENTS ONE OF THESE PINS.

RAD	STROKE	JME
63	4	69

CIRCLE, YEN
JME 48
(MOON-GATE)

GATE JME 143
(DOUBLE DOORS)

PICTURE OF
SOCKETED
PINS OF THE
SINGLE DOOR

PIN
DOOR
PIN

DOOR JME 69
(UPPER PIN MAY
BE OBLIQUELY
DRAWN)

KO; FURUI, OLD, ANCIENT.

OLD, ANCIENT 古 IS A COMPOSITE OF TEN 十 JME 10 AND MOUTH 口 JME 27. IT INDICATES SOMETHING ENDURING OR PASSED ON BY TEN 十 GENERATIONS OF MOUTHS 口 IS OLD, ANCIENT 古.

ORIENTALS RECKON A GENERATION AS THIRTY YEARS. TEN GENERATIONS IS THREE HUNDRED YEARS, A GREAT CYCLE OF THE ORIENTAL SIXTY YEAR CALENDAR CYCLE, OR FIVE LESSER CYCLES.

RAD	STROKE	JME
24	5	70

TEN JME 10

MOUTH JME 27

TEN
(GENERATIONS
OF)
MOUTHS

OLD, ANCIENT
JME 70

JME 71	STROKE 3	RAD 48

KŌ, KU; WORKER, ENGINEERING, CONSTRUCTION.

WORKER, ENGINEERING, CONSTRUCTION 工 IS A SMALL CARPENTER'S SQUARE OR A PLUMB LINE FROM THE CEILING OR HEAVEN TO THE FLOOR OR EARTH.   WORKER, ENGINEERING, CONSTRUCTION 工 WAS A COMPONENT IN LEFT 左 JME 18 AND A COMPONENT IN SKY 空 JME 65.

THE SQUARE OR PLUMB LINE IS ESSENTIAL TO A WORKER IN CONSTRUCTION OR ENGINEERING 工.

THE CONCEPT OF THE SQUARE OR PLUMB LINE AS APPLIED TO HEAVEN AND EARTH AS A DIVINE CONSTRUCTION JME 71

WORKER, ENGI-NEERING, CON-STRUCTION AS SUPERIMPOSED PLUMB LINE OR SQUARE

LEFT JME 18. WORKER, OR ENGINEERING CONSTRUCTION IS THE LOW COMPONENT

SKY JME 65. WORKER, OR ENGINEERING, CONSTRUCTION IS THE LOW COMPONENT

JME 72	STROKE 6	RAD 42

KŌ; HIKARI, LIGHT, BRILLIANCE; HIKARU, TO SHINE.

LIGHT, BRILLIANCE, TO SHINE 光 IS A COMPOSITE OF A WALKING MAN (ON TWO LEGS 儿) CARRYING A FIRE 火 (TORCH). THE BOTTOM PORTION OF THE KANJI FOR FIRE 火 HAS BEEN FLATTENED: 业. 业 CAN ALSO BE INTERPRETED AS RAYS OF LIGHT 业.

MAN IS PORTRAYED BY TWO LEGS WALKING (WHICH WILL CARRY THE FIRE, TORCH)

LIGHT, BRIL-LIANCE, TO SHINE (FIRE ABOVE, MAN CARRYING THE FIRE OR TORCH)

THE LOWER PART OF FIRE HAS BEEN FLAT-TENED AND RAISED FROM DOTS

DOTTED LINE SHOWS THE FUTURE POSITION OF THE LOWER PART OF FIRE

FIRE JME 13 BECOMES TOP COMPONENT IN LIGHT, BRILLIANCE, TO SHINE JME 72

KŌ, GYŌ, AN;   IKU, YUKU, TO GO;
OKONAU, TO DO, TO ACT;   OKONAI, ACT, DEED.

Rad	Stroke	JME
144	6	73

行

TO GO, TO DO, TO ACT, ACT, DEED 行 HAD ITS
ORIGIN AS A CROSSROADS 丯.

AT PRESENT, TO GO, TO DO, TO ACT, ACT,
DEED 行 ALSO SUGGESTS TWO FEET OR LEGS
IN THE ACT OR DEED 行 OF GOING OR DOING 行.

ADDITIONAL MEANINGS SUCH AS TO CONDUCT,
TO PRACTICE 行 DERIVE FROM THE CONCEPT OF TRAVELING THE
CORRECT (RIGHTEOUS) ROAD OR PATH.

CROSSROADS & NECESSARY TO GO, TO DO, TO ACT	LINES OF CROSSROADS SHIFT AND STRAIGHTEN	TO GO, TO DO, TO ACT	TO GO, TO DO, TO ACT SUGGESTS LEGS, FEET JME 29	CORRECT CONDUCT, FOLLOW LEADER

KŌ;   KANGAERU, TO THINK;
KANGAE, IDEA, THOUGHT, OPINION

Rad	Stroke	JME
125	6	74

考

TO THINK, IDEA, THOUGHT, OPINION 考 IS FOR
THE FILIAL CONFUCIAN TO THINK OR TO REFLECT
ON HIS (DEAD) FATHER.
EARTH 土 CARRIED ON A SLANTED STICK OR
BACK ノ CONNOTES BURDEN. THE SAME SLANTED
LINE IS SEEN IN AGED, OLD 老 JME 541 AND IN
FEW, LITTLE, SCARCE 少. THE OLD AND THE
LITTLE ARE THE BURDEN.
THE COMPONENT 丂 MAY BE THE ASTHMATIC GROAN OF FATHER OR
THE RASP 丂 OF THE BOWSTRING. LINKED HERE IS THE THOUGHT OF
HOW HE CARRIED YOU DURING YOUR FIRST THREE YEARS. THAT IS
WHY THE OFFICIAL MOURNING PERIOD FOR A PARENT WAS THREE
YEARS.

MOVEMENT
OF BOWSTRING

EARTH (BURDEN)	BENT SLANTED BACK OR STICK CARRYING	RASP OF BOWSTRING OR GROAN	THOUGHT, OPINION, IDEA	ASIAN COMPOUND BOW	FEW, LITTLE, SCARCE JME 93 (ALSO IS A BURDEN)

JME 75	Stroke 10	Rad 75

KŌ, (SCHOOL, TO CORRECT, TO PROOFREAD).

SCHOOL, TO CORRECT, TO PROOFREAD 校 IS A COMPOSITE OF A CAPPED 亠 (SCHOLAR'S BIRETTA) FATHER 父 JME 131 BY A TREE JME 15 INDICATING THE PRESENCE OF A SCHOOL (GROVES OF ACADÈME). THE CAPPED FATHER IS AT THE SCHOOL AND CORRECTING, PROOFREADING. THE CHINESE SCHOLAR AS A MEMBER OF THE LITERATI (CLASS) WORE AN IDENTIFYING CAP.

TREE, WOOD JME 15 GROVES OF ACADEME

SCHOOL, TO CORRECT, TO PROOFREAD JME 75

TO BE MIXED, TO ASSOCIATE WITH JME 212

SYMBOL FOR CAP, ROOF, OR DIRECTION (DEPENDS ON CONTEXT)

FATHER JME 131

JME 76	Stroke 10	Rad 189

KŌ; TAKAI, HIGH, EXPENSIVE.

HIGH, EXPENSIVE 高 SHOWS A TWO STORIED, BUILDING WHICH IS HIGH AND EXPENSIVE 高 COMPARED TO THE USUAL ONE STORIED STRUCTURE. 亠 IS THE ROOF. BELOW IT, 口 IS THE UPPER STORY. SET IN SURROUNDING STRUCTURE 冂, 口 IS ALSO THE LOWER STORY. HIGH ALSO DESCRIBES ALTITUDE OR PRICE IN ENGLISH.

SURROUNDING LOWER STORY AS PART OF STRUCTURE

LOWER STORY

HIGH, EXPEN-SIVE JME 76 (TWO STORY BUILDING)

UPPER STORY OF BUILDING (MOUTH JME 27)

ROOF OF BUILDING

GŌ; AU, TO FIT, TO SUIT, TO AGREE, TO BE TOGETHER.

TO FIT, TO SUIT, TO AGREE, TO BE TOGETHER 合 IS A COMPOSITE OF A LARGE ROOF 人 ABOVE WITH THE COMBINATION OF ONE ─ AND MOUTH 口 BELOW.

ONE MOUTH 吕 INDICATES UNIFORMITY OF OPINION AND/OR ECONOMIC AGREEMENT SINCE THE COMMON MOUTH MUST BE NOURISHED AND THIS IS ACCOMPLISHED BY AGREEING, BEING TOGETHER.

THE IDEALIZED CHINESE PATRIARCHAL FAMILY HAD FIVE 五 GENERATIONS UNDER "ONE ROOF."

RAD	STROKE	JME
30	6	77

LARGE ROOF (OR MT. PEAK DEPENDING ON THE CONTEXT	TO FIT, TO SUIT, TO AGREE, TO BE TOGETHER (ROOF, UNITY)	ONE JME 1 OVER MOUTH (UNITY)	FIVE JME 5 (GENERATIONS)	MEETING, TO MEET JME 54 SOUND VIBRATIONS FROM MOUTH

KOKU; TANI, VALLEY.

VALLEY 谷 IS A COMPOSITE OF TWO SEPARATED OBLIQUE LINES 八 AT THE TOP WHICH MEAN DIVIDE, DIVIDED 八 (REFER TO EIGHT 八 JME 8) SINCE VALLEYS DIVIDE OR SEPARATE MOUNTAINS, THE MOUNTAIN PEAK ABOVE 人 THE VALLEY 口 REPRESENTED BY A MOUTH 口 SINCE THE VALLEY MAY BE USED FOR INGRESS AND SINCE THE VALLEY BY ITS SHAPE AND FERTILITY HOLDS THE PEOPLE, JUST AS A MOUTH HOLDS FOOD, ETC.

RAD	STROKE	JME
150	7	78

DIVIDED, SEPARATED (REVIEW JME 8)	VALLEY JME 78 (DIVIDED MOUNTAIN VALLEYS)	MOUTH OR APERTURE UNDER MOUNTAIN	MOUTH OR APERTURE (MAY HAVE HOLDING FUNCTION

JME	Stroke	Rad
79	8	31

KOKU, (GOKU); KUNI, (GUNI), COUNTRY.

COUNTRY 国 HAS TWO COMPONENTS, JEWEL OR JADE 玉 REPRESENTING THE AUTHORITY OF THE RULER THROUGH HIS JADE SEAL 玉, AND AN ENCLOSURE 口 AS THE NATIONAL BORDER OR BOUNDARY. THE ENCLOSURE 口 IS THE SAME SHAPE AS MOUTH 口 JME 27, BUT IS LARGER AND IS ONLY USED TO ENCLOSE.

ENCLOSURE HERE USED AS NATIONAL BOUNDARIES

COUNTRY... AUTHORITY OF KING 王 WITHIN THE NATIONAL BOUNDARIES JME 79

JADE (SEAL) OF THE KING REPRESENTING HIS CONTROL, AUTHORITY (JME 64)

THE DOT ` INCREASES CONTROL BY THE KING 王 THROUGH THE SEAL 玉

THE KING JME 49 (MEDIATES FROM EARTH TO HEAVEN FOR HIS PEOPLE)

JME	Stroke	Rad
80	11	203

KOKU; KURO, (GURO), KUROI, BLACK.

BLACK 黒 IS A COMPOSITE. THE FOUR STROKES BELOW /\\\ REPRESENT A FIRE 火 JME 13 IN A COMPONENT FORM. OVER THE FIRE /\\\ IS A STOVE OF EARTH 土 (LIKE ADOBE). THE VERTICAL FLUE | LEADS TO A GRATED 田 CHIMNEY WHERE THE BLACK 黒 SOOT COLLECTS. THE BLACKNESS IS EMPHASIZED BY TURNING THE TOP OF THE GRATE TO US. SOOT WAS USED AS AN INGREDIENT OF BLACK CHINESE INK.

VERTICAL FLUE AND GRATE (NOTE MOUTHS) FOR BLACK SOOT TO MAKE THE BLACK INK

BLACK... EMPHASIS ON THE SOOT OF THE GRATE

EARTH JME 17 OF WHICH STOVE IS MADE

FIRE JME 13 UNDER THE EARTHEN STOVE

FIRE AS A COMPONENT JME 13

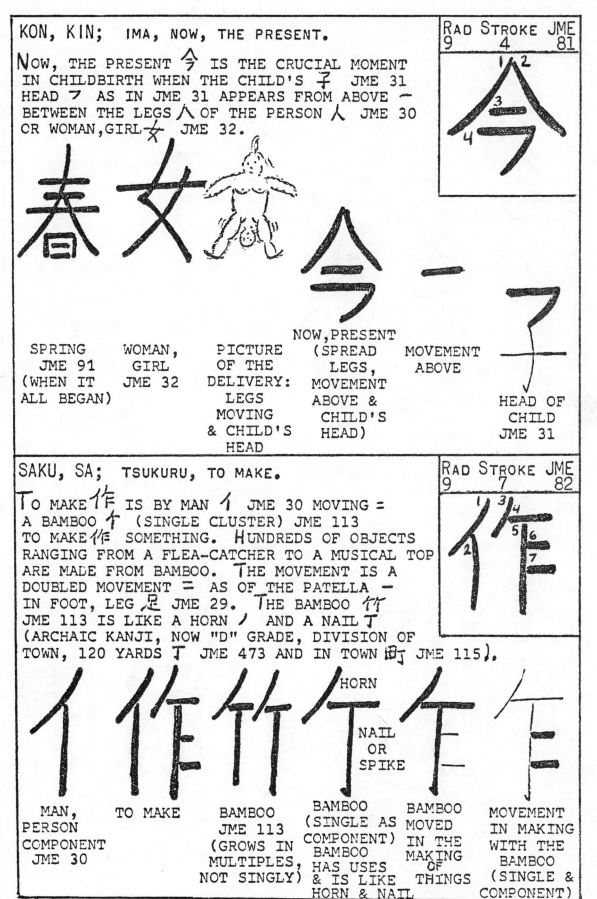

KON, KIN; IMA, NOW, THE PRESENT.

NOW, THE PRESENT 今 IS THE CRUCIAL MOMENT IN CHILDBIRTH WHEN THE CHILD'S 子 JME 31 HEAD ⴀ AS IN JME 31 APPEARS FROM ABOVE ⌐ BETWEEN THE LEGS 八 OF THE PERSON 人 JME 30 OR WOMAN, GIRL 女 JME 32.

RAD 9   STROKE 4   JME 81

SPRING
JME 91
(WHEN IT
ALL BEGAN)

WOMAN,
GIRL
JME 32

PICTURE
OF THE
DELIVERY:
LEGS
MOVING
& CHILD'S
HEAD

NOW, PRESENT
(SPREAD
LEGS,
MOVEMENT
ABOVE &
CHILD'S
HEAD)

MOVEMENT
ABOVE

HEAD OF
CHILD
JME 31

SAKU, SA; TSUKURU, TO MAKE.

TO MAKE 作 IS BY MAN 亻 JME 30 MOVING ⹀ A BAMBOO 乍 (SINGLE CLUSTER) JME 113 TO MAKE 作 SOMETHING. HUNDREDS OF OBJECTS RANGING FROM A FLEA-CATCHER TO A MUSICAL TOP ARE MADE FROM BAMBOO. THE MOVEMENT IS A DOUBLED MOVEMENT ⹀ AS OF THE PATELLA ⌐ IN FOOT, LEG 足 JME 29. THE BAMBOO 竹 JME 113 IS LIKE A HORN 丿 AND A NAIL 丁 (ARCHAIC KANJI, NOW "D" GRADE, DIVISION OF TOWN, 120 YARDS 丁 JME 473 AND IN TOWN 町 JME 115).

RAD 9   STROKE 7   JME 82

MAN,
PERSON
COMPONENT
JME 30

TO MAKE

BAMBOO
JME 113
(GROWS IN
MULTIPLES,
NOT SINGLY)

HORN

NAIL
OR
SPIKE

BAMBOO
(SINGLE AS
COMPONENT)
BAMBOO
HAS USES
& IS LIKE
HORN & NAIL

BAMBOO
MOVED
IN THE
MAKING
OF
THINGS

MOVEMENT
IN MAKING
WITH THE
BAMBOO
(SINGLE &
COMPONENT)

JME	STROKE	RAD
83	6	120

SHI; ITO, THREAD.

THREAD 糸 IS A PICTOGRAPH OF TWO SILKWORM COCOONS 8 WITH A LITTLE 小 THREAD UNWINDING BELOW. THE THREADS ARE UNWOUND FROM THE COCOONS AND TWISTED FOR STRENGTH AND USE. IN CLOUD 雲 JME 47 THE COMPONENT FOR COCOON WAS DESCRIBED AS SOMETHING GENERICALLY COILED OR LAYERED LIKE A PINE CONE OR A MOUTH SPEAKING. IT ALSO HAS THE MEANING OF PRIVATE OR SECRET WHICH APPLIES VERY WELL TO THE WRAPPED COCOON.

END VIEWS LESS THAN LIFE OF TWO SILK- WORM COCOONS

KANJI RE- PRESENTA- TION OF TWO SILK- WORM COCOONS

THREAD.... COCOONS ABOVE & LITTLE THREAD BELOW

LITTLE THREAD

SUPERIMPOSITION OF COCOONS AND UNWINDING THREAD ON KANJI FOR THREAD

JME	STROKE	RAD
84	9	61

SHI; OMOU, TO THINK, TO RECALL.

TO THINK, TO RECALL 思 IS A COMPOSITE OF FIELD 田 JME 40 AND HEART, MIND 心 JME 95. MIND, HEART 心 WAS ORIGINALLY A PICTOGRAPH SHOWING THE AURICLES AND VENTRICLES OF THE HEART. THE HEART, MIND 心 THINK OF, RECALL 思, THE FIELD 田 (ONE'S OLD COUNTRY HOME, THE FIELD ONE OWNS, ETC.) EVEN CITY PEOPLE OWNED FARMS IN CHINA AND JAPAN. LAND WAS REGARDED AS THE BEST INVESTMENT.

ANATOMICAL FRONT VIEW OF HEART

SUPER- IMPOSITION ON RIGHT AND LEFT AURICLES & VENTRICLES

SUPER- IMPOSITION ON AURICLES & VENTRICLES OF THE HEART IN OLD KANJI

OLD KANJI FOR HEART

TO THINK, TO RECALL JME 84

RICE FIELD JME 40

SHI; KAMI, (GAMI), PAPER.

RAD	STROKE	JME
120	10	85

PAPER 紙 IS A COMPOSITE OF THREAD 糸 (SILK)
JME 83 AND FAMILY, CLAN 氏 JME 620. FAMILY,
CLAN 氏 ORIGINATES FROM A KANJI FOR THE
FLOATING PATTERN OF A WATER PLANT WITH MANY
BRANCHES AND PARTS WHICH THUS RESEMBLES THE
FAMILY TREE OF A GREAT PATRIARCHAL FAMILY OR
CLAN 氏 . TO MAKE PAPER 紙 THE PARTICLES OF
WASTE SILK MADE OF THREADS 糸 ARE PLACED IN
A SOLUTION. AT THIS STAGE THEY RESEMBLE THE
BRANCHED WATER PLANT LIKE A GREAT CLAN WITH ITS MANY PARTS
AND PARTICLES (INDIVIDUAL MEMBERS). ORIGINALLY SILK WAS
USED FOR WRITING. SILK THREADS 糸 SPREAD IN THE WARP AND
WOOF OF THE SILK MATERIAL LIKE THE RAMIFICATIONS OF THE
CLAN RELATIONSHIP LINES IN A GENEALOGICAL CHART.

OLD MEANING
OF THIS KANJI
WAS SILK

REPRESENTS A
FLOATING WATER
PLANT SPREAD OUT
ON THE SURFACE OF
THE WATER

THREAD
JME 83

PAPER
JME 85

FAMILY,
CLAN
JME 620

JI, IDEOGRAPH, WORD, LETTER;
AZA, (VILLAGE) SECTION.

RAD	STROKE	JME
40	6	86

IDEOGRAPH, WORD, LETTER 字 IS A COMPOSITE
OF ROOF 宀 (JME 53 HAS ANOTHER EXAMPLE) AND
CHILD 子 JME 31. WITH THOUSANDS OF KANJI
TO LEARN, THE ORIENTAL CHILD 子 UNDER THE
ROOF 宀 (NOT OUT WORKING OR PLAYING) IS
NATURALLY STUDYING IDEOGRAPHS, WORDS,
LETTERS 字. JI, IDEOGRAPH 字 IS THE LAST
PART OF THE COMPOUND WORD KAN-JI. KAN IS
JAPANESE FOR HAN (HAN DYNASTY) AND KAN-JI MEANS HAN OR KAN
IDEOGRAPHS.

DIVIDER AT
TOP DIRECTS
FLOW OF RAIN
WATER. TILES
ARE AT THE
ENDS.

SUPERIMPOSED

CHILD
JME 31

IDEOGRAPH,
WORD, LETTER
JME 86
ROOF OVER
CHILD

ROOF.....
AS IN HOUSE,
HOME JME 53

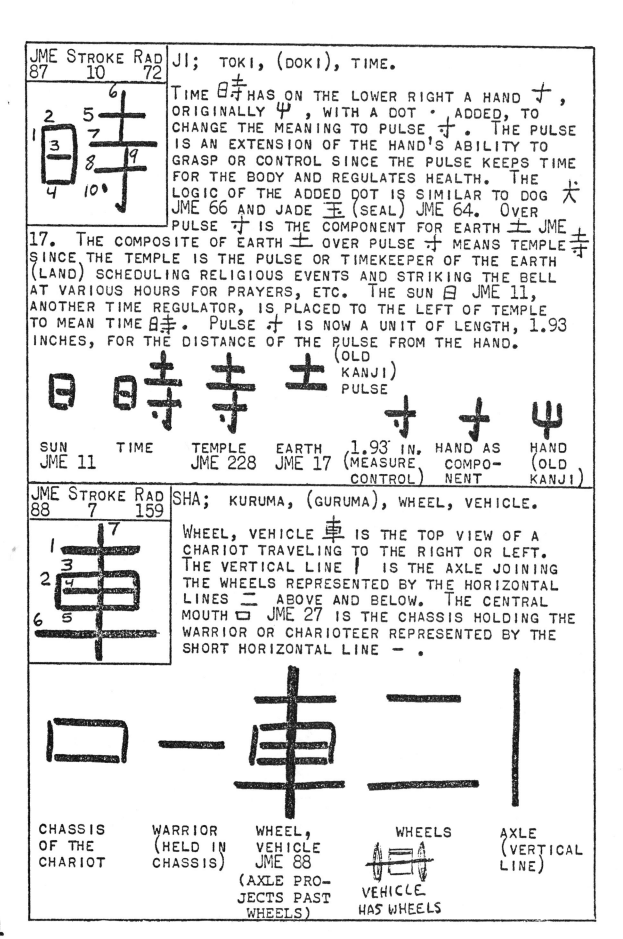

JME 87	STROKE 10	RAD 72

JI; TOKI, (DOKI), TIME.

TIME 時 HAS ON THE LOWER RIGHT A HAND 寸, ORIGINALLY ᕙ, WITH A DOT · ADDED, TO CHANGE THE MEANING TO PULSE 寸. THE PULSE IS AN EXTENSION OF THE HAND'S ABILITY TO GRASP OR CONTROL SINCE THE PULSE KEEPS TIME FOR THE BODY AND REGULATES HEALTH. THE LOGIC OF THE ADDED DOT IS SIMILAR TO DOG 犬 JME 66 AND JADE 玉 (SEAL) JME 64. OVER PULSE 寸 IS THE COMPONENT FOR EARTH 土 JME 17. THE COMPOSITE OF EARTH 土 OVER PULSE 寸 MEANS TEMPLE 寺 SINCE THE TEMPLE IS THE PULSE OR TIMEKEEPER OF THE EARTH (LAND) SCHEDULING RELIGIOUS EVENTS AND STRIKING THE BELL AT VARIOUS HOURS FOR PRAYERS, ETC. THE SUN 日 JME 11, ANOTHER TIME REGULATOR, IS PLACED TO THE LEFT OF TEMPLE TO MEAN TIME 時. PULSE 寸 IS NOW A UNIT OF LENGTH, 1.93 INCHES, FOR THE DISTANCE OF THE PULSE FROM THE HAND.

SUN JME 11	TIME	TEMPLE JME 228	EARTH JME 17	1.93 IN. (MEASURE CONTROL)	HAND AS COMPONENT	HAND (OLD KANJI)

(OLD KANJI) PULSE

JME 88	STROKE 7	RAD 159

SHA; KURUMA, (GURUMA), WHEEL, VEHICLE.

WHEEL, VEHICLE 車 IS THE TOP VIEW OF A CHARIOT TRAVELING TO THE RIGHT OR LEFT. THE VERTICAL LINE | IS THE AXLE JOINING THE WHEELS REPRESENTED BY THE HORIZONTAL LINES ニ ABOVE AND BELOW. THE CENTRAL MOUTH 口 JME 27 IS THE CHASSIS HOLDING THE WARRIOR OR CHARIOTEER REPRESENTED BY THE SHORT HORIZONTAL LINE ー.

CHASSIS OF THE CHARIOT	WARRIOR (HELD IN CHASSIS)	WHEEL, VEHICLE JME 88 (AXLE PROJECTS PAST WHEELS)	WHEELS VEHICLE HAS WHEELS	AXLE (VERTICAL LINE)

SHŪ; AKI, FALL, AUTUMN.

FALL, AUTUMN 秋 IS A COMPOSITE OF A STALK OF RIPE RICE 禾 ON THE LEFT AND FIRE 火 JME 13 ON THE RIGHT. IN RICE. 禾 , THE OBLIQUE LINE AT THE TOP ノ IS THE HEAVY GRAIN FILLED HEAD. THE VERTICAL LINE | IS THE STEM. THE LATERAL SHOOTS ARE THE HORIZONTAL LINE 一 . THE SLANTING LOWER LINES 八 ARE THE ROOTS. IN FALL, AUTUMN 秋 THE RICE 禾 IS RIPENED BY THE FIERY 火 HEAT.

TREE, WOOD JME 15 NOTE SIMILARITY TO RICE EXCEPT FOR HEAD

RICE AS RIPENED IN THE PADDY (FIELD)

FALL, AUTUMN JME 89 RICE ON LEFT IS RIPENED BY FIERY HEAT

FIRE JME 13

PICTURE

SHUTSU, SUI; DERU, TO COME OUT, TO EMERGE; DASU, TO PUT OUT, TO TAKE OUT, TO PULL OUT.

TO COME OUT, TO EMERGE, TO PUT OUT, TO TAKE OUT, TO PULL OUT 出 IS A COMPOSITE OF A VERTICAL LINE FOR MOVEMENT UP | AND A DOUBLING 凵 OF THE SYMBOL FOR OPEN VESSEL OR RECEPTACLE 凵 . THUS SOMETHING IS COMING OUT, EMERGING, BEING PUT OUT, TAKEN OUT, OR PULLED OUT 出 OF THE VESSELS OR RECEPTACLES WHICH ARE SHOWN DOUBLE 凵 .

OPEN VESSEL, RECEPTACLE

TWO OPEN VESSELS OR RECEPTACLES ONE OVER THE OTHER

TO COME OUT, TO EMERGE, TO PUT OUT, TO TAKE OUT, TO PULL OUT JME 90

VERTICAL LINE WHICH HERE SHOWS THE DIRECTION (UP) BY WHICH SOMETHING COMES OUT, IS PUT OUT

JME 91	Stroke 9	Rad 72

SHUN; HARU, SPRING.

IN SPRING 春 THE THICK FOLIAGE OF THE NEW SHOOTS 丰 IS STIMULATED AND PENETRATED BY THE SPREADING 人 RAYS OF THE SUN 日. NOTE THE SIMILARITY TO BLUE, GREEN 青 JME 36.

SPRING 春 IS ALSO INTERPRETED EROTICALLY. THE MATING TIME IS RELATED TO SPRING 春. THE PUBIC HAIR 丰 AND SPREAD LEGS 人 ARE ABOVE THE FEMALE APERTURE 口 WHICH IS OCCUPIED OR FILLED BY A SHORT HORIZONTAL LINE ―. NOTE THE ANALOGY TO THE CHARIOT CHASSIS 口 OCCUPIED BY THE WARRIOR ― IN WHEEL, VEHICLE 車 JME 88.

FOLIAGE   PUBIC HAIR

SUN RAYS SPREADING   SPREAD LEGS

SUN   APERTURE & INSERT

SPRING JME 91

SPREADING LEGS OR SUN RAYS

PUBIC HAIR OR THICK FOLIAGE OF SPRING

SUN OR INSERT & APERTURE

JME 92	Stroke 10	Rad 73

SHO; KAKU, TO WRITE.

TO WRITE 書 IS A COMPOSITE OF A HAND ヨ HOLDING A VERTICAL BRUSH | WHICH MOVES ― ON A FLAT WRITING SURFACE ―. THE SUN 日 JME 11 BELOW REPRESENTS AN INK-STONE 口 WITH A DEPRESSION ― WHICH HOLDS THE INK.

BLACK 黒書

INK-STONE & DEPRESSION

INK-STONE

DEPRESSION FOR INK

TO WRITE JME 92

FLAT WRITING SURFACE

MOVE-MENT OF THE BRUSH

HAND HOLDING THE BRUSH

HAND

SHŌ; SUKOSHI, SUKUNAI, LITTLE, FEW, SCARCE.

RAD	STROKE	JME
42	4	93

LITTLE, FEW, SCARCE 少 IS A LITTLE 小 JME 24 CARRIED AS ON A SLANTED STICK ノ, BOARD OR BACK, SHOULDERS. THE SLANTED STICK SYMBOL ノ APPEARED IN TO THINK, IDEA, THOUGHT, OPINION 考 JME 74. THE CONCEPT OF A LITTLE 小 ONE NECESSARILY BEING CARRIED SEEMS THE BASIS FOR LITTLE, FEW, SCARCE 少.

小

LITTLE, SMALL JME 24

ノ

SLANTED STICK, BOARD OR BACK, SHOULDERS

少

LITTLE, FEW SCARCE JME 93

SUPERIMPOSITION

SHIKI, SHOKU; IRO, COLOR.

RAD	STROKE	JME
139	6	94

COLOR 色 IS A COMPOSITE OF A COLORFUL 色 COILED STRIKING SNAKE 巴 AND A MAN BENDING OVER ク TO CATCH IT. THE EYES ⊂⊃ EXAGGER-ATED IN SIZE ALSO REPRESENT A DOUBLED ⊂⊃ MOUTH ⊡ DESCRIPTIVE OF THE EXPANSIBLE JAWS OF THE SNAKE 巴. THE SNOUT | IS THE VERTICAL LINE BETWEEN THE EYES OR MOUTHS ⊡.

MAN BENDS OVER TO CATCH SNAKE

SNOUT BETWEEN EYES OR MOUTHS

SNAKE IN THE KANJI POSITION

COLOR JME 94

SNAKE'S COIL ABBREVIATED

JME 95	Stroke 4	Rad 61

SHIN; KOKORO, (GOKORO), HEART, MIND, SPIRIT.

HEART, MIND, SPIRIT 心 IS A SIMPLIFIED REPRESENTATION OF THE AURICLES AND OF THE VENTRICLES OF THE HEART. THE ORIENTALS IN ANCIENT TIMES THOUGHT THAT THE MIND WAS LOCATED IN THE HEART 心. THE LANGUAGE OF THE WEST, SUCH AS "MY HEART TELLS ME SO" WOULD SEEM TO CONCUR. REVIEW TO THINK, TO RECALL 思 JME 84.

RIGHT AURICLE

RIGHT VENTRICLE

LEFT AURICLE

LEFT VENTRICLE

HEART JME 95

THE CHAMBERS OF THE HEART

KANJI FOR HEART SUPERIMPOSED ON THE CHAMBERS

OLD KANJI FOR HEART

JME 96	Stroke 6	Rad 146

SEI, SAI; NISHI, WEST.

WEST 西 SHOWS A BIRD 兀 RESTING IN ITS NEST 口 (MOUTH 口 JME 27) IN THE WEST 西. THE ASSOCIATION IS PROBABLY CREATED BY BIRDS 兀 RETURNING TO THEIR NESTS IN THE EVENING WHEN THE SUN SETS IN THE WEST 西.

NEST (MOUTH JME 27)

WEST JME 96

BIRD (ALIGHTING TO REST)

SEI; KOE, (GOE), VOICE, TONE, OUTCRY, CHIRP.

VOICE, TONE, OUTCRY, CHIRP 声 IS A COMPOSITE OF SUSPENDED / MUSICAL STONES 口口 STRUCK BY THE GENTLEMAN, MAN, FIGURE 士 JME 410, OR HUNG FROM HIS BELT OR GIRDLE FOR THEIR MUSICAL TINKLING SOUND.

| RAD 128 | STROKE 7 | JME 97 |

STONE JME 44

(JOINED) (SEPARATED) THE MUSICAL STONES

GENTLEMAN, MAN, FIGURE JME 410

VOICE, TONE, CHIRP, OUTCRY (OF THE MUSICAL STONES) SUSPENDED (FROM THE MAN'S BELT)

VOICE, TONE, OUTCRY, CHIRP SUSPENDED JME 97

MUSICAL STONES

SEKI; YŪ, EVENING.

EVENING 夕 IS THE CRESCENT MOON 月 JME 12 WITH THE LOWER PORTION CONCEALED BELOW THE HORIZON. REVIEW OUTSIDE, OTHER, FOREIGN 外 JME 56.

| RAD 36 | STROKE 3 | JME 98 |

MOON, MONTH JME 12

EVENING SUPERIMPOSED ON MOON, MONTH

EVENING JME 98

JME	STROKE	RAD
99	4	18

SETSU, SAI; KIRU, TO CUT.

TO CUT 切 IS A COMPOSITE OF SWORD 刀 JME 289 ON THE RIGHT AND SEVEN 七 (PIECES) ON THE LEFT. THE SEVEN 七 IMPLIES THE FIERCE, UNPLANNED CUTTING 切 WITH THE SWORD. THIS IS NOT THE CAREFUL BUTCHERING OF AN ANIMAL INTO TWO HALVES OR FOUR QUARTERS, ETC.

180 degree turn

EUROPEAN SEVEN GIVEN A 180 DEGREE TURN BECOMES SIMILAR TO THE KANJI SEVEN

SEVEN JME 7

TO CUT JME 99

SWORD JME 289

HAND, SWORD & MOVEMENT

SWASTIKA POWER

BLADE ANALOGY

SWORD AS A COMPONENT

JME	STROKE	RAD
100	11	173

SETSU; YUKI, SNOW.

SNOW 雪 IS A COMPOSITE OF RAIN 雨 JME 42 AND A HAND, BROOM, OR BRUSH 彐 WHICH CAN TAKE UP OR SWEEP AWAY THE SNOW 雪. SNOW 雪 IS LIKE CLOUD 雲 JME 47, BUT WITH HAND, BROOM, OR BRUSH 彐 SUBSTITUTED FOR THE CLOUD-PUFFING 云 MOUTH 厶.

OLD KANJI FOR HAND

THE HAND WHICH BRUSHES AWAY THE SNOW

SNOW JME 100

RAIN JME 42

CLOUD JME 47

90° TURN

HAND EVOLVED FROM OLD KANJI

THUMB AND OPPOSING INDEX FINGER ARE MOST IMPORTANT: SO TRIDENT RESULTS

SUMMER is
shaded head
& fan in hand

Japanese kanji
Chinesecharacters

ME   目
#25

MIMI

SEN, (ZEN); CHI, THOUSAND.

RAD	STROKE	JME
24	3	101

THOUSAND 千 IS REPRESENTED BY THE OFFICER WITH THE HORNED ╱ CREST WHO COMMANDS TEN ╋ HUNDREDS OR A THOUSAND 千 MEN. CENTRAL ASIAN ARMIES USED THE DECIMAL SYSTEM. THE MILLENION OVER A THOUSAND MEN COMMANDED TEN ╋ HORNS (BUGLES) ╱ OR CENTURIONS.

CENTURION (TUC)   HUNDRED JME 130   THOUSAND   MILLENION (TOMAN)

HORN   HEAD
        FORE-LEG
        BODY
HIND LEG
        TAIL

CATTLE, COW BULL, OX JME 62 (NOTE HORN(S) AS COMPONENT

HORNED HELMETED MILLENION TOMAN IN CENTRAL ASIA)

HORN(S) WORN ON HELMETS FROM SHIKOKU TO SCANDINAVIA (SHAPE IS FOR RIGHT HORN AND POSITION IS FOR LEFT HORN).

THOUSAND JME 101

TEN JME 10

ZEN; MAE, BEFORE, PREVIOUS, IN FRONT OF.

RAD	STROKE	JME
18	9	102

BEFORE, PREVIOUS, IN FRONT OF 前 IS A COMPOSITE OF THE HORNS 丷 OF A RAM 羊 WHICH ARE BEFORE, PREVIOUS TO, OR IN FRONT OF THE RAM 羊 ; OF THE SWORD 刂 JME 289 (IN THE COMPONENT FORM) WHICH IS BEFORE, PREVIOUS TO, OR IN FRONT OF 前 THE MAN FIGHTING; AND THE MOON 月 JME 12 WHICH IS BEFORE, PREVIOUS TO, OR IN FRONT 前 AS WE VIEW IT OR TRAVEL TOWARDS IT.

HORNS
HEAD
    FORELEGS
BODY
    HINDLEGS
    TAIL

RAM, SHEEP, EWE, LAMB

HEAD & HORNS OF A RAM AS A COMPONENT

MOON JME 12

BEFORE, PREVIOUS IN FRONT OF (AS A PICTURE)

SWORD JME 289

SWORD AS A COMPONENT

JME	STROKE	RAD
103	11	120

SO; KUMI, (GUMI), CLASS, GROUP, GANG, SET; KUMU, TO CONSTRUCT, TO UNITE WITH, TO ASSOCIATE.

CLASS, GROUP, GANG, SET (AS OF DISHES), TO CONSTRUCT, TO UNITE WITH, TO ASSOCIATE 組 IS A COMPOSITE OF THREAD, STRING 糸 JME 83 (USED TO UNITE AS IN TIEING) AND 且 ONCE MEANING A STAND 且 USED IN ANCESTOR, GRANDFATHER 祖 WORSHIP BY THE CLASSES (OF GENERATIONS), GROUP, "GANG", SET 組.

TO CONSTRUCT 組 IS ASSEMBLING, PUTTING TOGETHER 組 MATERIALS AND IS ANALOGOUS TO THE ASSOCIATION OF OF PEOPLE. THE RESEMBLANCE OF 且 TO EYE 目 MAKES IT EASY TO CONSIDER 且 AS THE ANCESTRAL 祖 EYE 目 . 且 NOW MEANS MOREOVER 且.

| GRANDCHILD JME 458 (NOTE THE STRING JME 83) | THREAD, STRING JME 83 | CLASS, GROUP, TO ASSOCIATE (STRUNG AS BY ANCESTRY) | GRAND-FATHER, ANCESTOR | ARCHAIC STAND. NOW IS BESIDES, MOREOVER. | EYE (HEAD, SKULL) |

JME	STROKE	RAD
104	6	72

SŌ; HAYA, HAYAI, QUICK, FAST, EARLY.

QUICK, EARLY, FAST 早 IS A COMPOSITE OF TEN 十 SUNS 日 MEANING WHAT HAPPENS (AS AGRICULTURALLY) IN TEN 十 SUNS 日 (DAYS).

THE RELATED KANJI GRASS, VEGETATION 草 JME 106 SUPPORTS THIS INTERPRETATION.

QUICK, FAST, EARLY JME 104

SUN

TEN

LIKE A TREE OR DRYAD, GRASS, VEGETATION RESEMBLES A HUMAN BEING SCARECROW JME 106

SŌ; HASHIRU, TO RUN.

TO RUN 走 IS A COMPOSITE OF FOOT, LEG 足 JME 29 WITH THE EARTH 土 JME 17 ACROSS WHICH ONE RUNS 走 SUBSTITUTED FOR THE PELVIS 口 (MOUTH 口 JME 27).

Rad	Stroke	JME
156	7	105

BONES OF PELVIS, LEG & FOOT

FOOT, LEG JME 29

TO RUN JME 105

SUBSTITUTION OF EARTH FOR PELVIS (MOUTH)

EARTH

FOOT, LEG AS A COMPONENT

SŌ; KUSA, (GUSA), GRASS, VEGETATION.

GRASS, VEGETATION 草 IS A COMPOSITE OF THE COMPONENT GRASS 十 DOUBLED 艹 , AND QUICK, FAST, EARLY 早 JME 104.

GRASS, VEGETATION 草 IS THE GRASS 艹 WHICH COMES UP QUICK, FAST, EARLY 早 JME 104 IN TEN 十 DAYS 日 (SUNS 日 JME 11).

Rad	Stroke	JME
140	9	106

QUICK, FAST EARLY JME 104

GRASS DOUBLED

GRASS SINGLE

PHYTOMORPH DRYAD SCARECROW

SUN, (DAY) JME 11

TEN JME 10

GRASS, VEGETATION JME 106

AFTER TEN SUNS SINK BELOW THE HORIZON GRASS GROWS THERE

JME 107	Stroke 7	Rad 75

SON; MURA, VILLAGE.

THE VILLAGE 村 IS A COMPOSITE OF TREES 木 AND PULSE 寸 ANALYZED IN TIME 日寺 JME 87. THE VILLAGE 村 IS WHERE THE PULSE 寸, THE ACTIVITY AND POLITICAL CONTROL EXIST FOR THE SURROUNDING COUNTRYSIDE. THE VILLAGE 村 ALSO HAS LARGE TREES 木 PARTICULARLY IN SUCH PLACES OF ACTIVITY AND POLITICAL CONTROL AS THE TEMPLE AND THE LOCAL COURT. THE SURROUNDING AGRICULTURAL LAND CANNOT BE WASTED ON TREES. BESIDES, THEIR SHADE AND ROOTS INTERFERE WITH CROPS.

TREE,WOOD
JME 15

VILLAGE
JME 107

ARCHAIC..
PULSE
(PRESENTLY
1.97 INCHES)

TEMPLE
JME 228

TIME
JME 87

JME 108	Stroke 6	Rad 36

TA; ŌI, MUCH, MANY, PLENTIFUL.

MUCH, MANY, PLENTIFUL 多 IS REPRESENTED BY EVENING 夕 DUPLICATED 夕夕 FOR MANY 多 JME 108 THE EVENINGS 夕 JME 98 OF ONE'S LIFE ARE MUCH, MANY, PLENTIFUL 多

MUCH,MANY
PLENTIFUL

EVENING
JME 98

OUTSIDE,OTHER
FOREIGN JME 56

MOON,MONTH
JME 12

DAN, NAN; OTOKO, MAN, MALE.

RAD	STROKE	JME
102	7	109

THE MAN, MALE 男 IS THE STRENGTH 力 JME 148 OF THE RICE FIELD 田 JME 40 FROM AN AGRICULTURAL STANDPOINT. STRENGTH 力 MAY BE VISUALIZED AS THE SET AND STRAINING LEGS OF A MAN 男 CARRYING THE RICE FIELD 田. STRENGTH IS ALSO A QUARTER OR QUADRANT OF THE SWASTIKA 卐 WHICH IS THE EMBODIMENT OF THE JUGGERNAUT OF ROLLING CRUSHING STRENGTH 力 JME 148.

RICE FIELD   SWASTIKA   STRENGTH   MAN,MALE MAN'S STRENGTH CARRIES FIELD

TO THINK   SUPERIMPOSITION NEW SHOES

CHI; IKE, POND, POOL.

RAD	STROKE	JME
85	6	110

POND, POOL 池 IS A COMPOSITE OF WATER 氵 JME 14 (AS A COMPONENT) AND SNAKE 也 IN A SLIGHTLY DIFFERENT FORM THAN WHEN WE HAD SNAKE 巴 AS A COMPONENT IN COLOR 色 JME 94. PONDS, POOLS 氵也 IN THE ORIENT HAVE THE IRIDESCENT COLOR 色 JME 94 OF A SNAKE 也 DUE TO PLANKTON AND IMPURITIES. CERTAIN SNAKES HAVE AFFINITY FOR PONDS, POOLS. THEIR SNOUTS ARE HIGH FOR BREATHING, LOWER JAWS INVISIBLE IN THE POND, POOL.

SNOUT
EYE EYE
MOUTHS
NO LOWER
JAW.
COILED

WATER AS A COMPONENT

POND,POOL SNOUT HIGH AS SNAKE BREATHES. LOWER JAW IS INVISIBLE IN THE WATER.

SNAKE AS A COMPONENT IN POND SNOUT HIGH. CAN'T SEE LOWER JAW.

SNAKE AS A COMPONENT IN COLOR. TROPICAL SNAKE MAY BE IN TREE.

COLOR JME 94

JME 111	Stroke 6	Rad 32

CHI, JI, EARTH, GROUND.

EARTH, GROUND 地 IS A COMPOSITE OF EARTH, SOIL 土 JME 17 AND THE COMPONENT SNAKE 也 AS IN POND, POOL 池 JME 110. THE SNAKE IS CLOSE TO THE SOIL 土 JME 17 OF THE GROUND 地, HIS LOWER JAW HIDDEN 也 AND HIS SNOUT RAISED "⼁" FOR BETTER VISION. THE SNAKE IS CLOSE TO THE EARTH AND THEREFORE SUITABLE FOR THIS KANJI. GENESIS SAYS, "ON THY BELLY SHALT THOU CRAWL...."

"THEY SHALL LICK THE DUST LIKE A SERPENT." MICAH

SNOUT, EYE EYE MOU-THS
SNAKE HEAD (COMPONENT IN COLOR 色)

RAISED SNOUT
EYE EYE MOU-THS
LOWER JAW MISSING (SNAKE COMPONENT IN EARTH 也)

土 EARTH, SOIL JME 17

地 EARTH, GROUND JME 111

也 SNAKE COMPONENT

池 POND, POOL JME 110

色 COLOR JME 94

JME 112	Stroke 8	Rad 111

CHI; SHIRU, TO KNOW; SHIRASERU, TO INFORM, TO TELL.

THE TARGET 口 (MOUTH 口 JME 27) WITH THE ARROW(S) 矢 KNOWS, INFORMS, TELLS 知 JME 112 THE RESULT OF THE SHOOTING. THE LEFT COMPONENT ARROW 矢 IS A PICTOGRAPH. THE POINT ⼁ IS LIKE THE HORN ⼁ OF CATTLE, COW, BULL, OX 牛 JME 62 WRITTEN AS AN OBLIQUE UPPER LEFT STROKE. THE GUIDING FEATHERS ARE THE TWO HORIZONTAL STROKES 二 BENT DOWN 矢. THE BODY ⼁ OF THE ARROW 矢 IS THE VERTICAL STROKE. THE NOTCH AND TAIL FEATHERS ARE THE BOTTOM TWO DIAGONAL STROKES 人. NOTE THE RELATIONSHIP OF TO KNOW, TO INFORM, TO TELL 知 TO MIDDLE, INSIDE, WITHIN, AMONG 中 JME 23 WHERE THE ARROW 矢 IS A VERTICAL LINE ⼁.

POINT IS HORN
GUIDING FEATHERS
SHAFT
NOCK:
TAIL FEATHERS
NOCK

PICTURE OF THE ARROW

矢 ARROW IN KANJI

知 TO KNOW, TO INFORM, TELL

口 TARGET (MOUTH JME 27)

中 MIDDLE, IN-SIDE JME 23

CHIKU; TAKE, (DAKE), BAMBOO.

BAMBOO 竹 SHOWS TWO CLUSTERS OF BAMBOO
LEAVES TO LEFT ⺮ AND TO RIGHT ⺮ . THE
BAMBOO HAS A CHARACTERISTIC LEAF PATTERN
PAINTED AS A CLUSTER OF THREE STROKES, ONE
FOR EACH OF THREE LEAVES.

Rad	Stroke	JME
118	6	113

Also note pattern in <u>Nandina</u>
<u>domestica</u>, Heavenly Bamboo.

STEREOTYPE
BAMBOO LEAF
PATTERN

BAMBOO

HORN   BAMBOO   NAIL
(SINGLE (ARCHAIC
CLUSTER) MEANING)

AN ALTERNATIVE EXPLANA-
TION IS THAT THE BAMBOO
COMBINES THE CHARACTER-
ISTICS AND PURPOSES OF
HORN AND NAIL

BAMBOO IS PAIRED BECAUSE THEY
ARE NEVER ALONE, BUT ALWAYS IN
CLUMPS OR GROUPS OR GROVES.
THEY ARE REGARDED AS TREES.

CHŪ; MUSHI, INSECT, WORM, BUG.

Rad	Stroke	JME
142	6	114

INSECT, WORM, BUG 虫 IS A COMPOSITE WITH THE
SAME EYE-MOUTH 田 COMPLEX AS IN THE SNAKE 巴
COMPONENT IN COLOR INCLUDING A VERTICAL LINE
PROBOSCIS ┃ WHICH IS EXTENDED DOWNWARDS FOR
THE BODY ┃ AND TWO BOTTOM STROKES FOR THE
FOOT-FEET ⼅ WHICH IS THE MIRROR IMAGE OF
THE FOOT COMPONENT ⼂ IN FOOT, LEG, PAW 足
JME 29. LIKE THE SNAKE 巴 , THE INSECT OR
BUG 虫 IS OFTEN IRIDESCENT. AWARENESS OF
THIS MAY BE SEEN IN THE KANJI FOR RAINBOW 虹 A COMPOSITE OF
INSECT, BUG 虫 ON THE LEFT AND WORKER, ENGINEERING,
CONSTRUCTION 工 TO THE RIGHT. THE EYE-MOUTH 田 COMPLEX
SHOWS BUG-EYEDNESS AND VORACIOUSNESS.

COLOR
JME 94

RAINBOW

FOOT,LEG
PAW
JME 229

INSECT
WORM,BUG

SUPER-
IMPOSED
INSECT

JME 115	Stroke 7	Rad 102

CHŌ; MACHI, TOWN.

TOWN 町 IS A COMPOSITE OF RICE FIELD 田 JME 40 AND STAKE, SPIKE, STUD, NAIL 丁.
THE HEAD ‾ OF THE NAIL 丁 IS AT THE TOP.
THE SHAFT Ⅰ IS THE VERTICAL LINE.
A TOWN DEVELOPS FROM THE SURVEYING OF A RICE FIELD 田 WITH STAKES 丁 TO CREATE A TOWN 町 DIVIDED INTO PLOTS FOR STORES, STREETS AND HOUSES. 町 IS ALSO USED FOR LINEAR AND SQUARE MEASURE OF LAND.

RICE FIELD IN PLOTS STAKED OUT AFTER A SURVEY

RICE FIELD PADDY JME 40

TOWN

NOW MEANS: "D" GRADE, DIVISION OF A WARD OR TOWN, 120 YARDS JME 473

JME 116	Stroke 8	Rad 168

CHŌ, HEAD (OF AN ORGANIZATION), CHIEF, DIRECTOR; NAGAI, LONG.

HEAD, CHIEF, DIRECTOR, LONG 長 IS A COMPOSITE OF THE LONG 長 STREAMING HAIR (HAIR 髟) OF THE HEAD, DIRECTOR, CHIEF 長 OF THE FAMILY, CLAN 氏 BELOW.

OR
NOTE THE VARIATIONS

PAPER JME 85

FAMILY CLAN JME 620

PEOPLE SUBJECTS JME 518

HEAD CHIEF DIRECTOR LONG

HAIR

CHŌ; TORI, (DORI), BIRD.

RAD	STROKE	JME
196	11	117

BIRD 鳥 IS A PICTOGRAPH OF A LONG TAILED
BIRD. THE LONG TAIL ⁊ SWEEPS AROUND THE
FOUR SHORT STROKES OR DOTS ⼩⼩ REPRESENTING
TWO FEET ⼋ AND TWO WINGS ⼃⼃ HOMOLOGOUS TO
THE FOUR LIMBS OF A QUADRUPED SUCH AS THE
HORSE 馬 JME 127. THE TOP OBLIQUE ⼃ LINE
IS THE BEAK ⼃. THE SUN 日 JME 11
COMPONENT IS FOR THE MOUTH 口 AND TONGUE OR
SONG 一 OF THE BIRD 鳥 OR FOR ITS EYE 一 AND
HEAD 口. THE LONG LOWER HORIZONTAL 一 LINE IS PLUMAGE.
NOTE HOW THE USE OF A SHORT OBLIQUE ⼃ LINE FOR BEAK ⼃
IN BIRD 鳥 JME 117, FOR HORN ⼃ IN CATTLE, COW, BULL, OX 牛
JME 62, AND FOR THE HEAD ⼃ OF RICE, GRAIN 禾 JME 89 IS
ANALOGOUS TO THE 'ORN IN ORNITHOLOGY, THE HORN, AND THE
'ORN IN CORN (BRITISH ENGLISH FOR WHEAT, GRAIN).

THE 'ORN ANALOGY
GRAIN　　　CATTLE
JME 89　　JME 62

BEAK
HEAD
PLUMAGE
TAIL
BIRD JME 117

HORSE 馬

BEAK
HEAD
WINGS
TAIL
LEGS
ANCIENT BIRD
SYMBOL

CHŌ; ASA, MORNING.

RAD	STROKE	JME
74	12	118

MORNING 朝 IS A COMPOSITE OF EARLY 早 JME 104
AND TEN 十 ABOVE FOR THE COMPLETENESS TEN 十
TENTHS OF THE SUN 日 JME 11 WITH THE
DISAPPEARING MOON 月 JME 12 ON THE RIGHT.
WITH THE EARLY 早 COMPLETE 十 SUN 日 OF THE
MORNING 朝, THE YANG FORCES OF THE SUN 日
COMPEL THE RETREAT OF THE YIN MOON 月 FORCES.

WAKE! For the Sun, who frighten'd into flight
The Moon before him from the Field of Night,
Drives Night along with her from Heav'n, and strikes

(Rubáiyát adapted)

YANG YIN

YANG (SUN)
AND THE
YIN (MOON)
FORCES.
SUN CHASES
MOON.

SUN, DAY
JME 11
(BELONGS
TO THE
YANG
FORCES)

TEN
JME 10
(COMPLETE,
FULL)

EARLY
JME 104

MORNING
JME 118

MOON
JME 12
(BELONGS
TO THE
FORCES OF
YIN)

IN THE EARLY MORNING, THE
YANG (SUN) FORCES IN FULL
STRENGTH COMPEL THE YIN
(MOON) FORCES TO FLEE.

JME 119	Stroke 4	Rad 1&37

TEN; AME, SKY, HEAVEN.

HEAVEN, SKY 天 IS GREAT, LARGE, BIG 大 JME 22 TOPPED BY THE HORIZONTAL LINE ー FOR HEAVEN AS IN KING 王 JME 49. "MONTANA, THE LAND OF THE BIG SKY" SHOWS THE SAME REACTION.

A MAN, PERSON 人 EXTENDS HIS ARMS ー IN THE GESTURE FOR GREATNESS 大 BENEATH THE "ETERNAL SKY."

UNLIKE EARTH 土, SKY, HEAVEN 天 HAS LEGS 八, WALKS IN THE PRECESSION OF THE EQUINOXES.

OUT-SPREAD ARMS	PERSON, MAN JME 30	BIG, LARGE, GREAT JME 22	SKY, HEAVEN JME 119	HORIZONTAL TOP LINE ABBREVIATION FOR HEAVEN (AS IN THREE JME 3)	KING JME 49 (CONNECTS HEAVEN, MANKIND, & EARTH).

JME 120	Stroke 5	Rad 15

TŌ; FUYU, WINTER.

WINTER 冬 IS A HAND 又 WITH A STICK ノ OR ALPENSTOCK AS THE PERSON WALKS 人 ON THE ICE 冫.

MAN WITH STICK WALKING ON ICE   LEGS   BODY & LEGS   BODY

STICK (AS IN HORN)

冫 ICE

BODY

LEGS

WINTER JME 120

HAND AS COMPONENT

HAND SUPER-IMPOSED

NOTE HOW THE IMPRESSIONS OF THE MAN WALKING ON THE ICE WITH THE STICK AND THE HAND HOLDING THE STICK CAN BE FUSED

TO; HIGASHI, EAST.

EAST 東 IS A COMPOSITE OF THE SUN 日 JME 11 RISING BEHIND A TREE 木 JME 15. THE EASTERN PROVINCES OF CHINA WERE HEAVILY FORESTED.

RAD	STROKE	JME
75	8	121

SUN, DAY JME 11	EAST (SUN RISING BEHIND TREE)	TREE	TREE JME 15

EAST JME 121	WEST JME 96	MIDDLE JME 23

DŌ; MICHI, ROAD, WAY, PATH.

ROAD, WAY, PATH 道 IS A COMPOSITE OF THE ELEVATED ANIMAL HORNS ⍴ FUSED ON THE RIGHT WITH THE KANJI COMPONENT FOR HEAD 首, AND ON THE LEFT THE COMPONENT 辶 MEANING TO GO FAST AND STOP SUDDENLY 辶 AND REPRESENTING A ROAD COMMENCING WITH THE DOT(S) ON THE UPPER LEFT AND WINDING ITS WAY TO THE LOWER RIGHT 辶 . THE HEAD 首 (LEADER) ELK ⍴ GOES FAST AND STOPS SUDDENLY 辶 ON THE ROAD, WAY, PATH 道 (AS DESCENDING THE CLIFF). MOST ROADS ORIGINATE AS ANIMAL TRAILS SUCH AS THE NARROW CROOKED COWPATH STREETS OF BOSTON.

RAD	STROKE	JME
162	12	122

EVOLVEMENT OF FOOT, LEG JME 29	TO GO FAST & PAUSE HAIR IS STREAMING AS MOVES	DEVELOPED FROM SYMBOL TO THE LEFT	ROAD, WAY PATH, TAO (SHAMAN LEADS)	FUSION OF ELK HORNS & HEAD	SHAMAN (SEE JME 239)

JME	STROKE	RAD
123	14	149

DOKU, (TOKU); YOMU, TO READ.

TO READ 読 IS A COMPOSITE OF WORDS 言 JME 392 (A MOUTH MAKING SOUND, VIBRATIONS) TO THE LEFT, AND A GENTLEMAN 士 JME 410 READING AT HIS DESK 兀 (COMPONENT FORM) ON THE RIGHT.

FACE OF GENTLEMAN

GENTLE-MAN JME 410

WORDS JME 392

TO READ (WORDS OF A GENTLEMAN AT HIS DESK)

GENTLE-MAN

DESK

MOUTH ☐ | | | ─

MOUTH SENDS OUT VIBRATIONS AS WORDS

GENTLEMAN AT HIS DESK

JME	STROKE	RAD
124	9	24

NAN; MINAMI, SOUTH.

SOUTH 南 IS A COMPOSITE DESCRIBING THE TROPICAL JUNGLE RAIN FORESTS TO THE SOUTH COMPLETELY 十 JME 10 (TEN TENTHS) SHIELDED 干 AS BY THE CURLING HORNS AND MASSIVE HEAD 丷 OF THE GOAT, RAM 羊 (NOTE JME 102). THE IMPLICATION IS THAT THE UNDERGROWTH WAS IMPASSIBLE LIKE A SHIELD 干 OR THE HORNS AND HEAD OF A RAM 羊 MAKING AN ENCLOSURE 冂.

TEN-TENTHS ENCLOSED

SOUTH

SHIELD

HORNS

GOAT AS COMPONENT

HORNS

GOAT, RAM (NOTE JME 102)

NYŪ; IRI, ENTERING, ATTENDANCE;
IRU, TO GO IN, TO ENTER; IRERU, TO PUT IN.

RAD	STROKE	JME
11	2	125

ENTERING, ATTENDANCE, TO GO IN, TO ENTER,
TO PUT IN 入 SHOWS A SINGLE LINE 丿 FORKING
INTO TWO LINES 八, AS WHEN ONE STREAM
GOES IN, ENTERS, IS PUT IN 入 THE LUNGS 八.
THE MAN IN ATTENDANCE 人 USED TO INHALE WITH A
SOFTLY SIBILANT SOUND. TO GO IN, TO ENTER
入 IS THE MIRROR IMAGE OF MAN, PERSON 人.
IN MAN 人 THE LONG STROKE IS TO THE LEFT 丿.
IN TO GO IN, TO ENTER 入 THE LONG STROKE IS ON THE RIGHT ╲.
THIS IS APT BECAUSE IT IS MAN, PERSON 人 THAT IS CONCERNED
WITH THE GOING IN, ENTERING, INHALING 入 OF THE AIR.

MIRROR IMAGES

MAN, PERSON JME 30	MAN, PERSON (LONG STROKE TO THE LEFT)	TO ENTER (LONG STROKE TO RIGHT)	ENTERING, ATTENDANCE, TO GO IN, TO ENTER	SUPERIMPOSITION OF GO IN AND LUNGS

NEN; TOSHI, YEAR.

RAD	STROKE	JME
51	6	126

YEAR 年 IS A FUSION OF THE ZODIAC OR THE
CALENDAR HORSE 午 JME 207 AND AN ARCHAIC
KANJI FOR TOOTH 牙. THE ZODIAC HORSE'S
TEETH 牙 TELL HIS YEAR 年 (YEARLING) OR AGE.
"DON'T LOOK A GIFT HORSE IN THE MOUTH".
THE ZODIAC HORSE 午 CURRENTLY MEANS NOON 午
JME 207 (THE HOUR OF THE HORSE: NOON HOUR).
THE CURRENT KANJI FOR HORSE IS 馬 JME 127.
THE CURRENT KANJI FOR TOOTH IS 歯 JME 414.
KEEP UP WITH THE TIMES.

(ZODIAC HORSE) NOON JME 207	YEAR JME 126	TOOTH AS COMPONENT	TOOTH EQUINE PERMANENT INCISORS APPEAR AT 2.5 TO 3 YEARS. AGE MAY BE APPRAISED IF YOU CHECK TEETH SURFACE WEAR.	HORSE JME 127 / TOOTH, TEETH JME 414

CROWN
VISIBLE TOOTH
GUM LINE
ROOTS

JME 127	Stroke 10	Rad 187

BA; UMA, HORSE.

HORSE 馬 IS A PICTOGRAPH. THE FOUR SHORT STROKES OR DOTS ⺣ ARE LEGS. THE LONG CURVED STROKE ⁊ ENCLOSING THE LEGS IS THE BODY AND TAIL. THE MANE ⧧ IS OUTSTRETCHED FLYING TO THE RIGHT AS THE HORSE 馬 GALLOPS TO THE LEFT. THE NECK IS THE VERTICAL LINE TO THE LEFT OF THE MANE | . THE HEAD IS THE HORIZONTAL LINE ABOVE ⎯ THE MANE. NOTE HOW THE LEGS ARE LIKE THE BIRD'S FEET AND WINGS ⺣ IN THE LONG TAILED BIRD 鳥 JME 117.

MONGOLIAN PONY OF ALTAI PLAINS HAS ERECT MANE (EXAGGERATED), NO FETLOCK

ARCHAIC KANJI FOR HORSE

HORSE JME 127 LEGS ARE "COMPACTED" INTO BODY

BIRD JME 117

JME 128	Stroke 7	Rad 199

BAKU; MUGI, BARLEY, WHEAT, OATS, RYE.

BARLEY, WHEAT, OATS, RYE 麦 IS A COMPOSITE. THE TOP COMPONENT IS LAYERS OF PLANT LIFE . THE LOWER COMPONENT SHOWS A HAND 又 HOLDING SICKLE OR KNIFE ⁄ TO CUT OR HARVEST THE BARLEY, WHEAT, OATS, RYE 麦 . WE HAD THE UPPER COMPONENT FOR LAYERS OF PLANT LIFE 㞢 IN SPRING 春 JME 91 AND IN BLUE, GREEN, UNRIPE, INEXPERIENCED 青 JME 36.

KNIFE, SICKLE

EXISTENCE, LIFE, TO BE BORN JME 34 GRAIN HEAD ON FOLIAGE

BLUE

SPRING JME 91

GROWING GRAIN (LAYERS OF PLANT LIFE)

BARLEY, WHEAT,

SUPER-IMPOSED

HAND & KNIFE

HAN; NAKABA, HALF.

HALF ⼲ IS THE TOP VIEW OF A HORNED ⌣
QUADRUPED = CARCASS ⼲ SPLIT INTO TWO
HALVES ⼲ BY THE VERTICAL CENTER LINE ⏐ .
THE HORNS, HEAD, BODY, LEGS, AND TAIL OF
THE CARCASS ARE READILY RECOGNIZABLE. TWO
HORNS ⌣ REMAIN FOR THE SYMMETRY OF THE
HALVES. NOTE HOW THE CONSTRUCTION OF THE
KANJI HALF ⼲ IS A COMPROMISE WITH THE HORSE,
BULL, COW'S HEAD AND EWE, SHEEP, RAM'S HORNS.

Rad	Stroke	JME
24	5	129

RAM, SHEEP, EWE
LAMB

HALF JME 129
(A QUADRUPED
CUT IN HALVES)

NOON JME 207
ZODIAC HORSE

CATTLE, COW,
BULL, OX
JME 62

HYAKU, (BYAKU), HUNDRED.

HUNDRED 百 LIKE THOUSAND ⼂ JME 101 HAS A
MILITARY ORIGIN. NOMADIC CENTRAL ASIAN
ARMIES USED A DECIMAL NOTATION. HUNDRED 百
WAS SIMPLIFIED FROM LEADER, CHIEF 酋 OR 酋
HUNDRED IS A COMPOSITE OF ONE — JME 1 FOR
A CREST LIKE A HORSE'S MANE, WHITE 白
JME 37 WHICH HAS COLLATERAL MEANINGS SUCH AS
ELDER, UNCLE, PRINCE IN SINO-JAPANESE....
PROBABLY FOR THE WHITE HAIR OF THE AGED
LEADER, AND THE MOUTH ⼝ JME 27 WHICH SPEAKS WORDS — OF
COMMAND.

Rad	Stroke	JME
106	6	130

HUNDRED
JME 130

CENTURION
FRONT

CENTURION
PROFILE

CREST

WHITE

MOUTH

WORDS

HUNDRED
JME 130

WHITE
JME 37

JME	Stroke	Rad
131	4	88

FU; CHICHI, FATHER.

FATHER 父 REPRESENTS THE HAND 又 HOLDING THE STICK 乂. FATHER IS THE DISCIPLINARIAN. "SPARE THE ROD AND SPOIL THE CHILD." ONE CAN ALSO VISUALIZE THE HULKING (FROM THE CHILD'S POINT OF VIEW) FIGURE OF THE FATHER WITH SHOULDERS ⌒, BODY, ⌄ LEGS 乂.

FATHER   STICK IN HAND   STICK   HAND   SUPER-IMPOSITION

SUPERIMPOSITION FATHER, FRONT VIEW   SUPERIMPOSITION FATHER, SIDE VIEW   FATHER

JME	Stroke	Rad
132	9	182

FŪ; KAZE, WIND.

THE WIND 風 IS THE SHELTERING WING 几 CARRYING SWARMS OF ANTENNAED OR HORNED ノ INSECTS OR BUGS 虫 (SUCH AS LOCUSTS, ETC.). THE WING 几 IS OPEN AT THE BOTTOM 几 SINCE THE INSECTS 虫 ARE RELEASED ON THE FIELDS BY THE WIND 風.

PSALMS: "...HE DID FLY UPON THE WINGS OF THE WIND..."
EXODUS: "....THE EAST WIND BROUGHT THE LOCUSTS...."

ANTENNA
EYES
MOUTH
LOCUST
BODY
LEGS

WINGED WIND CARRIES HORNED OR ANTENNAED INSECT(S)

RADIUS
ULNA
HUMERUS
DIGITS
DIGITS

BONES OF BIRD'S WING WITH INSECT LOCUST INSET

FUN, (PUN), MINUTE (OF TIME); BUN, BU, PART;
WAKARU, TO UNDERSTAND, TO COMPREHEND;
WAKERU, TO DIVIDE, TO SPLIT, TO DISTRIBUTE;
WAKARERU, TO SPLIT, PART, BRANCH OFF.

A PART, TO DIVIDE, TO DISTRIBUTE, TO SPLIT 分
IS A COMPOSITE OF EIGHT 八 JME 8 FOR EASY
DIVISION AND THE SWORD 刀 JME 99 THAT
DIVIDES, SEPARATES 分 THE PARTS 分.
  分 ALSO MEANS MINUTE 分, A PART OF THE
HOUR.

Rad	Stroke	JME
18	4	133

EIGHT, A NUMBER FOR VERY EASY DIVISION

MINUTE, PART, UNDERSTAND, COMPREHEND, DIVIDE, SPLIT (TO DIVIDE, ETC. IS TO ANALYZE & UNDERSTAND)

SWORD JME 99

BOAT, SHIP JME 266 WITH IDEAL FAMILY OR CREW OF EIGHT

TABLE SETTING FOR THE IDEAL FAMILY OF EIGHT

BUN, COMPOSITION, ESSAY, SENTENCE.

A COMPOSITION, ESSAY, SENTENCE 文 IS A
COMPOSITE OF THE SYMBOL FOR A SCHOLAR'S
BIRETTA 亠 REPRESENTING DIRECTION, CONTROL,
AUTHORITY (THE SCHOLARS, LITERATI, WERE THE
CIVIL SERVANTS) AND THE LONG-NAILED HAND 乂
OF THE SCHOLAR 亠 (LIKE A BIRD'S CLAW) WHICH
DID THE COMPOSITION, ESSAY, SENTENCE 文.
AN ORIENTAL LEGEND SUGGESTS THAT KANJI WERE
CREATED BY COPYING OR IMITATING THE PRINTS
OF BIRD CLAWS ON THE BEACH SAND. LIKE OTHER KANJI,
COMPOSITION, ESSAY, SENTENCE 文 SUGGESTS CLAW MARKS,
WRINKLES, OR CROSSING LINES. COMPOSITION, ESSAY, SENTENCE
文 CAN ALSO BE VIEWED AS THE BODY AND LEGS 乂 OF THE
FATHER 父 JME 131 WHO IS A SCHOLAR 亠.

Rad	Stroke	JME
67	4	134

SCHOLAR'S BIRETTA

SYMBOL OF DIRECTION, CONTROL

ESSAY, SENTENCE, COMPOSITION

FATHER JME 131

SUPERIMPOSITIONS

JME 135	Stroke 6	Rad 119

BEI, (AMERICA, RICE); MAI, (RICE); KOME, RICE.

RICE 米 IS A COMPOSITE OF GRAINS 丷 OF RICE 米 SPREAD ABOUT A TEN 十 JME 10 FOR COMPLETENESS, FULLNESS (TEN TENTHS). RICE WAS REGARDED AS THE COMPLETE FOOD MUCH AS EUROPE PREVIOUSLY REGARDED BREAD. SINCE AMERICA IS THE GREAT GRAIN PRODUCING COUNTRY AND THE SECOND SYLLABLE "ME" HAS NEARLY THE SAME SOUND AS THE MAI OF RICE, THIS SYMBOL WAS CHOSEN FOR AMERICA.

RICE GRAINS

(AMERICA), RICE

TEN JME 10 (INDICATES COMPLETENESS)

GRAINS OF RICE CENTERED ON TEN TO INDICATE A "COMPLETE" FOOD

JME 136	Stroke 8	Rad 77

HO, (PO), A STEP, A PACE; ARUKU, AYUMU, TO WALK, TO STEP.

A STEP, A PACE, TO WALK, TO STEP 歩 IS A COMPOSITE OF LITTLE 少 JME 93 AND TO STOP 止 JME 220. ONE WALKS, STEPS 歩 WITH LITTLE 少 STOPS 止 FOR EACH PACE, STEP 歩.
TO STOP 止 IS LEG, FOOT 足 WITH THE PELVIS 口 (MOUTH 口) OMITTED AND THE FOOT 人 COMPONENT ALTERED FOR GREATER GROUND CONTACT TO ⊥ (A SCREECHING HALT).

LEG, FOOT JME 29

TO STOP JME 220 (NOTE THE FLAT, SKID-ING HALT; PELVIS IS NO LONGER NEEDED TO RAISE LEGS)

A STEP, A PACE

LITTLE JME 93

LITTLE, SMALL JME 24

BO; HAHA, MOTHER.

MOTHER 母 IS A PAIR OF DIVIDED — NIPPLED ⸵
BREASTS 母 TURNED VERTICALLY 母 FROM THE
NATURAL POSITION 毌 FOR WRITING EASE.
NOTE THE SIMILARITY OF THE ENGLISH MAMA TO
THE LATIN MAMMA (MEANING BREAST). MAMMALS
FEED THE YOUNG AT THE MOTHER'S BREAST.
REVIEW SEA, OCEAN 海 JME 55 WHERE THE
NIPPLES ⸵ MAY BE DRAWN AS ONE STROKE |
SUGGESTING A DIFFERENT DERIVATION, OR ASSO-
CIATION.

Rad	Stroke	JME
80	5	137

OLD FORM FOR MOTHER
HORIZONTALLY PLACED
BREASTS

ARCHAIC KANJI
MAMMI-   STEATO-   MOTHER   BOAT,SHIP   SEA, OCEAN
FEROUS   PYGOUS   VERTICAL   JME 266   JME 55
                              BREASTS

HŌ, (PŌ), DIRECTION, WAY, SIDE, SQUARE;
KATA, (GATA), PERSON;
-KATA, MANNER, WAY, CARE OF (WITH ADDRESS).

DIRECTION, WAY, SIDE, SQUARE, PERSON,
MANNER, WAY, CARE OF.... 方 IS A COMPOSITE
OF THE SCHOLAR'S BIRETTA 亠 (SYMBOLIZING
CONTROL OR AUTHORITY) AND A SQUARE, BOAT,
QUADRANT 刀 OF THE SWASTIKA JUGGERNAUT 卐. TO
CONTROL 亠 THE SQUARE, BOAT 刀 GIVES SIDES,
DIRECTIONS 方 CREATES A SQUARE 方 (AS WITH EARTH'S EAST,
WEST, SOUTH, NORTH, AND CENTER OR THE BOAT'S FORE, AFT,
PORT, STARBOARD, AND AMIDSHIPS. DIRECTION 方 THUS MERGES
WITH SIDE, SQUARE 方 AND ALSO WITH THE PERSON 方 DIRECTING.

Rad	Stroke	JME
70	4	138

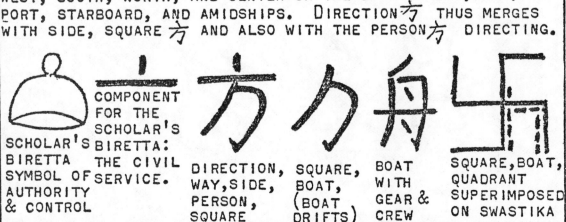

SCHOLAR'S   COMPONENT
BIRETTA   FOR THE
SYMBOL OF   SCHOLAR'S
AUTHORITY   BIRETTA:
& CONTROL   THE CIVIL
            SERVICE.   DIRECTION,   SQUARE,   BOAT   SQUARE,BOAT,
                          WAY,SIDE,   BOAT,   WITH   QUADRANT
                          PERSON,   (BOAT   GEAR &   SUPERIMPOSED
                          SQUARE   DRIFTS)   CREW   ON SWASTIKA

JME 139	Stroke 5	Rad 21

HOKU, (BOKU); KITA, NORTH.

NORTH 北 SHOWS TWO MEN OR PERSONS SITTING BACK TO BACK ON THE LEFT AND ON THE RIGHT. THEY WOULD BE MIRROR IMAGES IF IT WERE NOT FOR CONVENIENT DIRECTION AND ORDER IN STROKING SEQUENCE. THE PERSONS TO THE LEFT 土 AND TO THE RIGHT 匕 ILLUSTRATE THE ENMITY ("HE TURNED HIS BACK ON ME") AND DIFFERENCE IN MODE OF LIFE BETWEEN THE NOMAD TO THE NORTH AND THE CHINESE AGRICULTURIST, ONCE DELIBERATELY SEPARATED BY THE GREAT WALL BECAUSE OF THE TRADITIONAL ENMITY BETWEEN ABEL THE HERDSMAN AND CAIN THE FARMER (GENESIS 4). REFER TO JME 43 FOR A MAN IN A SITTING, FOETAL, OR MUMMY POSITION 匕.

MAN IN A SITTING, FOETAL OR MUMMY POSITION

FLOWER JME 43

NORTH

MEN SITTING BACK TO BACK

JME 140	Stroke 6	Rad 30

MEI, MYŌ, NAME, FAME; NA, NAME.

NAME, FAME 名 IS A COMPOSITE OF MOUTH 口 JME 27 AND EVENING 夕 JME 98. IN THE EVENING (DARKNESS), ONE'S MOUTH CALLS OUT ONE'S NAME FOR IDENTIFICATION OR AS A PASSWORD IN A MILITARY SETTING. NAME IS EQUIVALENT TO FAME. ONE'S NAME 名 IS MENTIONED AS A RESULT OF ONE'S FAME 名; ONE'S FAME RESULTS FROM THE MENTIONING OF ONE'S NAME.

MOON

MOON JME 12

EVENING JME 98

NAME, FAME

MOUTH SPEAKS OF NAME & FAME

MOUTH JME 27

MEI, MYŌ, (BRIGHT); AKARUI, LIGHT, BRIGHT;
AKIRAKA, BRIGHT, CLEAR; AKERU, TO DAWN.

BRIGHT, LIGHT, CLEAR, TO DAWN 明 IS A
COMPOSITE OF SUN 日 AND MOON 月 AS THE
BRIGHT 明 HEAVENLY BODIES WHICH MAKE BRIGHT,
CLEAR 明. WITH THE MEANING OF BRIGHT,
BRILLIANT, 明 IS THE MING 明 (1368-1644)
DYNASTY OF CHINA AND MEIJI 明 (1868-1912)
(ERA) OF JAPAN.

RAD	STROKE	JME
72	8	141

SUN,
DAY
JME 11

LIGHT,BRIGHT,CLEAR,
TO DAWN UNITES THE
SUN AND MOON, THE
SYMBOL WAS CHOSEN
FOR THE MEIJI (ERA) OF
JAPAN AND THE MING
DYNASTY OF CHINA

MOON,
MONTH
JME 12

MOON

MŌ; KE, HAIR, WOOL, FUR, FEATHERS.

HAIR, WOOL, FUR, FEATHERS 毛 IS A PICTOGRAPH
OF A FEATHER (MUCH LIKE A HAND WITH THE
FEATHER'S BARBS, ETC. AS FINGERS), BUT WITH
THE LOWER END CURVED TO SHOW IT IS ROOTED OR
CLINGING LIKE A SNAKE'S 色 TAIL 乚. HAIR,
WOOL, FUR, FEATHERS 毛 CAN ALSO BE INTER-
PRETED AS A HAND 手 CARESSING THE SINUOUS
SNAKY 色 (MEDUSA) HAIR 毛.

RAD	STROKE	JME
82	4	142

EARTH,GROUND
JME 111

COW,
BULL
JME 62

HAIR,
WOOL,
FUR,
FEATHERS

SHEEP

HAND
JME 28

HAIR,WOOL,
FUR,FEATHERS

COLOR
JME 94

(NOTE ANALOGOUS FORM OF
SNAKES' TAILS & FEATHER)

OLD SYMBOL
FOR HAND

FEATHER

JME 143	Stroke 8	Rad 169

MON, GATE; KADO, GATE.

GATE 門 IS A PICTOGRAPH OF DOUBLE DOORS 叩. REVIEW SPACE, ROOM, TIME, INTERVAL, DISTANCE 間 JME 58. THE GATE 門 MAY BE VISUALIZED AS SWINGING BAR DOORS. THE GATE COMPOSED OF DOUBLE DOORS WAS TRADITIONALLY THE ENTRANCE THROUGH THE COMPOUND WALL. THE ORIENTAL ARCHITECTURAL STYLE LIKE THE SPANISH ENCLOSED ITS LIVING AREAS AND BUILDINGS.

PICTURE OF A GATE TO SHOW MODIFICATION FOR THE KANJI

GATE (PAIRED OR DOUBLE DOORS)

SPACE, ROOM, TIME, INTERVAL, DISTANCE JME 58 (NOTE HOW GATE JME 143 IS A COMPONENT HERE)

DOOR JME 69

DOOR JME 69

JME 144	Stroke 8	Rad 36

YA; YO, YORU,

EVENING, NIGHT 夜 IS A COMPOSITE OF THE SCHOLAR'S BIRETTA 亠 (FOR SCHOLAR OR DIRECTION), A MAN 亻, EVENING 夕 (AS A SIMPLER KANJI 夕 JME 98), MOON 夕, AND A MAN, PERSON WALKING 夂. IN THE ORIENT, MOON-VIEWING WAS A CULTURAL, SOCIAL, AND EVEN RELIGIOUS AFFAIR WITH A RITUALISTIC OVERTONE. EVENING, NIGHT 夜 SHOWS THE SCHOLAR 亠 OR MAN 亻 STROLLING 夂 IN THE EVENING 夕 VIEWING THE MOON 夕.

SCHOLAR'S BIRETTA

PERSON, MAN (AS COMPONENT)

EVENING, NIGHT

MAN WALKING

MOON JME 12

EVENING JME 98

THE SCHOLAR OR MAN IS WALKING ON A MOONLIGHT EVENING
....a braw moonlicht nicht.

YŪ; TOMO, FRIEND.

FRIEND 友 IS A COMPOSITE OF CLASPED HANDS, ONE HAND TO THE LOWER RIGHT 又, AND THE OTHER TO THE UPPER LEFT ナ. THE UPPER LEFT HAND ナ WAS IN LEFT 左 JME 18 AND IN RIGHT 右 JME 19. THE LOWER RIGHT COMPONENT 又 IN FRIEND 友 IS THE HAND THAT USUALLY HOLDS SOMETHING AS IN BARLEY 麦 JME 128 AND SUMMER 夏 JME 52. THE CLASPING OF HANDS INDICATES FRIENDSHIP BETWEEN FRIENDS 友.

OLD SYMBOL FOR HAND

HAND AS A COMPONENT (THREE FINGERS CLOSED)

FRIEND

HAND AS A COMPONENT

THERE IS A SUGGESTION OF WALKING WHILE HAND IN HAND

YŌ, BUSINESS; MOCHIIRU, TO USE.

BUSINESS, TO USE 用 REPRESENTS THE GUTS OR INTESTINES ‡ IN THE ABDOMINAL CAVITY 冂. THE INTESTINES ‡ IN THE CAVITY 冂 USE 用 THE FOOD TO OUR BENEFIT. THE COMPLEXITY OF THE COILED INTESTINES IS SIMILAR TO THE COMPLEXITY OF BUSINESS 用. IN ENGLISH, WE MAY TELL A LITTLE CHILD, "DO YOUR BUSINESS," WHEN ENCOURAGING HIM TO EMPTY HIS BOWELS OR INTESTINES. WHEN FOOD IS PRESENT, THE SMALL INTESTINE MOVES AND CHURNS WITH CONTRACTIONS, RELAXATIONS.

WHEEL, VEHICLE JME 88

INTESTINES COILING & TURNING LIKE THE WHEELS OF A VEHICLE

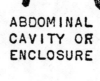

BUSINESS, TO USE

ABDOMINAL CAVITY OR ENCLOSURE

ABDOMINAL CAVITY WITH COLON AND SMALL INTESTINE

JME 147	Stroke 7	Rad 9

RAI; KURU, TO COME.

TO COME 来 IS A PICTOGRAPH SHOWING THE COMING 来 OF THE GRAIN ON A CEREAL PLANT. THE TWO SHORT OBLIQUE LINES ∨ ARE THE GRAIN AS IN THE GRAINS OR NUGGETS ∨ OF GOLD JME 金 16. THE TOP HORIZONTAL LINE ─ EMPHASIZES THE COMING 来 OF THE YIELD.

GOLD, MONEY
JME 16
(NOTE GRAINS
OR NUGGETS
OF GOLD)

RICE
JME 135

TO COME

GRAIN,
RICE (AS
IN FALL,
AUTUMN
JME 89)

K'uai k'uai mu-tze!

Cut the wheat now!

JME 148	Stroke 2	Rad 19

RIKI, RYOKU; CHIKARA, STRENGTH, POWER.

STRENGTH, POWER 力 WAS A COMPONENT IN MAN, MALE 男 JME 109. THERE, STRENGTH, POWER 力 WAS VISUALIZED AS THE LEGS 迫 OF A MAN "PUTTING HIS SHOULDER TO THE WHEEL" OR STRAINING TO MOVE SOMETHING. STRENGTH, POWER 力 IS ALSO A QUADRANT OF THE SWASTIKA 卐 WHICH IS THE EMBODIMENT OF THE JUGGERNAUT OR CRUSHING STRENGTH.

SUPERIMPOSITION

LEGS SHOW THE
FORM OF THE
KANJI STRENGTH

STRENGTH,
POWER

MAN, MALE
JME 109
(THE STRENGTH
OF THE FIELD)

RITSU; TATSU, TACHI, (DACHI), TO STAND.

TO STAND 立 IS A PERSON 大 WITH HEAD ` ,
ARMS ─ , AND LEGS \/ CLEARLY DELINEATED
STANDING 立 ON THE HORIZONTAL BASELINE ─ .
REVIEW SIX 六 JME 6 AND SOUND 音 JME 50.

Rad 117	Stroke -8	JME 149

OLD SYMBOLS FOR MAN

SIX
JME 6
AS IT MAY
DERIVE FROM
MAN

TO STAND

BASELINE
OR EARTH
(AS IN
THREE
JME 3)

RIN; HAYASHI, (BAYASHI), GROVE, WOODS.

GROVE, WOODS 林 IS A DOUBLING OF THE KANJI
FOR WOOD, TREE 木 JME 15. A KANJI MAY BE
DOUBLED TO INDICATE INCREASE IN QUANTITY
(NUMBERS) OR QUALITY (SIZE, ETC.). TREE,
WOOD 木 JME 15 WAS TRIPLED TO BECOME FOREST
森 JME 41.

Rad 75	Stroke 8	JME 150

TREE, WOOD
JME 15

GROVE, WOODS
JME 150

FOREST
JME 41

JME	STROKE	RAD
151	13	149

WA; HANASHI, (BANASHI), STORY; HANASU, TO SPEAK.

STORY, TO SPEAK 話 IS A COMPOSITE. THE LEFT COMPONENT MEANS SPEECH, WORDS, TO SAY 言 JME 392. IT HAS A MOUTH 口 BELOW AND SPEECH VIBRATIONS ≡ ABOVE. THE RIGHT COMPONENT IS TONGUE 舌 JME 827. TONGUE HAS A MOUTH 口 BELOW, A VERTICAL LINE FOR THE BODY | OF THE TONGUE, A SHORT HORIZONTAL LINE FOR THE MOVEMENT — OF THE TONGUE, AND A TOP OBLIQUE LINE FOR THE TIP ノ OF THE TONGUE (ANALOGOUS TO THE POINT ノ OF THE ARROW 矢 JME 112; THE HORN ノ OF THE BULL, COW 牛 JME 62; ETC.).

| VIBRATIONS FROM MOUTH ARE WORDS, SPEECH | SPEECH WORDS TO SAY | STORY TO SPEAK | TONGUE JME 827 | MOUTH | ANALOGY OF KANJI & TONGUE |

JME	STROKE	RAD
152	11	61

AKU, EVIL, BADNESS; WARUI, BAD, EVIL.

EVIL, BAD, BADNESS 悪 IS A COMPOSITE OF HEART, MIND, SPIRIT 心 JME 95 BELOW AND THE SYMBOL ORIGINALLY SHOWING TWO HUNCHBACKS STANDING FACING EACH OTHER 亞 . FOR EASY WRITING, THIS SYMBOL FOR TWO HUNCHBACKS IS NOW 亜 . HUNCHBACKS WERE REGARDED AS UGLY AND, BY EXTENSION, EVIL. THE HEART 心 COMPONENT BELOW EMPHASIZED THE EVIL, BAD, BADNESS 悪 OF THE MIND, SPIRIT, HEART 心 .

| HUNCHBACKS FACING EACH OTHER | (FOR EASIER AND FASTER WRITING) | EVIL BADNESS BAD, EVIL | HEART MIND SPIRIT JME 95 |

HAT
HEAD
HUMP
LEGS
FEET

AN; YASUI, INEXPENSIVE, EASY.

INEXPENSIVE, EASY 安 IS A COMPOSITE OF A
WOMAN 女 JME 32 UNDER A ROOF 宀. THE
DOMESTIC LIFE WITH A WOMAN 女 UNDER A ROOF 宀
IS SUPPOSED TO BE INEXPENSIVE, EASY 安
COMPARED TO THAT OF A SPENDTHRIFT BACHELOR.
WE HAD ROOF 宀 AS A COMPONENT IN HOUSE,
HOME 家 JME 53 AND IN IDEOGRAPH, LETTER,
WORD 字 JME 86.

Rad	Stroke	JME
40	6	153

ROOF.......
AS IN HOUSE,
HOME JME 53

INEXPENSIVE,
EASY JME 153

WOMAN, GIRL,
FEMALE JME 32

SUPERIMPOSITION

AN; KURAI, DARK.

DARK 暗 IS THE STANDING 立 OF A SUN 日 OR
HEAVENLY BODY OVER ANOTHER SUN 日 OR
HEAVENLY BODY PRODUCING DARKNESS 暗 (OR
ECLIPSE). ONE SUN 日 OR HEAVENLY BODY
STANDS 立 OVER (OR SHUTS OFF) THE SOUND 音
(OR EFFECT) OF THE OTHER HEAVENLY BODY.

Rad	Stroke	JME
72	13	154

SUN
JME 11

DARK
JME 154

SOUND
JME 50

DARK
(AS FROM AN ECLIPSE)

JME	STROKE	RAD
155	13	117

1; IDEA, MIND, WILL, MEANING.

IDEA, MIND, WILL, MEANING 意 IS REPRESENTED BY A MAN 亠 (SIX 六 JME 6) STANDING 立 JME 149 (ERECTNESS, PROBITY) MAKING SOUNDS 音 JME 50 FROM HIS HEART, MIND, SPIRIT 心 JME 95.

SOUND
JME 50

IDEA, MIND,
MEANING,
WILL

HEART, MIND,
SPIRIT
JME 95

JME	STROKE	RAD
156	4	57

IN; HIKI, (BIKI), PULLING, DRAWING; HIKU, TO PULL, TO DRAW.

TO PULL, TO DRAW, PULLING, DRAWING 引 IS A COMPOSITE OF A BOW 弓 ON THE LEFT AND THE ARROW 丨 ON THE RIGHT. THE BOW 弓 IS THE DOUBLE-ARCHED MODEL OF THE ASIAN STEPPES. BOW 弓 AND THE ARROW 丨 CONVEY THE IMPRESSION OF TO PULL, TO DRAW, PULLING, DRAWING 引.

DOUBLE CURVED
ASIAN BOW
AND ARROW

BOW

PULLING,
DRAWING,
TO PULL,
TO DRAW
JME 156

ARROW
(IN A
COMPONENT
FORM)

MIDDLE, INSIDE,
WITHIN, AMONG
JME 23
(THE ARROW
IS STRIKING
THE TARGET)

UN, LUCK; HAKOBU, TO CARRY, TO TRANSPORT.

LUCK, TO CARRY, TO TRANSPORT 運 IS A COMPOSITE OF A CANOPIED ⌐ WAGON, VEHICLE, CHARIOT 車 JME 88 TRAVELLING FROM THE DISTANCE INTO THE FOREGROUND 辶 (UPPER LEFT TO FRONT RIGHT). TO CARRY, TO TRANSPORT 運 IS LUCK 運 FOR THE PERSON INVOLVED (WHETHER IT IS HIS PACK, LUGGAGE, OR PERSON). THE MOVEMENT COMPONENT 辶 WAS PART OF ROAD, WAY, PATH 道 JME 122.

RAD	STROKE	JME
162	12	157

"AND THE CAISSONS GO ROLLING ALONG"

CANOPY

(A CAISSON IS A BOX OR CHEST FOR AMMUNITION OR A TWO-WHEELED VEHICLE FOR ARTILLERY AMMUNITION).

TO GO AND TO PAUSE, TO STOP & GO, MOVEMENT

TO TRANSPORT, TO CARRY, LUCK JME 157

CANOPIED WAGON, VEHICLE, CHARIOT (SURREY WITH A FRINGE, COVERED WAGON)

CHINESE WAR CHARIOT

CAISSONS

EKI, STATION.

STATION 駅 IS A COMPOSITE OF HORSE 馬 JME 127 ON THE LEFT AND SHAKU 尺 REPRESENTING A FOOT ON THE RIGHT. (SHAKU 尺 IS A LINEAR MEASURE EQUAL TO .995 FEET). THE STATION (ORIGINALLY A GOVERNMENT POST-STATION OR RELAY STATION WITH HORSES) WAS WHERE FRESH HORSES 馬 WAITED AT A CERTAIN DISTANCE IN SHAKU 尺 (FEET). A SHAKU IS A PICTOGRAPH OF A BODY STEPPING OUT TO MEASURE (AS IN PACES).

RAD	STROKE	JME
187	14	158

HORSE JME 127

STATION

SHAKU (.995 FEET)

BODY STEPS OUT AS FOR MEASUREMENT IN PACES

HUMAN BODY AS OF THE MERCHANT, SHOPKEEPER (SEE SHOP 屋 JME 161)

JME	STROKE	RAD
159	13	31

EN; SONO, (ZONO), GARDEN.

A GARDEN 園 IS AN ENCLOSURE 囗 WITH EARTH 土 AND GOWNED 朩 PEOPLE 袁 (THE MOUTHS OR HEADS 口 ABOVE AND THE RIPPLES OR FOLDS 朩 OF THE GOWNS BELOW. THIS FOUR-SIDED ENCLOSURE WAS A COMPONENT IN COUNTRY 国 JME 79.

EARTH, SOIL
JME 17

PICTOGRAPH
OF A
PERSON

GARDEN SCENE

ENCLOSURE   GARDEN   EARTH, SOIL
                                   & GOWNED
                                   PERSON

JME	STROKE	RAD
160	13	162

EN, ON; TŌI, FAR, DISTANT.

FAR, DISTANT 遠 IS A COMPOSITE OF THE MOVEMENT COMPONENT 辶, EARTH 土, AND A GOWNED PERSON 袁 (OR PERSONS) FAR OFF OR DISTANT 遠. NOTE THAT WITHOUT THE MOVEMENT COMPONENT 辶, FAR, DISTANT 遠 IS THE SAME AS GARDEN 園 JME 159 WITHOUT THE ENCLOSURE 囗. REMOVING THE ENCLOSURE 囗 IMPLIES A FAR, DISTANT 遠 GOWNED PERSON 袁 MOVING 辶 ON THE EARTH 土 IN A GARDEN 園 ENVIRONMENT.

MOVEMENT,   FAR, DISTANT   PERSON WITH   FAR, DISTANT SCENE
GO & STOP   EARTH, SOIL
                                 BACKGROUND

OKU; YA, SHOP.

SHOP 屋 IS A COMPOSITE OF HUMAN BODY 尸 AND
TO REACH, TO ARRIVE 至 JME 796. GOODS REACH
OR ARRIVE 至 AT THE SHOP 屋 WHERE THE HUMAN
BODY 尸 LAYS 一 (THEM HORIZONTALLY) SECRETLY
AND PRIVATELY ム (AS IN A COCOON) ON THE
SOIL OR EARTH 土 (FLOOR). THE HUMAN BODY 尸
(OF THE SHOPKEEPER) HAS A MOUTH OR HEAD 口
ABOVE A VERTICAL LINE / FOR THE BODY.
THE BODY 屋 ALSO SUGGESTS A DOOR 戸 AS FOR
THE SHOP 屋. SHOPKEEPER'S BODY 尸 STANDS IN DOOR 戸 WAY.
HE SAYS, "COME IN!"

RAD 44 STROKE 9 JME 161

DOOR JME 69

HUMAN BODY
(AS OF THE SHOPKEEPER OR CORPSE IN A COFFIN)

SUPER-IMPOSITION
(DOOR HAS PINS IN SOCKETS, NOT HINGES)

SHOP

TO REACH, ARRIVE JME 796

CORPSE IN THE COFFIN (SUPER-IMPOSED)

ON, (WARM).

WARM 温 IS A COMPOSITE OF THE SUN 日
WARMING 温 WATER ⺡ IN A DISH 皿. THE TWO
VERTICAL LINES IN THE CENTRAL PART OF THE
DISH 皿 INDICATE A TROUGH OR CONCAVITY ‖
FOR HOLDING WATER ⺡ ETC.

RAD 85 STROKE 12 JME 162

WATER (COMPONENT)

WARM

SUN OVER DISH

PICTURE OF SUN WARMING WATER IN A DISH

JME	STROKE	RAD
163	4	21

KA, KE; BAKERU, TO ASSUME THE FORM OF, TO CHANGE INTO, TO CHANGE, TO BE TRANSFORMED; BAKASU, TO BEWITCH.

TO ASSUME THE FORM OF, TO CHANGE INTO, TO CHANGE, TO BEWITCH 化 SHOWS THE CHANGE IN POSITION OR FORM OF A MAN. THE LEFT COMPONENT イ SHOWS THE MAN STANDING; THE RIGHT COMPONENT ヒ SHOWS THE MAN SITTING, PERHAPS IN A MUMMY-LIKE FOETAL (DECEASED) POSITION, THE RESULT OF BEWITCHMENT ヒ.

TO ASSUME THE FORM OF, TO CHANGE INTO 化 WAS A COMPONENT IN FLOWER 花 JME 43 AND WAS DISCUSSED THERE.

THE STANDING MAN CHANGES, ASSUMES THE FORM OF A SITTING MAN

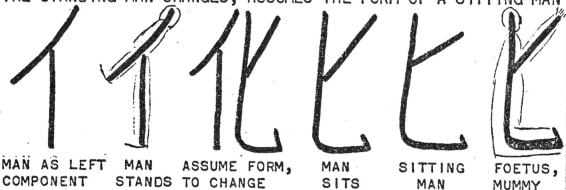

| MAN AS LEFT COMPONENT | MAN STANDS | ASSUME FORM, TO CHANGE | MAN SITS | SITTING MAN | FOETUS, MUMMY |

JME	STROKE	RAD
164	9	115

KA, COURSE, BRANCH (AS OF STUDY, KNOWLEDGE).

COURSES, BRANCHES 科 (OF KNOWLEDGE) RANGE FROM RICE 禾 (GROWING) TO THE GREAT DIPPER 斗 (ASTRONOMY). THE RICE 禾 AS THE LEFT COMPONENT IS THE GROWING PLANT. THE GREAT DIPPER IS REPRESENTED BY SEVEN STARS 斗. THE CROSS 十 HAS FIVE STARS AT ITS ENDS AND CENTER; THE TWO DOTS OR SHORT STROKES ARE THE REMAINING TWO STARS ⸚. THE GREAT DIPPER COMPONENT ALSO IS A MEASURING DEVICE FOR GRAIN OF STANDARD SIZE. THUS COURSE, BRANCH 科 ALSO IMPLIES THAT COURSES, BRANCHES 科 OF STUDY WILL EVENTUALLY MEASURE OUT 斗 GRAIN 禾 (TO THE STUDENT).

FROM AGRONOMY TO ASTRONOMY

| GRAIN, RICE (AS IN FALL, AUTUMN JME 89) | COURSE, BRANCH | TO MEASURE (19.04 QTS.) | SEVEN STARS (CONNECTED) | THE DIPPER |

KA; NI, LOAD, BURDEN.

LOAD, BURDEN 荷 IS REPRESENTED BY A MAN 亻
WHOSE MOUTH 口 IS EXCLAIMING 丁 IN THE
CUSTOMARY CADENCE (UNDER A LOAD OF
GRASS 艹 (STRAW). REVIEW WHAT, HOW MANY 何
JME 51. ORIENTAL FARMERS, PORTERS, ETC.
CHANTED WHILE CARRYING LOADS.

RAD	STROKE	JME
140	10	165

LOAD,
BURDEN

亻
MAN AS
LEFT
COMPONENT

荷
LOAD,
BURDEN

可
MOUTH
EXCLAIMING
IN CADENCE

艹
GRASS
(STRAW,
HAY AS A
LOAD)

KA; UTA, SONG; UTAU, TO SING.

SONG, TO SING 歌 IS A COMPOSITE OF A MOUTH 口
EXCLAIMING 丁 IN CADENCE DOUBLED 哥 (REVIEW
LOAD, BURDEN 荷 JME 165), AND A MAN, PERSON
INHALING INTO A COVER 欠 (LUNGS). THUS THE
MAN 人 INHALES INTO THE COVER, WRAPPER 勹
(LUNGS) SO HIS MOUTH 口 CAN EXCLAIM 丁 IN
SONG 歌. THE COMPONENT MAN 人 MAY HAVE
BEEN ENTER 入 JME 125 FOR THE AIR ENTERING 入
THE MAN'S 人 LUNGS 勹 SINCE THE COMPONENT 入
ENTER IS SOMETIMES WRITTEN MAN 人 AS AN ERROR OR AMBIGUITY.
OR THE MAN 人 MAY HAVE A WRAPPER, COVER 勹 AS HE WALKS AND
SINGS 歌.

RAD	STROKE	JME
76	14	166

何
WHAT?,
HOW MANY?
JME 51

哥
SONG,
ELDER
BROTHER

歌
SONG,
TO SING

欠
LACK, WANT
(AIR ENTERS
LUNGS FOR
SINGING)

LUNGS
WANT,
LACK
AIR FOR
SINGING

欠
AS
HE
SINGS,
MAN WALKS
UNDER COVER

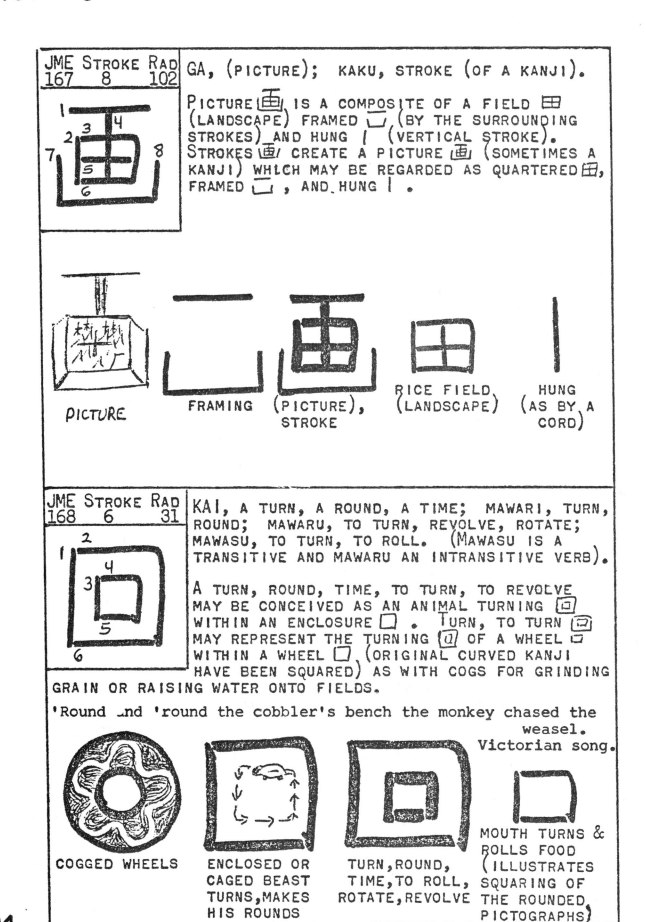

JME 167	Stroke 8	Rad 102

GA, (PICTURE); KAKU, STROKE (OF A KANJI).

PICTURE 画 IS A COMPOSITE OF A FIELD 田 (LANDSCAPE) FRAMED ⊔ (BY THE SURROUNDING STROKES) AND HUNG | (VERTICAL STROKE). STROKES 画 CREATE A PICTURE 画 (SOMETIMES A KANJI) WHICH MAY BE REGARDED AS QUARTERED 田, FRAMED ⊔ , AND HUNG | .

PICTURE   FRAMING   (PICTURE),   RICE FIELD,   HUNG
                                 STROKE   (LANDSCAPE)   (AS BY A
                                                                    CORD)

JME 168	Stroke 6	Rad 31

KAI, A TURN, A ROUND, A TIME; MAWARI, TURN, ROUND; MAWARU, TO TURN, REVOLVE, ROTATE; MAWASU, TO TURN, TO ROLL. (MAWASU IS A TRANSITIVE AND MAWARU AN INTRANSITIVE VERB).

A TURN, ROUND, TIME, TO TURN, TO REVOLVE MAY BE CONCEIVED AS AN ANIMAL TURNING 回 WITHIN AN ENCLOSURE 口 . TURN, TO TURN 回 MAY REPRESENT THE TURNING 回 OF A WHEEL 口 WITHIN A WHEEL 口 (ORIGINAL CURVED KANJI HAVE BEEN SQUARED) AS WITH COGS FOR GRINDING GRAIN OR RAISING WATER ONTO FIELDS.

'Round and 'round the cobbler's bench the monkey chased the
                                                     weasel.
                                              Victorian song.

COGGED WHEELS   ENCLOSED OR   TURN, ROUND,   MOUTH TURNS &
                   CAGED BEAST   TIME, TO ROLL,   ROLLS FOOD
                   TURNS, MAKES   ROTATE, REVOLVE   (ILLUSTRATES
                   HIS ROUNDS   SQUARING OF
                                                       THE ROUNDED
                                                       PICTOGRAPHS)

KAI, (GAI), SEA SHELL.

THE SEA SHELL 貝 IS AN EYE 目 (WHICH IT OFTEN RESEMBLES) MOUNTED ON SHORT LEGS (TO SHOW MOBILITY).
AS A KANJI COMPONENT, SEA SHELL 貝 MEANS MONEY. SHELLS 貝 , ESPECIALLY COWRIE, WERE WIDELY USED IN THE ANCIENT WORLD AS A MEDIUM OF EXCHANGE. WE STILL SPEAK OF "SHELLING OUT" MONEY AND OF "CLAMS" AS UNITS OF VALUE.

RAD	STROKE	JME
154	7	169

LITTLE LEGS, PERHAPS OF CRAB TENANT, CIRCULATE THE COWRIE

EAR

EAR
JME 26
("CONCHA" MEANS THE EXTERNAL EAR)

EYE
JME 25

SEA SHELL
(THE EAR-SHELL IS A FLATTENED UNIVALVE SHELL)

ABALONE
IS AN EAR-SHELL (GENUS HALIOTIS)

KAI, (WORLD).

WORLD 界 IS A FIELD 田 OR EXPANSE (AS MEASURED OUT OR WITH LATITUDE AND LONGITUDE LINES) WHICH SEPARATE ノ丶 PEOPLE ‖.
WORLD 界 ALSO SUGGESTS THE FIELD 田 (OF THE WORLD) BALANCED ACCORDING TO ANCIENT LEGEND ON A MOUNTAIN PEAK OR A GREAT TORTOISE 亻丁.
(Tectonic plates contain the earth just as the hexagonal plates of the carapace and rectangular plates of the plastron contain the tortoise.)

RAD	STROKE	JME
102	9	170

RICE FIELD (MAY ALSO REPRESENT DIAGRAMMED TORTOISE SHELL OR CARAPACE)

WORLD

MAY REPRESENT A GREAT TORTOISE OR A MOUNTAIN

FIELD OR EXPANSE OF THE WORLD BALANCED ON THE GREAT TORTOISE OR THE MOUNTAIN

JME	Stroke	Rad
171	12	169

KAI; HIRAKU, TO OPEN.

TO OPEN 開 SHOWS A GATE 門 JME 143 WITH A PAIR OF HANDS 廾 REMOVING THE BAR — (THAT LOCKS OR BARS THE GATE).

LEFT PANEL OF GATE

TO OPEN

RIGHT PANEL OF GATE

RIGHT PANEL OR DOOR OF GATE

BAR

HANDS

BAR

HANDS

HANDS ARE REACHING FOR THE BAR

HANDS OPENING GATE BY REMOVING THE BAR

JME	Stroke	Rad
172	12	120

KAI; E, PICTURE.

PICTURE 絵 IS THE MEETING 会 JME 54 (COMING TOGETHER) OF THE THREADS 糸 JME 83 THAT COMPOSE THE PICTURE 絵. THE PICTURE MAY BE WOVEN AS IN A TAPESTRY. HOWEVER, A LINE CAN BE PEN-DRAWN OR BE A NAUTICAL LINE (CORD, ROPE) RELATED TO THREAD.

PICTURE OF TWO COCOONS AND THREADS.

THREADS JME 83

PICTURE (MEETING OF THREADS OR "LINES")

MEETING JME 54

ROOF OF MEETING HOUSE

VIBRATIONS = AND VAPOROUS BREATH 云 OF MOUTHS ᕼ OF THOSE MEETING

KAKU, ANGLE; TSUNO, HORN (ANIMAL HORN).

RAD 148	STROKE 7	JME 173

ANGLE, HORN 角 IS A PICTOGRAPH OF A
STRIATED 土 HORN 角 (LIKE AN ENCLOSURE: 冂
EMPTY INSIDE) WITH A MAN BENDING OVER ク
(AS TO INSPECT OR DEHORN). THE BASE OF THE
HORN 用 IS LEFT OPEN TO SUGGEST THE HORN IS
HOLLOW (AND USED FOR POURING, AS A CONTAINER
AND DRINKING-HORN). NOTE THE SIMILARITY OF
THE BODY OF THE HORN 用 TO THE BODY OF THE
FISH 田 JME 190 WHOSE SCALES ARE RELATED TO
HORN. A MAN IS ALSO BENDING OVER ク THE FISH 魚 AND OVER ク
THE SNAKE COMPONENT 巴 IN COLOR 色 JME 94. A HORN IS
USUALLY IN AN ANGLED POSITION: THUS ALSO MEANS ANGLE 角.
NOTE THE RELATIONSHIP OF CORNER (THE MEETING PLACE OF
ANGLES) AND HORN.

STRIATIONS OR
GROWTH MARKS
ON HORNS

ENCLOSURE   ANGLE, HORN

MAN BENDING
OVER TO
INSPECT OR
POLL (CUT
OFF OR CUT
SHORT) HORN

KATSU, (LIFE, ACTIVITY, ENERGY).

RAD 85	STROKE 9	JME 174

LIFE, ACTIVITY, ENERGY 活 IS USED IN
COMPOUNDS RELATED TO THAT MEANING. LIFE,
ACTIVITY, ENERGY 活 IS A COMPOSITE OF THE
WATER COMPONENT 氵 AND TONGUE 舌 JME 151.
WHILE THE TONGUE 舌 HAS SALIVA 氵 , THERE
IS LIFE, ACTIVITY, ENERGY 活 .

DROPS   SALIVA   LIFE, ENERGY   TONGUE
                    ACTIVITY   JME 151

JME 175	Stroke 12	Rad 40

KAN, THE COLDEST PART OF THE YEAR; SAMUI, COLD.

COLD 寒 IS A COMPOSITE OF A MAN 八 (LEGS) STORING FUEL 茻 (PLANT LIFE DOUBLED) UNDER HIS ROOF 宀 (IN HIS HOUSE) FOR THE COLD 寒 OF THE ICE 冫 (WATER COMPONENT DROPS 冫 CONGEALED AND ONLY TWO IN NUMBER).

WINTER
JME 120

ICE

八
LEGS
OF MAN

茻
FUEL
PILED UP

寒
COLD,
THE COLDEST
PART OF THE
YEAR

宀
ROOF
(AS IN
HOUSE,
HOME
JME 53)

JME 176	Stroke 13	Rad 61

KAN, FEELING, EMOTION, THOUGHT.

FEELING, EMOTION, THOUGHT 感 IS THE MIND, HEART 心 OF THE POPULATION 口 (ONE MOUTH FOR ECONOMIC UNITY) IN A DEFENSIVE POSTURE (WITH WEAPONS 戈 ON THE CLIFFS 厂 (MOUNTAIN DEFENSE LINE).

BLADE
CROSSPIECE
HAND
STOCK
WEAPON

DOT IS FOR EXTENDED RANGE OF WEAPON IN REACHING OR HURLING

PICTURE
OF CLIFFS
OR MESAS.

厂
CLIFF
(WALLED
CITY
COMPO-
NENT)

口
ONE
MOUTH
(ECONOMIC
UNITY OR
SOURCE OF
SUSTENANCE)

戈
WEAPONS
(THE DOT
REPRESENTS
THE EXTENSION
OF POWER
THROUGH THROWING)

感
FEELING,
EMOTION,
THOUGHT

心
MIND,
HEART
JME 95

GAN; KISHI, (GISHI), BANK, SHORE, COAST.

BANK, SHORE, COAST 岸 SHOWS THE SHIELD 干 OF CLIFFS 厂 AND MOUNTAINS 山 AT THE BANK, SHORE, COAST 岸. SHIELD 干 WAS A COMPONENT IN GOLD, MONEY 金 JME 16. CLIFF 厂 WAS A COMPONENT IN STONE 石 JME 44.

RAD	STROKE	JME
46	8	177

SUPERIMPOSED VIEW
OF LARGE SHIELD
WHICH CAN BE RESTED
ON THE GROUND

SHIELD   CLIFF   BANK,   MOUNTAIN
                          SHORE,   JME 38
                          COAST

GAN; IWA, ROCK, CLIFF, CRAG.

THE ROCKS, CLIFFS, CRAGS 岩 ARE THE STONES 石 JME 44 OF THE CLIFFS 厂 (COMPONENT FORM) OF THE MOUNTAINS 山 JME 38.

RAD	STROKE	JME
46	8	178

BANK, SHORE   STONE   MOUTH   CLIFF   ROCK,   MOUNTAIN
COAST   JME 44   REPRE-   AS A   CLIFF, CRAG   JME 38
JME 177   SENTING   COMPONENT
                            A STONE

JME 179	Stroke 18	Rad 181

GAN, KAO, FACE.

FACE 顔 COMPOSITES HEAD 頁 AS THE RIGHT COMPONENT, AND A FUSION OF STAND 立 JME 149 (AS A FACE) WITH BODY 尸 (COMPONENT FORM AS IN SHOP 屋 JME 161 BUT LACKING THE LINES FOR MOUTH, HEAD) AND HAIR 彡 (AS A COMPONENT ADDED). THE HAIR 彡 (COMPONENT FORM) AS HEAD AND FACIAL HAIR (AND BEARD) COVERS PART OF THE BODY.

HUMAN BODY ABBREVIATED LACKING THE HEAD, MOUTH (CLIFF GIVES IMPRESSION)

STAND; (USED AS CAPPED FACE OR HEAD)

FACE

HEAD

SEMI-PICTURE OF HEAD

JME 180	Stroke 10	Rad 149

KI, (CHRONICLE).

CHRONICLE 記 IS A COMPOSITE OF SPEECH 言 JME 123 AND JME 151 (SHOWING THE MOUTH 口 BELOW AND SOUND VIBRATIONS 𡆥 ABOVE), AND TURN, CYCLE 己. NOTE HOW TURN, CYCLE 己 RESEMBLES THE YIN AND YANG ☯ SYMBOL WITH ITS DUALITY AND SUGGESTION OF OPPOSITES AS OF THE SEASONS, THE SPRING AND AUTUMN ANNALS, DYNASTY AND DISORDER, RISE AND DECLINE, WAX AND WANE, AND THE WHEEL OF TIME.

VIBRATIONS FROM THE MOUTH 口

SPEECH JME 123

CHRONICLE

TURN, CYCLE

I, MYSELF, ONESELF JME 777 (PRONOUN TURNS REFLEXIVELY)

KI; OKIRU, TO GET UP, TO RISE;
OKOSU, TO RAISE, SET UPRIGHT, (TRANSITIVE
VERB).

TO GET UP, TO RISE, TO RAISE, TO SET
UPRIGHT 起 COMPOSITES TO RUN 走 JME 105 AS
THE LEFT COMPONENT, AND TURN, CYCLE 己 AS
THE RIGHT COMPONENT. ONE GETS UP, RISES,
RAISES, SETS UPRIGHT 起 ON TURNING 己
(UNCURLING) AND RUNNING 走.

Rad	Stroke	JME
156	10	181

| EARTH, SOIL JME 17 | FOOT, LEG JME 29 | TO RUN JME 105 | TO GET UP, TO RAISE, TO RISE, SET UPRIGHT | TURN, CYCLE, AS COMPONENT I, MYSELF, ONESELF JME 777 |

KI; KAERU, TO RETURN, TO COME BACK,
TO LEAVE.

TO RETURN, TO COME BACK, TO LEAVE 帰 IS A
COMPOSITE OF A DUSTING BRUSH 帚 COMPOSED OF
A HAND 彐 HOLDING A COVERED 冖 CLOTH 巾 AS
THE RIGHT COMPONENT; AND TWO VERTICAL
STROKES ｜｜ AS AN ABBREVIATION OF THE EARLIER
LEFT COMPONENT COMPOSED OF EARTH LAYERS 𠂤
(NOTE THE TWO STORY EFFECT) AND TO STOP 止
JME 220. THE DUSTING BRUSH OR FEATHER
DUSTER REPRESENTS THE WIFE FOR WHOM IT IS TRADITIONAL TO
MAKE STOPS 止 OR VISITS AT HER PARENTAL HOME 𠂤 TO WHICH
SHE 帚 (THE DUSTING BRUSH) RETURNS, COMES BACK ｜｜帚.

Rad	Stroke	JME
58	10	182

| TO STOP | BLDG. & STOP | TO RETURN, COME BACK, LEAVE | HAND & DUSTER | *HAND GRIPS DUSTER* |

JME	STROKE	RAD
183	12	74

KI, GO, (TIME, PERIOD, TERM).

TIME, PERIOD (OF TIME), TERM (OF SCHOOL) IS A COMPOSITE. THE LEFT COMPONENT IS A WINNOWING DEVICE OR SIEVE 其 TAKING A CERTAIN LENGTH OF TIME 期 TO WINNOW OR SIFT GRAIN. THE RIGHT COMPONENT MOON 月 ALSO INDICATES TIME 其月, PARTICULARLY IN HER PHASES.

SIEVE HANDLES

SIEVE, GRATER (NOTE THE EYES)

EYE JME 25

WINNOWING DEVICE, SIEVE

SIEVE (HOLES IN SIEVE LIKE EYES IN NET)

TIME, PERIOD, TERM

MOON, MONTH JME 12

JME	STROKE	RAD
184	9	40

KYAKU, KAKU, GUEST.

GUEST 客 SHOWS UNDER A ROOF 宀 THE HAND 又 OF A GUEST 客 HOLDING A FAN 宀 FUSED WITH THE IMPRESSION OF THE GUEST 客 SEATED 口 (AS ON A STOOL, STONE, BOX) WITH LEGS TO EITHER SIDE 八 AND BODY ABOVE 夂.

PICTURE OF THE GUEST UNDER THE ROOF, SEATED AND FANNING

ROOF (AS IN HOUSE, HOME JME 53)

GUEST

SITTING GUEST & HAND HOLDING FAN

SEAT (AS STONE IN STONE JME 44

KYŪ, (STUDY).

STUDY 究 GIVES THE IMPRESSION OF SOMETHING "TUMBLED" OR POLISHED IN A HOLE 穴 UNTIL IT IS NINE- 九 SIDED (NINE 九 JME 9) OR NEARLY ROUND. IN THE KANJI AS IN ENGLISH THERE IS THE ANALOGY OF STUDY 究 POLISHING A PERSON AND ROUNDING OFF HIS ROUGH CORNERS JUST AS STONES ARE TUMBLED IN A HOLE (UNDER WATER).

RAD	STROKE	JME
116	7	185

POLISHED EGGHEAD STUDYING IN HIS DEN OR HOLE

 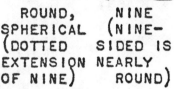

ROUND, SPHERICAL (DOTTED EXTENSION OF NINE)

NINE (NINE- SIDED IS NEARLY ROUND)

(STUDY)

HOLE (AS IN SKY JME 65

ROOF (AS IN HOUSE, HOME JME 53

KYŪ; ISOGU, TO HURRY.

TO HURRY 急 IS A BRUSH OR HAND ヨ SWEEPING ACROSS OR CLUTCHING THE HEART, MIND 心 OF A MAN BENDING OVER ク TO CATCH SOMETHING. THE MAN BENDING OVER ク AS TO CATCH SOMETHING IS A COMPONENT IN FISH 魚 JME 190 AND HORN, ANGLE 角 JME 173 AND THE SNAKE COMPONENT IN COLOR 色 JME 94. A MAN BENDING OVER ク TO CATCH SOMETHING IS IN A HURRY 急 AND IT IS AS THOUGH A BRUSH OR HAND ヨ SWEPT ACROSS HIS HEART, MIND 心 .

RAD	STROKE	JME
61	9	186

RIGHT AURICLE

LEFT AURICLE

LEFT VENTRICLE

RIGHT VENTRICLE

SUPERIMPOSED HEART

HEART, MIND JME 95

TO HURRY

HAND OR BRUSH SWEEPING ACROSS OR CLUTCHING HEART

MAN BENDING OVER AS TO CATCH SOMETHING

JME 187	Stroke 9	Rad 120

KYŪ, CLASS, GRADE, RANK.

CLASS, GRADE, RANK 級 IS A COMPOSITE OF THREAD 糸 JME 83 ON THE LEFT AND A HAND 彐 GRASPING A BODY 尸 ON THE RIGHT. THE COMPOSITE REFERS TO GRASPING 彐 THE BODY 尸 OF THE THREAD 糸, STRANDS OF THREAD BEING TWISTED FOR DIFFERENT CLASS, GRADE, RANK 級. THE HAND 彐 PUTS SILK THREADS 糸 (CLOTHES) ON THE BODY, CORPSES 尸 OF CERTAIN RANK, CLASS, GRADE 級.

CORPSE IN A COFFIN (SUPER-IMPOSITION)

STORE-KEEPER BODY (SUPER-IMPOSITION) JME 161

THREAD JME 83

CLASS, GRADE, RANK

BODY OF GRADES OF THREAD AS ANALOGOUS TO HUMAN BODY SHOWN

HAND

JME 188	Stroke 11	Rad 96

KYŪ, GLOBE, SPHERE, BALL, BULB.

GLOBE, SPHERE, BULB, BALL 球 IS A COMPOSITE OF JEWEL, ROUND OBJECT 玉 JME 64 (WITHOUT THE DOT) ON THE LEFT AND A HAND 十 (ONCE) ASKING FOR 扌 (DOT) WATER 氺 ON THE RIGHT, JUST AS ONE ASKS FOR A BALL 球 ETC. IN PRIMITIVE SURROUNDINGS, IT IS WATER 氺 THAT IS ASKED FOR 扌 WITH THE OUTSTRETCHED HAND 十. IN ANCIENT TIMES, THE KINGS 王 WHO CONTROLED IRRIGATION AND WATER- 氺 ING RIGHTS WERE ASKED FOR 扌 WATER 氺.

JEWEL, JADE SEAL, ROUND OBJECT
JADE SEAL AND KING ARE INTERCHANGEABLE AS COMPONENTS IN CERTAIN KANJI

KING JME 49

GLOBE, BALL, SPHERE, BULB

WATER AS COMPONENT

WATER JME 14 RESEMBLES COMPONENT FORM ABOVE

HAND

ASKING FOR (AS A COMPONENT WITH HAND)
DOT EXTENDS SCOPE AND MEANING OF THE HAND: THE CUPPED HAND ASKS FOR, BEGS WITH DOT COMPONENT. PREVIOUS DOTTED HAND BECAME PULSE 扌 IN VILLAGE 村 JME107

KYO, KO, (PAST); SARU, TO LEAVE, DEPART, MOVE AWAY.

TO LEAVE, TO DEPART, TO MOVE AWAY 去 IS A COMPOSITE OF EARTH 土 JME 17 AND SOMETHING COILED UP ム BELOW THE EARTH 土 HIBERNATING, DORMANT, OR BURIED AWAITING RESURRECTION OR REVIVAL. THE SOMETHING COILED UP ム UNDER THE EARTH 土 HAS LEFT, DEPARTED, MOVED AWAY 去. IT IS IN THE PAST 去.

Rad	Stroke	JME
28	5	189

BODY RESTS ON THE EARTH

TO REACH, TO ARRIVE (IS TO COIL ON EARTH: REST)

EARTH-MOUND OVER GRAVE

COILED BODY

TO LEAVE, DEPART, MOVE AWAY

BODY IS COILED UNDER THE EARTH

SOIL, EARTH JME 17

GYO; UO, SAKANA, FISH.

FISH 魚 IS A PICTOGRAPH OF THE BODY 田, FINS AND TAIL 灬 OF A FISH 魚 WITH A MAN BENDING OVER ク TO CATCH THE FISH 魚. AS IN OTHER KANJI, THE CONCEPTION OF THE MAN BENDING OVER ク IS FUSED WITH WHAT HE CATCHES OR BENDS OVER. IN THE FISH 魚 IT IS THE MOUTH ク; IN THE HORN 角 THE TIP ク; IN COLOR 色 THE FANGS ク OF THE SNAKE IN A COMPONENT.

Rad	Stroke	JME
195	11	190

HORSE JME 127

BIRD

TAIL & FINS LIKE LIMBS OF BIRD, HORSE

FISH

BODY OF SCALES

MAN BENDING OVER TO GET OR CATCH: ALSO THE PART THAT MAY BE CAUGHT OR HOOKED OR WRAPPED.

JME	STROKE	RAD
191	11	66

KYŌ; OSHIERU, TO TEACH.

TO TEACH 教 IS A COMPOSITE OF THE HAND WITH WITH THE ROD 攵 ON THE RIGHT ENCOURAGING THE CHILD 子 ON THE LEFT WITH LEARNING BURDENING HIM LIKE A LOAD OF EARTH 土 ON A SLANTED STICK ／ OVER HIS SHOULDER AS THE CHILD 子 IS TAUGHT 教 FILIAL PIETY, FILIAL DUTY 孝 JME 781.

SUPERIMPOSITION OF CHILD CARRYING HIS BURDEN OF PIETY OR FILIAL DUTY LIKE A LOAD OF EARTH

FILIAL PIETY, DUTY (MOST IMPORTANT: LIKE WEIGHT OF EARTH ON SHOULDERS OF CHILD)

TO TEACH

HAND WITH ROD

HAND WITH ROD

JME	STROKE	RAD
192	11	57

KYŌ, GŌ; TSUYOI, STRONG.

STRONG 強 IS A COMPOSITE OF THE COMPOUND BOW 弓 ON THE LEFT AND AN INSECT 虫 ON THE RIGHT UNDER A CLOUD ム OR THE GENESIS OF EXPANSION. THE BOW IS THE ESSENCE OF STRENGTH TO THE PRIMITIVE MIND. SO IS THE INSECT SUDDENLY APPEARING IN IMMENSE CLOUDS OR SWARMS DEVOURING EVERYTHING IRRESISTABLY.

ASIAN COMPOUND BOW

BOW (TO PULL, TO DRAW 引 JME 156)

STRONG

INSECT JME 114

CLOUD OF OR EXPANSION POTENTIAL OF INSECTS AS PLAGUE OR HORDE

KYŌ; HASHI, (BASHI), BRIDGE.

BRIDGE 橋 HAS WOOD, TREE 木 JME 15 ON THE LEFT AND HIGH 高 ON THE RIGHT WITH THE CAP OR ROOF 亠 REPLACED BY SKY, HEAVEN 夭 JME 119. A BRIDGE 橋 IS A HIGH 高 STRUCTURE WITHOUT A ROOF 亠 UNDER HEAVEN OR SKY 夭 AND MADE USUALLY OF WOOD 木. ORIENTAL BRIDGES 橋 WERE FREQUENTLY BUILT HIGH 高 AND ARCHED TO FACILITATE PASSAGE OF SHIPS.

ARCHES WERE SOMETIMES CONTINUED UNDER THE STREAM AS A DOUBLE ARCH SO THEY WERE 360° WITH GREAT RESULTANT STRENGTH AND STABILITY

RAD	STROKE	JME
75	16	193

BRIDGE

TREE, WOOD JME 15

BRIDGE

HIGH (LACKING CAP); ROOF COMPONENT

SKY, HEAVEN JME 119

DOUBLE ARCH (IS A CIRCLE)

KYOKU, DEPARTMENT, OFFICE, BUREAU.

DEPARTMENT, OFFICE, BUREAU 局 IS A PICTOGRAPH OF A TWO STORY BUILDING. TWO STORY BUILDINGS AS PRIVATE RESIDENCES WERE RARE IN THE ORIENT; TWO STORY BUILDINGS WERE USUALLY OFFICIAL OR GOVERNMENT OFFICES, DEPARTMENTS, BUREAUS 局, ETC.

RAD	STROKE	JME
44	7	194

PICTURE OF TREE & BRIDGE

BRIDGE JME 193

HIGH JME 76

LOWER STORY

DEPT., OFFICE, BUREAU

UPPER STORY (AS HEAD IN HUMAN BODY 尸: BATS IN THE BELFRY)

JME 195	Stroke 7	Rad 162

KIN; CHIKAI, NEAR.

NEAR 近 IS THE MOVEMENT 辶 OF AN AXE 斤.
(THE MOVEMENT 辶 OF AN AXE 斤 IS NEAR 近 THE
WOODCUTTER).   AXE 斤 IS A PICTOGRAPH.
MOVEMENT 辶 IS AS IN FAR, DISTANT 達 JME 160
AND ROAD, WAY, PATH 道 JME 122. 達

MOVEMENT,
GO & STOP,
ETC. AS
IN ROAD,
PATH

MOVING
(GOES &
STOPS)
AXE

AXE
(PICTO-
GRAPH)

PICTURE
OF AXE

JME 196	Stroke 14	Rad 167

GIN, SILVER.

SILVER 銀 HAS GOLD, MONEY 金 JME 16 ON THE
LEFT AND 日 FOR THE WHITE 白 JME 37 (TOP
OBLIQUE STROKE LOST) MULTI-BRANCHED K (AS
IN CHIEF, DIRECTOR, LONG 長 JME 116 AND
PAPER 紙 JME 85) VEINS OF SILVER 銀 IN ITS
NATURAL STATE. GOLD, MONEY 金 JME 16 IS
OFTEN USED AS A COMPONENT TO INDICATE
METALS AND METALLIC THINGS.

GOLD, MONEY
METALLIC
COMPONENT

SILVER

WHITE
VEINS
OF SILVER

VEINS OF
SILVER

WHITE JME 37
(LOSES ITS
HORN OR RAY
AS COMPONENT
IN SILVER)

KU, PAIN, SUFFERING, ANXIETY;
KURUSHII, PAINFUL; NIGAI, BITTER.

PAIN, SUFFERING, ANXIETY 苦 RESULT WHEN THE
GRASS ⺾ IS OLD 古 JME 70. THIS SITUATION
IS BITTER AN AND PAINFUL 苦 FOR THE NOMADIC
HERDSMAN WHO DEPENDS ON THE GRASS ⺾ .

RAD	STROKE	JME
140	8	197

EGYPTIAN
HIEROGLYPH
FOR MOUTH

MOUTH

TEN
JME 10

OLD,
ANCIENT
(PASSED
ON OR TOLD
BY TEN
MOUTHS OR
GENERATIONS)

PAIN,
SUFFERING,
ANXIETY,
PAINFUL,
BITTER
(GRASS OLD
OR DEAD)

GRASS IN
COMPONENT
FORM
(NOTE IN
GRASS,
VEGETATION
JME 106)

KUN, MR.; KIMI, YOU (FAMILIAR AS BETWEEN
                             FRIENDS).

RAD	STROKE	JME
30	7	198

LIKE MR. AND ITS EUROPEAN EQUIVALENTS SUCH
AS HERR, SENOR, SIGNOR, MONSIEUR, ETC., KUN
君 AND KIMI 君 ORIGINALLY REFERRED TO A
GENTLEMAN OR LORD. MR., YOU 君 IS A HAND ⺕
HOLDING A STICK ノ (MEANING TO RULE OR TO
GOVERN), AND A MOUTH 口 WHICH COMMANDS.

MOUTH'S
TONE OF
COMMAND

STICK, SCEPTER,
SHEPHERD'S CROOK,
BATON OF MARSHAL
OR CONDUCTOR

MOUTH

MR., YOU
(HAND HOLDS
SCEPTER OR
STICK; MOUTH
COMMANDS)

HAND
HOLDING
STICK OR
SCEPTER

HAND

OLD SYMBOL
FOR HAND

JME 199	Stroke 5	Rad 10

KEI, KYŌ; ANI, ELDER BROTHER.

ELDER BROTHER 兄 IS A WALKING 儿 MOUTH 口.
IN THE CONFUCIAN RELATIONSHIP OF ELDER
BROTHER 兄 TO YOUNGER BROTHER, THE ELDER HAD
THE AUTHORITY AND DUTY TO INSTRUCT THE
YOUNGER BROTHER.

SEE JME 159
AND JME 160

MOUTH
JME 27
(MOUTH-
HEAD-
PELVIS
CONCEPT)

ELDER
BROTHER
(BIG-MOUTH)

LEGS,
WALKING

PICTURE
OF OLDER
BROTHER

JME 200	Stroke 7	Rad 59

KEI, GYŌ; KATACHI, -GATA, FORM, SHAPE.

FORM, SHAPE 形 HAS AN ALIGHTING BIRD 开 (AS
IN WEST 西 JME 96 OR THE FORM, SHAPE 形 OF
A SHINTO TORII 开 GATEWAY, LITERALLY
BIRD-PLACE) ON THE LEFT AND HAIR 彡 AS A
COMPONENT (FROM HAIR 髪) ON THE RIGHT.
THE HAIR 彡 OF THE HEAD, SIDEBURNS, BEARD,
MOUSTACHE, ETC. GIVES FORM SHAPE 形. THE
ALIGHTING BIRD 开 IN WEST 西 OR AS SHOWN BY
THE TORII ALSO HAS REMARKABLE FORM, SHAPE 形.

WEST
JME 96
(BIRD ON
NEST)

GATEWAY,
TORII
(LITERALLY
"BIRDPLACE")

FORM,
SHAPE

HAIR

CRYPTOMERIA,
JAPANESE
CEDAR (HAS
DOWNSWEEPING
BRANCHES
LIKE HAIR)

HAIR AS
COMPONENT
(THE HAIR
GIVES
FORM &
SHAPE,
APPEARANCE)

FORM & SHAPE ARE BEST DEPICTED BY
THE ALIGHTING BIRD, TAIL & WINGS
SPREAD, AS IN TORII; AND THE HAIR

VOLUME THREE: KANJI 201-300

兄

OLDER BROTHER

is a head-mouth
on two legs in the
Japanese _kanji_ or
Chinese characters

KEI; HAKARU, TO MEASURE.

ONE MEASURES 計 BY SPEECH 言 JME 392 IN TENTHS AND TENS 十 JME 10 WHICH ARE THE BASIS OF MEASURING 計 . THE TEN 十 JME 10 ALSO REPRESENTS THE FIVE DIRECTIONS: NORTH, EAST, SOUTH, WEST, CENTER AND IS PART OF THE DIPPER 斗 (AS IN GREAT DIPPER 〰)USED TO MEASURE 計 .

RAD	STROKE	JME
149	9	201

言 — SOUND VIBRATIONS FROM MOUTH

言 — WORDS, SPEECH JME 392

計 — TO MEASURE

十 — TEN JME 10 SYMBOL FOR DIRECTIONS & DECIMALS

斗 — TO, (UNIT OF MEASUREMENT; 19.04 QT.) SYMBOLIZES A DIPPER OR GREAT DIPPER

斗 — 7 STARS OF THE GREAT DIPPER

KETSU; KIMERU, TO DECIDE; KIMARU, TO BE DECIDED.

TO DECIDE, TO BE DECIDED 決 IS A COMPOSITE OF A MAN 人 WITH A THUMB RING ㄊ ,(AN INCOMPLETE CIRCLET WAS USED), WORN IN ARCHERY ON THE RIGHT AND THE WATER COMPONENT 氵 TO THE LEFT. THE THUMB RING ㄊ IS THE UPPER PART OF A BOW 弓 AND THUS IMPLIES ARCHER THE MEANING IS "WHEN THE ARROW IS ON THE STRING, IT MUST FLY." ANOTHER MEANING OF TO DECIDE, TO BE DECIDED 決 IS DIVERTING 人 AND FLOODING WITH WATER 氵 A WALLED CITY 凵 . THE THUMB RING ㄊ SHAPE IS THAT OF THE EMBRASURES IN THE WALL. ONE MUST DECIDE WHEN TO RELEASE THE ARROW OR THE DAMMED WATER. CITY WALL EMBRASURES WERE USED LIKE LOOPHOLES.

RAD	STROKE	JME
85	7	202

氵 — WATER AS COMPONENT

決 — TO DECIDE, TO BE DECIDED

人 — MAN, PERSON DIVERSION

弓 — BOW

凵 — OPEN VESSEL, CONTAINER

ㄊ — ARCHER'S THUMB RING

CITY WALL EMBRASURES

JME	STROKE	RAD
203	9	109

KEN, PREFECTURE.

PREFECTURE 県 IS REPRESENTED BY A HEAD (HUMAN AND INVERTED) STRUNG 糸 (BOTTOM OF STRING, THREAD 糸) UP. HEADS OF CRIMINALS WERE STRUNG UP BY THE GATES OF THE PRINCIPAL CITY OF THE PREFECTURE AS A WARNING AND A SIGN OF STRICT GOVERNMENT. (TRAFFIC CHECKED BY RADAR).

HEAD

HEAD

PREFECTURE
THE HEAD AND THE
STRING HAVE BEEN
INVERTED TO SHOW
DEATH (LIKE THE
DEAD FISH WITH
WHITE BELLY UP)

STRUNG UP CHOPPED
(LOWER OFF HEAD
PART OF STRUNG UP
THREAD
JME 83
MODIFIED)

JME	STROKE	RAD
204	9	112

KEN, (STUDY).

STUDY 研 IMPLIES A SHAPE 开 (FROM SHAPE, FORM 形 JME 200 SUBJECTED TO A GRIND-) STONE 石 FOR POLISHING AS IN STUDY 究 JME 185. WE SPEAK OF A HARD-WORKING STUDENT OR A COURSE OF STUDY AS A "GRIND."

SHAPE
OF BIRD

PURE
SHINTŌ
GATE

RYŌBU
SHINTŌ
GATE

WEST
JME 96

(STONE)
MOUTH
JME 27

CLIFF

STONE
JME 44
(CLIFF &
STONE)

STUDY
(FIGURE IS
POLISHED
AS BY THE
GRINDSTONE)

BIRD
ALIGHTING,
SHINTŌ
GATEWAY

FORM,
SHAPE
JME 200

GEN, ORIGIN; HARA, (WARA), FIELD, MEADOW.

FIELD, MEADOW 原 IS REPRESENTED BY A WHITE
白 JME 37 LITTLE 小 JME 24 (ORIGINALLY
WATER 水 JME 14) STREAM FROM A CLIFF 厂
TO SUPPLY A FIELD, MEADOW 原. SUCH A
FIELD, MEADOW 原 IS THE ORIGIN 原 OF A
HOMESTEAD OR FAMILY.

RAD	STROKE	JME
27	10	205

CLIFF AS A
COMPONENT

FIELD, MEADOW

WHITE
LITTLE
(STREAM)

RIVER
JME 39

WATER
JME 14

KO, (STOREHOUSE, WAREHOUSE).

STOREHOUSE, WAREHOUSE 庫 IS A SHED 广
ORIGINALLY USED TO SHELTER A VEHICLE, WHEEL
車 JME 88.

RAD	STROKE	JME
53	10	206

CART IN SHED

CLIFF (MAY
GIVE SHELTER)

SHED
ORIGINALLY A
LEAN-TO

STOREHOUSE,
WAREHOUSE

VEHICLE, WHEEL
JME 88

JME 207	Stroke 4	Rad 24

GO, (NOON), (ZODIAC HORSE).

NOON 午 IS THE DOUBLE HOUR OF THE ZODIAC HORSE 午 FROM 11 AM TO 1 PM. THE TWELVE DOUBLE HOURS LIKE THE TWELVE YEARS OF THE ZODIAC CYCLE ARE NAMED FOR ANIMALS. NOON 午 (THE ZODIAC HORSE) IS A COMPOSITE OF THE HORN, THE SICKLE ノ (THE HORN AS AN ANIMAL'S WEAPON OR THE POINT OF A SPEAR, AND THE SICKLE AS A KNIFE) AND THE SHIELD 干 (A COMPONENT IN GOLD, MONEY 金 JME 16 AND SOUTH 南 JME 124). APPARENTLY THE ZODIAC HORSE WAS A WARHORSE REPRESENTED BY WEAPONS ノ AND SHIELD 干.

ZODIAC HORSE (HORNED) HAS EQUINE SHAPE: COMPOSITE OF ARMS

HORN, BUGLE (IN JAPAN & ELSEWHERE, WAR HORSES SOMETIMES WORE HORNS & ARMOR)

ZODIAC HORSE, NOON (COMPOSITE OF HORN & SHIELD)

SHIELD

CATTLE, COW, BULL, OX JME 62

HORSE JME 127

JME 208	Stroke 9	Rad 60

GO, KŌ, AFTERWARDS; USHIRO, BEHIND, THE BACK, THE REAR; NOCHI, AFTER, LATER.

BEHIND, AFTER, LATER, THE BACK, THE REAR 後 IS A COMPOSITE. THE LEFT COMPONENT IS MAN DOUBLED TO MEN 彳 BY THE ADDITION OF A STROKE. THE MEN 彳 COME AFTER, LATER 後 FOLLOWING BEHIND 後 IN THE BACK, THE REAR 後. THE UPPER RIGHT COMPONENT IS TWO COCOONS 幺 (AS IN THREAD, STRING 糸 JME 83) AFTER, BEHIND, LATER 後 THAN ONE ANOTHER. THESE TWO COMPONENTS ALSO SYMBOLIZE THE SUCCESSION OF GENERATIONS. ON THE LOWER RIGHT IS A MAN WALKING SLOWLY 夊 WHO COMES AFTER, BEHIND, LATER 後 (BRINGING UP THE REAR 後).

MEN WALK ONE AFTER, BEHIND, LATER

PAIRS OF COCOONS AS PICTURE & COMPONENT OF KANJI: (ONE COCOON IS AFTER, BEHIND, LATER)

SUPERIMPOSITION

MAN WALKS SLOWLY WITH FAN (AFTER, BEHIND, IN THE REAR)

GO, WORD, SPEECH; KATARI, NARRATIVE;
KATARU, SPEAK, TALK, NARRATE.

WORD, SPEECH, NARRATIVE, SPEAK, TALK,
NARRATE 語 IS A COMPOSITE OF WORD, SPEECH 言
JME 392 ON THE LEFT (MOUTH 口 AND SOUND
VIBRATIONS) AND THE MOUTH 口 SPEAKING IN
FIVE 五 (ALL) DIRECTIONS ON THE RIGHT. THE
MEANING 吾 IS FROM COMMANDING BY MOUTH
A SQUAD OF FIVE 五 MEN.

Rad	Stroke	JME
149	14	209

WORD, SPEECH
JME 392

WORD, SPEECH,
NARRATIVE,
SPEAK, TALK,
NARRATE

MOUTH SPEAKING
IN 5 DIRECTIONS
(MOUTH SPEAKING
SQUAD LEADER OF 5)

KANJI
FIVE

ARABIC
FIVE

NOTE THE
SIMILARITY
ABOVE

KŌ; OYAKE, PUBLIC.

PUBLIC 公 IS A DIVISION 八 OF WHAT WAS
PRIVATE, SECRET, HIDDEN 厶 (AS IN A COCOON
厶) SO THAT IT EXPANDS 厶 IN PUBLIC , USE.
THE SYMBOL 厶 AS IN A CLOUD 雲 OR THE CONE
厶 OF A PINE TREE IS CAPABLE OF IMMENSE
EXPANSION. YET AS A COCOON 厶 (HALF OF
THE TWO COCOONS 玄 IN THREAD, STRING 糸),
IT SUGGESTS PRIVATE, SECRET, HIDDEN 厶 WITH
A FUTURE IN TRANSFORMATION. WHAT IS PUBLIC
SUCH AS A PARK OR PUBLIC BUILDING IS USUALLY SPREAD OUT.
THE COCOON 厶 UNWOUND EXPANDS INTO THREAD AND BECOMES
PUBLIC 公,

Rad	Stroke	JME
12	4	210

EIGHT JME 8
(IMPLIES TO
DIVIDE,
DIVISION)

PUBLIC

PRIVATE, HIDDEN,
SECRET AS IN A
COCOON, BUT READY
TO BECOME PUBLIC

THREAD JME 83
(EARLY MEANING
SILK: THREAD
FROM COCOON)

JME	Stroke	Rad
211	5	53

KŌ; HIROI, WIDE; HIROGARU, TO SPREAD,(I.V.); HIROGERU, TO SPREAD, (T.V.); HIROMARU, TO BE SPREAD, TO BE DIFFUSED.

WIDE, TO SPREAD, TO BE SPREAD, TO BE DIFFUSED 広 IS REPRESENTED BY THE COCOON ム IN THE SHED 广 WHICH IS UNWOUND AND SPREADS, IS SPREAD, IS DIFFUSED 広 AS THREAD 糸 AND EVENTUALLY AS SILK CLOTH FOR CLOTHING, ETC.

THE COCOON UNDER THE SHED IS SPREAD WIDE AS IT IS UNWOUND

THREAD JME 83

| SHED (AS A LEAN-TO) | WIDE,TO SPREAD, TO BE SPREAD, TO BE DIFFUSED | COCOON (AS IN THREAD) IMPLIES PRIVATE, SECRET,HIDDEN | PUBLIC JME 210 |

JME	Stroke	Rad
212	6	8

KŌ; MAJIRU, TO MIX, MINGLE, TO BE MIXED; MAJIWARU, TO ASSOCIATE, KEEP COMPANY.

TO MIX, MINGLE, ASSOCIATE, KEEP COMPANY 交 IS WHAT THE FATHERS 父 JME 131 WEARING THE BIRETTA OR SCHOLARS' CAP 亠 DO. THERE IS ALSO IMPLIED A MIXING, MINGLING 交 BY THE CROSSING OF LINES ✕ (AS WITH THE LETTER X) JUST AS IN COMPOSITION, ESSAY, SENTENCE 文 JME 134 WITH THE MIXED, MINGLED, ASSOCIATED, COMPANY KEEPING 交 LINES OF THE KANJI.

THE FATHERS WHO ARE SCHOLARS MIX, MINGLE, ASSOCIATE, KEEP COMPANY (AS THEY ENJOY) COMPOSITIONS, ESSAYS, SENTENCES

| SUPER-IMPOSITION | FATHER JME 131 | MIX,MINGLE, TO BE MIXED, TO ASSOCIATE, KEEP COMPANY | COMPOSITION, ESSAY, SENTENCE JME 134 | SCHOLARS' CAP OR BIRETTA (SUGGESTS DIRECTION, CONTROL, THE CIVIL SERVICE) |

KŌ; MUKAU, TO FACE, TO CONFRONT;
MUKU, TO TURN TOWARD, BE SUITED.

TO FACE, TO CONFRONT, TO TURN TOWARD, TO BE
SUITED 向 WAS A PICTOGRAPH OF A WINDOW 向.
IN THE EARLY DAYS, WINDOWS WERE MADE OF
TRANSLUCENT HORN ノ. NOTE THE SIMILARITY OF
WINDOW 向 TO THE LOWER STORY 向 IN HIGH 高
JME 76.
THE WINDOW 口 (APERTURE, MOUTH) OF HORN ノ IN
THE ENCLOSURE 冂 (BUILDING) FACES, CONFRONTS,
TURNS, IS SUITED TO 向 THE LIGHT

RAD 30	STROKE 6	JME 213

ノ
HORN

向
TO FACE,
TO CONFRONT,
TURN TOWARD,
BE SUITED

冋
ENCLOSURE
OR LOWER
STORY OF
BUILDING
WITH A
WINDOW

高
HIGH
JME 76

高
STYLE
OF
BUILDING

KŌ, Ō; KI, YELLOW.

YELLOW 黄 IS A PICTOGRAPHIC TIGER 亩 AS IN
THE ZODIAC TIGER 寅 WITH MEN STANDING OVER
卄 HIM. YELLOW 黄 IS THUS THE BRILLIANT
SATURATED RUFOUS FAWN OF THE TIGER, A
MEMORABLE COLOR. NOTE THICK, HEAVY FOREFEET OF
THE TIGER.

RAD 201	STROKE 11	JME 214

SUPER-
IMPOSED

寅
ZODIAC
TIGER
(TIGER
UNDER ROOF
OF DEN, CAVE)

宀
ROOF OF
DEN OR
CAVE

亩
TIGER
AS A
COMPONENT ON TIGER

黄
YELLOW
(HUNTERS
ON TIGER)

卄
MEN
(WITH ARMS
LINKED &
NUMEROUS
AS TWENTY)
(OR RAISING
JOINED HANDS
IN TRIUMPH)

JME 215	Stroke 5	Rad 141

GŌ, NUMBER, ISSUE (AS OF A MAGAZINE).

THE NUMBER, ISSUE 号 (AS OF A MAGAZINE) IS THE MOUTHED 口 (SOUND, TWANG) OF A BOW 弓 (ONLY LOWER PART 丂 SHOWN) STRING VIBRATION 一. THE CONCEPT IS THE NEWSBOY SHOUTING: "EXTRA! EXTRA!" THIS BOW 丂 COMPONENT WAS IN TO REFLECT, THINK, IDEA, THOUGHT, OPINION 考 WHERE IT REPRESENTED THE LAST ASTHMATIC GROANS OF THE DECEASED FATHER, A CONSTANT REFLECTION, IDEA 考 OF THE DEVOUT CONFUCIAN SON IMBUED WITH FILIAL PIETY. IN TO REFLECT, IDEA 考, THE LINE FOR THE BOWSTRING MOVEMENT OR VIBRATION IS SLANTED DIFFERENTLY ╱ TO SUIT THE TOTAL COMPOSITION 考.

REFLECT, IDEA
JME 74

MOUTH (CALLING OUT THE NUMBER, OR ISSUE)

NUMBER, ISSUE

SOUND, TWANG

BOWSTRING MOVEMENT

PULLING, DRAWING, TO PULL, DRAW
JME 156

ASIAN BOW

BOW

JME 216	Stroke 10	Rad 75

KON, ROOT, RADICAL, (MATH.), PERSEVERANCE, STAMINA; NE, ROOT.

ROOT, RADICAL, (MATH.) 根 DERIVE (AS IN ENGLISH) FROM THE PLANT ROOT OR SOURCE CONCEPT. THE ROOTS 根 WHICH HAVE PERSEVERANCE 根 (AS IN PROBING UNDER THE GROUND) ARE A COMPOSITE OF TREE 木 ON THE LEFT, WHITE 白 (LACKING THE HORN OR RAY ╱) ON THE UPPER RIGHT, AND MULTI-BRANCHED 氏 AS IN FAMILY, CLAN 氏 JME 620 AND SILVER 銀 JME 196 AND PERSON(S) AS COMPONENTS IN GARDEN 園 JME 159 AND FAR, DISTANT 遠 JME 160. THE FORM OF THE BRANCHES OR ROOTS VARIES, THE CONCEPTION IS ALIKE.

TREE
JME 15

ROOT, RADICAL, PERSEVERANCE, STAMINA

WHITE ROOTS

SILVER

FAMILY, CLAN

GARDEN
JME 159

FAR, DISTANT
JME 160

SAI, TALENT, SUFFIX AS YEARS OF AGE.

RAD	STROKE	JME
64	3	217

TALENT, "YEARS OLD" 才 IS A PICTOGRAPH OF
A TREE 木 PRUNED AND THINNED 才 SO THAT
THE "DEADWOOD," AND EXCESS GROWTH IS
REMOVED AS WITH FRUIT TREES. THIS IS DONE
AT CERTAIN STAGES IN TIME OR "YEARS OLD" 才.
THE PROCESS WITH TREES IS REGARDED AS
ANALOGOUS TO THAT IN EDUCATING OR DEVELOPING
PEOPLE TO THEIR TALENT(S) 才.

TREE, WOOD
JME 15
(COMMON WOOD)

TALENT,
YEARS OF AGE
(TREE ANNUALLY
PRUNED & THINNED
LEAVING BEST GROWTH)

HAND
(COMPONENT)

ACTION OF THE
PRUNING KNIFE
WHICH TRIMS &
PRUNES TREES

SAI; HOSOI, SLENDER, NARROW;
KOMAKAI, FINE, DETAILED, MINUTE.

RAD	STROKE	JME
120	11	218

SLENDER, NARROW, FINE, DETAILED, MINUTE 細
IS THE APPEARANCE OF A RICE FIELD OR PADDY 田
WHICH IS LIKE THREADS, STRANDS 糸. SUCH
FIELDS ARE PARTICULARLY SEEN ON THE TERRACED
MOUNTAIN SIDES WHERE THE RETAINING WALLS IN
THE DISTANCE CURVE LIKE WINDING THREADS 糸.

TERRACED RICE PADDIES
ON THE MOUNTAINSIDE

THREAD,
STRING
JME 83

SLENDER,
NARROW,
FINE,
DETAILED,
MINUTE

RICE FIELD
OR PADDY
JME 40

JME	Stroke	Rad
219	14	118

SAN, (ZAN), CALCULATION, RECKONING.

CALCULATION, RECKONING 算 SHOWS AN ABACUS OF BAMBOO 竹 JME 113 WITH TWO HANDS 廾 BELOW MANIPULATING THE BEADS. THE BEADS, WHICH ARE NOT REPRESENTED IN THE KANJI, ARE STRUNG ON THE RODS WITHIN THE FRAME. BEADS OF THE ABACUS ARE AN IMPROVEMENT ON THE QUIPU OR KNOTS ON CORDS OF ANCIENT TIMES BECAUSE THE BEADS SLIDE. HOWEVER, KNOTS WERE PERMANENT.

"MOBILE QUIPU"

USUALLY OF BAM-BOO (JME 113)

QUIPU ABACUS

ABACUS FRAME

HANDS READY TO MANIPULATE ABACUS BEADS

CALCULATION, RECKONING

JME	Stroke	Rad
220	4	77

SHI; TOMARU, TO STOP; TOME, (DOME), A STOP; TOMERU, TO STOP, BRING TO A STOP.

TO STOP, BRING TO A STOP, A STOP 止 SHOWS A FOOT, LEG 足 JME 29 WITH THE ARCH 人 FLATTENED 丄 AND THE PELVIS 口 REMOVED. THE ARCHED FOOT IS A FOOT RUNNING (ON ITS TOES). MOVEMENT OF THE LEG MAY BE CONSIDERED TO BE INITIATED BY THE MUSCLES OF THE BUTTOCK AREA BY THE PELVIS. STOPPING MEANS THIS PART IS NO LONGER NEEDED. THE ARCH 人 HAS COME TO A "SCREECHING" FLAT-FOOTED STOP 丄.

FOOT, LEG JME 29

PELVIS REMOVED

FOOT FLATTENS FOR "SCREECHING" STOP

TO STOP, BRING TO A STOP

THIGH
KNEE
KNEE
SHANK
FOOT

FOOT (THIGH, KNEE, SHANK & FOOT)

TO RUN JME 105

CORRECT, RIGHT JME 46

TO GET UP, TO RISE JME 181

TO WALK JME 136

SHI, (WORK); TSUKAERU, TO SERVE.

TO SERVE 仕 IS WORK 仕 . TO SERVE 仕 SHOWS THE MAN イ JME 30 WHO SERVES 仕 AS A PERSON, MAN, FIGURE 士 JME 410 (ORIGINALLY THE KNIGHT OR SCHOLAR WHO SERVED THE LORD OR GOVERNMENT).

RAD	STROKE	JME
9	5	221

MAN, PERSON (AS LEFT COMPONENT)

WORK TO SERVE JME 221

MAN, FIGURE JME 410 (ORIGINALLY JAP. KNIGHT, FIGURE CH. SCHOLAR)

FACE OF MAN, FIGURE

MAN, FIGURE (KNIGHT) INVERTS INTO

SHIELD (REFLECTING THE KNIGHT'S FACE)

SHI, CITY; ICHI, MARKET.

CITY, MARKET 市 IS A COMPOSITE OF THE SCHOLAR OR CIVIL SERVANT'S BIRETTA 亠 (INDICATING AUTHORITY, CONTROL, DIRECTION) AND A CLOTH HANGING OR DRAPE 巾 (PICTO-GRAPHIC) AS ABOUT A MARKET BAZAAR, FOR CITY 市 STREET SIGNS, IN CITY OFFICES.

RAD	STROKE	JME
50	5	222

SCHOLARS' CAP OR BIRETTA FOR AUTHORITY, DIRECTION, CONTROL, CIVIL SERVICE

CITY, MARKET

CLOTH HANGING OR DRAPE (AS IN DUSTCLOTH, DUSTER. IN TO RETURN JME 182

DUSTER

JME 223	Stroke 6	Rad 78

SHI, DEATH; SHINU, TO DIE.

DEATH, TO DIE 死 IS A COMPOSITE OF THE EVENING 夕 (OF LIFE) OR SUNKEN MOON OR BODY BELOW THE HORIZON 一 AND A MAN 人 IN THE MUMMY OR INVERTED FETAL POSITION ヒ , AS IN FLOWER 花 JME 43 AND TO CHANGE, TO BE TRANSFORMED 化 JME 163.

EVENING JME 98

DEATH, TO DIE

MUMMY (SITTING AS IN OLD BURIAL JARS)

FLOWER JME 43

TO CHANGE, TO TRANSFORM (STANDING MAN BECOMES THE SITTING MAN)

JME 224	Stroke 8	Rad 9

SHI; TSUKAU, TO USE.

TO USE 使 SHOWS THE MAN イ USED IN VARIOUS CAPACITIES AS AN OFFICIAL 吏 . THE PICTOGRAPH OF THE MAN イ USED 使 IS A COMPOSITE OF A MOUTH 口 FOR CARRYING MESSAGES AND THE KANJI MEANING TEN SHAKU 丈 (10 x 0.995 FT.), A PICTOGRAPH OF A BIG MAN イ SUITABLE FOR USE 使 . NOTICE HOW THIS BIG MAN STRUTS.

MAN, PERSON (AS LEFT COMPONENT)

TO USE

MOUTH

TEN SHAKU

AN OFFICIAL

SHI; HAJIMARU, TO BEGIN, (I.V.);
HAJIMERU, TO BEGIN, (T.V.).

TO BEGIN 始 IS THE PURSED UP, COILED
MOUTH ム OF A WOMAN 女 READY TO BEGIN
HER TIRADE, ETC., COMFORTABLY SEATED ON
A STOOL, STONE OR BOX 口.

RAD	STROKE	JME
38	8	225

WOMAN, GIRL,
FEMALE
JME 32

TO BEGIN

THE "PURSED-UP"
MOUTH (SEATED
ON A STOOL, ETC.
READY TO BEGIN)

PICTURE OF
THE WOMAN'S
MOUTH ABOUT
TO BEGIN

SHI; YUBI, FINGER.

FINGER 指 IS A COMPOSITE OF HAND 扌 (THE
ABBREVIATED COMPONENT FORM OF HAND 手 JME 28)
TO POINT OR INDICATE ヒ (VISUALIZE AS A
SITTING PERSON ヒ IN PROFILE WITH HAND /
EXTENDED TO INDICATE, AND A MOUTH SPEAKING 日
TO SUPPLEMENT THE POINTING ヒ (COMMANDS 旨).
IT IS THE FINGER 指 THAT IS SIGNIFICANT
WHEN THE SITTING MAN'S ヒ HAND 扌 IS
EXTENDED AS HE SPEAKS 日.

RAD	STROKE	JME
64	9	226

MAN SITS:
ARM INDICATES,
FINGER POINTS

YEARS OF AGE,
TALENT
JME 217

COMPONENT HAND,
ARM (INDICATES
DIRECTIONALLY
LIKE PRUNE TREE)

FINGER

MOUTH SPEAKS
(SUPPLEMENTS
ARM & FINGER)

COMMANDS
(COMPOSITE OF
SPEAKING &
POINTING WHILE
SITTING)

JME 227	STROKE 6	RAD 15

SHI, JI; TSUGI, NEXT;
TSUGU, TO RANK NEXT TO, COME NEXT.

NEXT, TO RANK NEXT TO, COME NEXT 次 IS A
COMPOSITE OF BREATHE 欠 (THE BREATH
ENTERING 人 JME 125 THE WRAPPING OR COVERING
勹 OF THE LUNGS) AND OF TWO 二 JME 2 (WHICH
HAS BECOME TWO DOTS 冫) FOR THE SUCCESSION
OF BREATHS. "AT THE NEXT BREATH...." IS AN
ENGLISH PHRASE. THE CONCEPT OF NEXT 冫欠 MAY
INVOLVE ICINESS 冫 IF THERE IS FEAR IN THE
ANTICIPATION. 勹 HAS THREE MEANINGS OR A THREEFOLD MEANING:
1. A MAN REACHING DOWN TO CATCH OR BRING SOMETHING "IN".
2. THE MOUTH OF A FISH, ETC. WHICH WRAPS ITSELF AROUND THE
HOOK. 3. A WRAPPING AS A PACKAGE, BOAT, ETC.

ICE (AS
COMPONENT)

NEXT,TO RANK
NEXT TO,COME
NEXT

TO BREATHE

TWO LUNGS
FED BY ONE
AIRSTREAM

ONE FLOW OF
AIR ENTERS
TWO LUNGS
ENCLOSED BY
BODY

JME 228	STROKE 6	RAD 41

JI; TERA, (DERA), TEMPLE.

TEMPLE 寺 IS A COMPOSITE OF PULSE 寸 (A HAND
寸, ORIGINALLY 屮, AND A DOT • TO SHOW THE
EXTENSION OF HAND 寸 AS A CONTROLLING
FACTOR), AND THE SURROUNDING EARTH 土 JME 17.
THE PULSE 寸 REGULATES THE BODY JUST AS THE
TEMPLE 寺 IS THE PULSE BEAT OF THE EARTH
BY ITS REGULATION OF ACTIVITIES IN FESTIVALS,
CEREMONIES AND BY THE TEMPLE BELL WHICH
SERVES AS A CLOCK. (THE MEANING OF PULSE 寸
LATER BECAME A UNIT OF LENGTH (1.193 IN.) BECAUSE THE
STANDARD OF LENGTH SERVES TO REGULATE AND THE PULSE 寸 IS
ABOUT THAT FAR FROM THE HAND.

TEMPLE
AND SOUND OF
BELLS

EARTH,SOIL
JME 17

TEMPLE

OLD KANJI
FOR PULSE

1.93 INCHES
MEASURE,
CONTROL

TIME JME 87
(TEMPLE KEEPS
TIME AS PULSE
OF EARTH AS
DOES THE SUN)

JI, SHI; MIZUKARA, SELF, ONESELF, IN PERSON.

RAD	STROKE	JME
132	6	229

SELF, ONESELF, IN PERSON 自 IS THE COMPONENT FOR A HEAD 自 WITH THREE STROKES LACKING. HOWEVER, THE COMPONENT FOR HEAD MAY TAKE VARIOUS FORMS. EXAMPLES ARE IN PREFECTURE 県 JME 203 AND IN SUMMER 夏 JME 52. ABOVE IS THE COMPONENT FOR HORN ノ WHICH THE NOSE RESEMBLES. (RHINOPLASTY).

HORN (IS LIKE NOSE: RHINO & RHINECTOMY, ORIENTALS POINT TO NOSE TO MEAN SELF OR ONESELF JUST AS IN "COUNT NOSES")

SELF, ONESELF, IN PERSON (ANCIENT KANJI FOR NOSE)

EYE JME 25 (ABACUS FRAME, HEAD, SHELL COMPONENT, ETC.)

PICTURE OF SELF (FACE WITH NOSE CLOSE ENOUGH TO TOUCH)

SUMMER JME 52

PREFECTURE JME 203

JI; KOTO, THING, MATTER, AFFAIR, FACT.

RAD	STROKE	JME
6	8	230

THING, MATTER, AFFAIR, FACT 事 IS REPRESENTED BY A HAND ⺕ WITH A STYLUS OR PEN | OFFICIALLY, FOR ALL UNITEDLY 口 (AS ONE MOUTH), RECORDING THINGS, MATTERS, AFFAIRS, AND FACTS 事 .

ONE MOUTH (ECONOMIC, POLITICAL UNITY OR CONFORMITY)

THING, MATTER, AFFAIR, FACT

HAND GRASPS A (VERTICAL) STYLUS

JME	STROKE	RAD
231	9	64

JI; MOCHI, DURABILITY;
MOTSU, TO HAVE, TO HOLD.

DURABILITY, TO HAVE, TO HOLD 持 IS A
COMPOSITE OF A HAND 扌 (COMPONENT FOR ARM,
HAND 手 JME 28), AND OF TEMPLE 寺 WHICH HAS,
HOLDS 持 (PROPERTY, ENDOWMENTS) AND IS
DURABLE 持 . THERE IS AN ANALOGY TO LA MAIN
MORTE (THE DEAD HAND) OF THE MEDIEVAL CHURCH
WHICH DURABLY HAD AND HELD 持 WHAT IT WAS
BEQUEATHED, INDEFINITELY OR IN PERPETUITY.

HAND, ARM (AS A COMPONENT)	TO HAVE, TO HOLD DURABILITY (TEMPLE HAS & HOLDS LAND, ETC. WITH DURABILITY)	TEMPLE JME 228 (THE PULSE OF THE LAND)	TIME JME 87 (THE TEMPLE IS THE PULSE OF THE LAND LIKE THE SUN)

JME	STROKE	RAD
232	9	40

SHITSU, ROOM;
MURO, STOREROOM, CAVE, GREENHOUSE.

ROOM, STOREROOM, CAVE, GREENHOUSE 室 ARE
ROOFED 宀 PLACES WHERE GOODS ARE STORED —
(AS LYING HORIZONTALLY) SECRETLY, PRIVATELY
厶 (AS IN A COCOON) ON THE EARTH, SOIL 土 .
THE GOODS ARE LAIN AWAY 云 WHEN THEY REACH,
ARRIVE 至 JME 796. CAVES 室 WERE USED AS
STOREROOMS 室 , OFTEN BECAUSE OF THEIR LOW
TEMPERATURES.

ROOF (NECESSARY TO PROTECT WHAT IS STORED)	ROOM, CAVE, STOREROOM, GREENHOUSE	TO REACH, ARRIVE JME 796	BODY COILED UP ON THE GROUND UNDER THE ROOF IN THE ROOM, CAVE.	SHOP JME 161

JITSU, TRUTH, REALITY; MI, FRUIT, NUT;
MINORU, TO BEAR FRUIT.

Rad	Stroke	JME
40	8	233

TRUTH, REALITY, FRUIT, NUT, TO BEAR FRUIT 実
IS A PICTOGRAPH OF A MAN 人 LADEN WITH NUTS,
FRUIT 圭 UNDER HIS ROOF 宀. THE ENGLISH
CONCEPT OF A PROJECT OR ENTERPRISE BEARING
FRUIT (ABSTRACT) IS ALSO JAPANESE.
NOTE THE SIMILARITY OF TRUTH, REALITY,
FRUIT, NUT, TO BEAR FRUIT 実 JME 233 TO
SPRING 春 JME.91. ABSTRACTLY FRUIT PRODUCED IS
ALSO TRUTH OR REALITY 実. "BY THEIR FRUITS YE SHALL KNOW
THEM."

春	青	生	実	人	宀
SPRING	BLUE,	EXISTENCE,	FRUIT,	PERSON,	ROOF
JME 91	GREEN	LIFE, BORN	NUT,	MAN	
SUN THROUGH	JME 36	JME 34	BEAR	JME 30	
THICK	MOON	PLANTS &	FRUIT		
FOLIAGE	LIGHT	YIELD			
	THRU				
	PLANTS				

SHA, (JA), COMPANY, CORPORATION, FIRM;
YASHIRO, A SHINTO SHRINE.

Rad	Stroke	JME
113	7	234

COMPANY, CORPORATION, FIRM, SHINTO SHRINE 社
IS A COMPOSITE OF THE COMPONENT FORM 礻 OF
TO SHOW, TO POINT OUT 示 JME 622 AND OF SOIL
EARTH 土 REFERRING TO THE LOCAL DEITIES OF
THE PHYSICAL TERRAIN (LIKE THE ROMAN MANES).
TO SHOW, POINT OUT 示 JME 622 REPRESENTS
HEAVEN'S 二 (OR SUN, MOON AND STARS' 三)
ILLUMINATION 小 (THREE SPREADING RAYS) WHICH
SHOW, POINT OUT 示 TO MAN ON EARTH. THE PRIESTS OF THE
SHINTO SHRINE 社 WERE A COMPANY 社 (IN THE SENSE OF A
GROUP) AND THIS MEANING WAS EXTENDED TO COMPANY, FIRM,
CORPORATION 社.

神	示	未	礻	社	土
GOD	TO SHOW,	KANJI	COMPONENT	COMPANY,	EARTH,
JME 257	POINT OUT	BECOMES	FORM OF	CORPORA-	SOIL
	JME 622	COMPONENT	JME 622	TION, FIRM,	JME 17
		COMPONENT JME 622		SHINTO	
				SHRINE	

JME	Stroke	Rad
235	8	125

SHA; MONO, PERSON.

THE PERSON 者 TALKS 曰 (CHANTS) AS HE CARRIES ノ LIFE'S BURDEN OR LOAD OF EARTH 土, HIS EARTHLY BURDEN, ON HIS HEAD. (HOD CARRIER).

LIFE'S BURDEN
LOAD OF EARTH

PERSON

TALKS, CHANTS

TO THINK, IDEA,
THOUGHT, OPINION
JME 74

PERSON
JME 235

TO TEACH JME 191
ROD IN HAND BY
BURDENED CHILD

JME	Stroke	Rad
236	10	57

JAKU; YOWAI, WEAK;
YOWARU, WEAKEN, BECOME WEAK, BE PERPLEXED.

WEAK, WEAKEN, BECOME WEAK, BE PERPLEXED 弱
IS A PICTOGRAPH OF TWO YOUNG BIRDS 弱 WHO
BY THEMSELVES ARE IN THAT CONDITION. THE
TWO STROKES AT THE TOP ココ ARE IN EACH CASE
THE HEAD. THE SCRAWNY NECKS ARE THE SHORT ||
VERTICAL STROKES. BELOW ARE THE WINGS WITH
PINFEATHERS 冫冫. THE YOUNG BIRDS HAVE A
GAWKY, AWKWARD, ADOLESCENT APPEARANCE. NOTE
THAT THEY ARE DRAWN AS BOWS 弓弓 WITH PINFEATHERS. THUS HERE
BOW DOES NOT SYMBOLIZE STRENGTH AS IT DID IN STRONG 強
JME 192 AND TO PULL 引 JME 156. PICTOGRAPHICALLY, BOTH BOW
AND YOUNG BIRD ARE
DOUBLE-ARCHED.

WINGS

PIN-
FEATHERS

WEAK, WEAKEN,
BECOME WEAK,
PERPLEXED

BOW

BIRD SKELETON
LIGHT BONES
FOR FLIGHT
ARE FRAGILE

SHU, SU; NUSHI, OWNER, MASTER.

OWNER, MASTER 主 IS AN EXTENSION ` OF
KINGSHIP 王 JME 49 TO THE OWNER, MASTER 主
(OF THE HOUSEHOLD, PATRIARCHAL FAMILY, ETC.)
NOTE THE ANALOGY IN THE USE OF THE DOT TO
SHOW EXTENSION OF SCOPE OR POWER IN OWNER,
MASTER 主 AND OTHER DOTTED KANJI.

RAD	STROKE	JME
8	5	237

犬
DOG
JME 66

` DOT
(EXTENDS
SCOPE OR
POWER: IN
KING BY
JADE SEAL
IMPRINT ON
WRITTEN
COMMANDS
OR THROUGH
HOUSEHOLD
MASTERS OR
OWNERS)

主
OWNER,
MASTER
(LOCAL
EXTENSION
OF KINGSHIP)

王
KING
JME 49
(CONNECTS
HEAVEN,
EARTH,
& MAN)

玉
JEWEL,
ROUND OBJECT,
JADE SEAL
(JADE SEAL
SYMBOLIZES
KING'S POWER)

SHU; TORU, TO TAKE.

TO TAKE 取 IS A COMPOSITE OF EAR 耳 JME 26
AND HAND 又 ORIGINALLY ψ . TO TAKE 取 IS
ASSOCIATED WITH THE HAND 又 WHICH TAKES, AND
THE HANDLES AS OF A BOWL WHICH ARE TAKEN.
THE EARS 耳 CLOSELY RESEMBLE THE HANDLES OF
A BOWL OR URN. A SMALL BOY CAN BE TAKEN
BY THE EAR 耳 (WITH THE HAND 又). IN WAR,
WHEN THE ENEMY WAS TAKEN 取 (KILLED), HIS
EAR 耳 WAS TAKEN 取 (BY THE HAND 又) AS
EVIDENCE. HIDEYOSHI'S CONQUEST OF KOREA HAS AS MEMENTOS
EAR-MOUNDS MADE FROM THE EARS 耳 TAKEN 取 IN BATTLE. THE
VIETNAM WAR IS RUMORED TO HAVE CONTINUED THE PRACTICE.

RAD	STROKE	JME
128	8	238

BOWL WITH
HANDLES AS
EARS
(JUG EARED)

EAR

TO TAKE

HAND
(COMPONENT)

TO TAKE
(HAND TAKES
THE EAR)

JME	STROKE	RAD
239	9	185

SHU; KUBI, NECK.

NECK 首 IS A FUSED KANJI FROM THE COMPONENT ⍍ FOR BIGHORN, RAM, SHEEP 羊 AND HEAD 自 . THE ABILITY OF THE NECK 首 OF THE ELK OR MOOSE TO WITHSTAND THE SHOCK OF THE COLLISION OF THEIR HORNED ⍍ HEADS 自 CAUSES THIS FUSION TO REPRESENT THE NECK 首 . OUR ENGLISH TERM "BULL-NECKED" SHOWS SIMILAR THINKING. WEIGHT AND STRENGTH OF HORNS DESCRIBES INVISIBLE NECK 首.

BEFORE, PREVIOUS, IN FRONT OF JME 102

NECK LIKE AN ELK OR MOOSE (SHAMAN CONCEPT)

NECK (THE ELK'S HEAD HAS THE NECK)

HORNS
HEAD
BODY FORELEGS
HINDLEGS
TAIL

RAM (SEE JME 102)

JME	STROKE	RAD
240	8	29

JU; UKE, RECEPTACLE, POPULARITY; UKERU, TO RECEIVE.

RECEPTACLE, POPULARITY, TO RECEIVE 受 IS A COMPOSITE OF A HAND ⺥ ABOVE, A HAND BELOW 又 AND A CROWN OR CAP 冖 BETWEEN. WHAT IS POPULAR 受 IS RECEIVED 受 BY A HAND 又 FROM A HAND ⺥ (OR PASSED FROM HAND TO HAND). A RECEPTACLE 受 AS WELL AS A CAP OR CROWN 冖 CAN BE EVIDENCE OF POPULARITY 受.

ANOTHER HAND COMPONENT (LOOKS LIKE SCRATCH MARKS FROM BEING EAGERLY RECEIVED)

TO CARRY, TO TRANSPORT JME 157 (VEHICLE COVER LIKE A CAP, CROWN, ETC.)

RECEPTACLE, POPULARITY, TO RECEIVE

TO TAKE (HAND AS COMPONENT AS IN TO RECEIVE, RECEPTACLE)

PICTURE OF HANDS PASSING A CAP OR A RECEPTACLE

RAD	STROKE	JME
120	11	241

SHŪ; OWARI, END; OWARU, TO COME TO AN END, TO END; OERU, TO END, TO FINISH, COMPLETE.

END, TO COME TO AN END, TO END, TO FINISH, TO COMPLETE 終 IS A COMPOSITE OF WINTER 冬 JME 120 AND THREAD, STRING 糸 JME 83. WITH WINTER 冬 THE THREAD 糸 (OF TIME, OF THE SEASONS) ENDS, FINISHES, IS COMPLETE 終. WINTER SYMBOLIZES DEATH OR THE END; SPRING SYMBOLIZES BIRTH, LIFE. WE SPEAK OF THE THREAD OF LIFE, THE THREAD OF TIME.

TWO COCOONS OF THE SILKWORM, THREADS DANGLING

THREAD, STRING JME 83

END, TO END, TO FINISH, TO COMPLETE, TO COME TO AN END

WINTER JME 120 (MAN WITH STICK WALKS ON ICE)

RAD	STROKE	JME
162	11	242

SHŪ, WEEK.

WEEK 週 HAS THREE COMPONENTS: EARTH, SOIL 土 JME 17; MOVEMENT OR GO AND STOP 辶 ; AND TURN, ROTATE, ROLL 回 JME 168. THE LAST COMPONENT 回 IS WRITTEN IN AN OLDER FORM 囘 WITHOUT THE BOTTOM STROKE — .
THE WEEKS 週 MOVE OR GO AND STOP 辶 AS THE EARTH 土 TURNS, ROTATES, ROLLS 回 IN ITS ENCLOSURE 冂 OF ATMOSPHERE.

MOVEMENT, TO GO AND STOP

WEEK

TURN, ROTATE, ROLL, A TURN, A ROUND, A TIME

EARTH JME 17 (IN ITS ATMOSPHERIC ENCLOSURE OR WRAPPER)

JME 243	STROKE 12	RAD 172

SHŪ; ATSUMERU, TO GATHER, COLLECT, (T.V.);
ATSUMARU, TO GATHER, ASSEMBLE, TO FLOCK,
TO SWARM, (I.V.).

TO GATHER, COLLECT, ASSEMBLE, FLOCK, SWARM
集 IS A COMPOSITE OF A SHORT-TAILED BIRD 隹
(ORIGINALLY 隹) REPRESENTING MANY SHORT-
TAILED BIRDS ON A TREE 木 JME 15. NOTE
TO ADVANCE, TO PROGRESS 進 JME 259.
SHORT-TAILED BIRDS 隹 COLLECT, GATHER,
FLOCK, OR ASSEMBLE 集 IN TREES.

TREE
CONCEPT

TREE
JME 15

TO GATHER,
COLLECT,
ASSEMBLE,
TO FLOCK,
TO SWARM

SHORT-TAILED
BIRD

HEAD
EYE
BREAST
WINGS
AND
FEATHERS
OLD SYMBOL
FOR SHORT-
TAILED BIRD

JME 244	STROKE 9	RAD 9

JŪ, DWELLING; SUMU, TO LIVE, TO DWELL,
TO RESIDE, TO INHABIT.

DWELLING, TO LIVE, TO DWELL, TO RESIDE,
TO INHABIT 住 SHOWS THE MAN 亻 JME 30
WHO LIVES, DWELLS, RESIDES, INHABITS
THE DWELLING 住 AS THE OWNER OR MASTER 主
JME 237.

MAN, PERSON
JME 30
(COMPONENT)

DWELLING,
TO LIVE,
DWELL,
RESIDE,
INHABIT

OWNER,
MASTER
JME 237

KING
JME 49

DOT
SHOWS THE
EXTENSION OF
THE POWER OF
THE KING TO
THE MASTER,
OWNER

JŪ, CHŌ; OMOI, HEAVY, WEIGHTY, SERIOUS;
KASANERU, TO PILE UP, PUT ONE UPON ANOTHER;
KASANERU, TO BE PILED UP (AS IN LAYERS);
KASANE, A PILE, A HEAP, A LAYER OF CLOTHING.

RAD	STROKE	JME
166	9	245

HEAVY, WEIGHTY, SERIOUS, TO PILE UP, PUT ONE
UPON ANOTHER, TO BE PILED UP, A PILE, A HEAP,
A LAYER OF CLOTHING 重 ARE REPRESENTED BY A
CAISSON 車 (AS IN TO CARRY, TO TRANSPORT 連
JME 157) FOR MILITARY SUPPLY WHICH IS
DOUBLE-WHEELED 壬 FOR THE HEAVY, PILED UP
HEAPED 重 ARMS, CLOTHING, ETC. THE SUPPLY TRAIN CONTENTS
ARE A WEIGHTY, SERIOUS 重 PROBLEM FOR THE MILLENION 千.
THIS HEAVY PILED UP CAISSON IS RESTING

CAISSONS
(JME 157)

HORN
(MILITARY
AS BUGLE)

RI, MILES
JME 332

MILLENION

EARTH, SOIL
(HEAVY HEAP)   COMMANDS

HEAVY,
WEIGHTY,
SERIOUS,
HEAP

VEHICLE,
WHEELS,
CHARIOT
JME 88

WARE-
HOUSE
JME
206

TO CARRY,
TRANSPORT,
LUCK
JME 157

SHO, (JO); TOKORO, (DOKORO), PLACE.

RAD	STROKE	JME
63	8	246

PLACE 所 IS AN AXE 斤 BY THE DOOR 戸 (AS IN
PRIMITIVE WOODED SURROUNDINGS FOR PROTECTION
AND CONVENIENCE). LIKE SPEARHEADS, AXES 斤
WERE STANDARDIZED AND USED AS WEIGHTS OR
UNITS OF VALUE. METAL WAS PRECIOUS. THUS
THE MODERN MEANING OF AXE 斤 IS A WEIGHT
CALLED KIN 斤 EQUAL TO 1.323 POUNDS.

AXE IS
HANGING
BY PICTURED
DOOR

DOOR
JME 69

PLACE

KIN
1,3 LBS.
(AXE)

NEAR
JME 195

PRIMITIVE
AXE

JME 247	STROKE 12	RAD 72

SHO; ATSUI, HOT.

HOT 暑 IS A COMPOSITE OF A PERSON 者 JME 235 UNDER THE HOT 暑 SUN 日 JME 11. THE PERSON 者 IS ALSO HOT 暑.

日
SUN
JME 11

暑
HOT
JME 247
(HOT SUN ON
HOT PERSON)

者
PERSON
JME 235

HOT SUN
HOT PERSON
(CARRIES EARTH)

JME 248	STROKE 7	RAD 19

JO; TASUKERU, TO HELP, TO AID, TO RESCUE; TASUKARU, TO BE SAVED, TO BE RESCUED.

TO HELP, AID, RESCUE, BE SAVED, BE RESCUED 助 IS A COMPOSITE OF STRENGTH 力 JME 148 AND THE ANCESTRAL TABLET OR EYE OF THE ANCESTOR 且. THE EYE OF THE ANCESTOR IS AMONG THE EARLIEST KANJI. THE PEOPLE BELIEVED THAT IF THEY WERE FAITHFUL TO THEIR DEAD ANCESTORS WITH SACRIFICES, THE DEAD ANCESTORS WOULD HELP, AID, AND RESCUE THEM. IF NEGLECTED, THE SPIRITS OF THE ANCESTORS WOULD SEEK VENGEANCE.

ANCESTRAL
TABLET
(FORM LIKE
TOMBSTONE)

EYE
JME 25

(ANCESTRAL
EYE, TABLET)
NOW MEANS
"MOREOVER"

TO HELP, AID,
TO RESCUE,
TO BE SAVED,
BE RESCUED

STRENGTH,
POWER
JME 148

SHŌ, (BRIGHT).

BRIGHT 昭 IS A COMPOSITE OF SUN 日 AND CALL, SUMMON 召 . CALL, SUMMON 召 IS A COMPOSITE OF KNIFE 刀 (CUTTING UP A KILLED ANIMAL FOR FOOD) AND THE MOUTH 口 CALLING OR SUMMONING 召 (TO EAT). THE SUN 日 CALLS OR SUMMONS 召 TO ITS BRIGHTNESS 昭 . THE CONCEPT INVOLVES HELIOTROPISM.

RAD	STROKE	JME
72	9	249

PUEBLO PETROGLYPH SUN SYMBOL

EGYPTIAN HIEROGLYPH SUN SYMBOL

SUN, DAY JME 11

(BRIGHT)

TO CALL, SUMMON

SHŌ; KATSU, TO WIN, TO CONQUER, TO DEFEAT.

TO WIN, TO CONQUER, TO DEFEAT 勝 IS A COMPOSITE OF THE MOON 月 JME 12 WHICH WAXES AND WANES LIKE EMPIRES (ACCORDING TO THE THREE KINGDOMS OR SAN KUO), AND THE STRENGTH 力 JME 148 OF FIRE 火 JME 13 (THE RAVAGER OR DESTROYER) SHOWN FUSED WITH TWO LINES 二 LIKE FOUR LEGS OF THE COW 牛 OR GOAT 羊 TO INDICATE THE RAPID RUNNING MOVEMENT OF THE WINNING, CONQUERING, DEFEATING FIRE.

RAD	STROKE	JME
130	12	250

COW JME 62

GOAT JME 102

MOON JME 12 WAXES & WANES AS EMPIRES

TO WIN, CONQUER, TO DEFEAT (RAVAGES & DESTROYS)

FIRE JME 13 (RAVAGES & DESTROYS)

TWO LINES AS FOR FOUR LEGS OF THE COW OR GOAT

STRENGTH, POWER JME 148

JME	STROKE	RAD
251	9	4

JŌ; NORU, TO RIDE; NOSERU, TO PLACE ON, CARRY, GIVE A RIDE TO.

TO RIDE, PLACE ON, TO CARRY, TO GIVE A RIDE TO 乗 HAS A FUSED CENTRAL COMPONENT LIKE THE CHASSIS AND AXLE 申 OF A CHARIOT 車 JME 88. THE KANJI FOR RICE, GRAIN 禾 AS IN JME 89 IS ALSO A FUSED COMPONENT BECAUSE THE HEADS ON THE STALKS BOB UP AND DOWN AS THO RIDING, AND BECAUSE THE MOVEMENT OF THE HEADED STALKS UNDER THE WIND SUGGESTS THE MOVEMENTS OF HORSES OR CHARIOTS SWEEPING BY.

CHARIOT TOP VIEW PICTURE

CHARIOT JME 88

TO PLACE ON, CARRY, GIVE A RIDE TO

RICE, GRAIN (AS IN JME 89)

CENTER, MIDDLE (NOTE ROD TO PLACE ON, CARRY, RIDE) JME 554

JME	STROKE	RAD
252	12	32

JŌ; BA, PLACE.

PLACE IS IS A COMPOSITE AND FUSION OF A CHAMELEON 易 JME 545 SUNNING 日 JME 11 ON THE EARTH 土 UNDER THE WARM SUN ABOVE THE HORIZON LINE 一 . TO BASK IN THE WARM SUN IS A FAVORITE ACTIVITY OF THE CHAMELEON AND HE HAS A FAVORITE PLACE FOR IT. THE KANJI FOR CHAMELEON HAS A NEW MODERN MEANING.

易經 I CHING

The I Ching is the Book of Changes or chameleon book because the chameleon changes color in mimicry.

SOIL, EARTH JME 17

PLACE

(EASY), DIVINATION JME 545 CHAMELEON PICTOGRAPH

NOTE HOW PICTURE IS SIMILAR TO THE KANJI

SUN OVER THE HORIZON IN DAYTIME, AT NOON

HORIZON (ALSO SUGGESTS CHAMELEON IS LYING FLAT)

SHOKU; FOOD; TABERU, TO EAT; KUU, TO EAT.

FOOD, TO EAT 食 IS A COMPOSITE OF A LARGE ROOF 人 AS IN JME 54 INDICATING THAT THE FOOD IS PREPARED OR READY TO EAT, WHITE 白 JME 37 FOR THE COLOR OF RICE (THE BASIC FOOD) AND THE MULTI-BRANCHED 𧘇 LIKE A WATER PLANT REFERRING TO THE FAMILY BRANCHES OR MEMBERS WHO WILL EAT 食 THE FOOD 食. MULTI-BRANCHED 𧘇 WAS IN LONG, CHIEF 長 JME 116 WHERE IT HAD THE SAME INFERENCE.

| RAD 184 | STROKE 9 | JME 253 |

会
MEETING, TO MEET JME 54

人
LARGE ROOF (OVER THE FOOD PREPARED AS IN A RESTAURANT)

白
WHITE JME 37

食
TO EAT

𧘇
MULTI-BRANCHED FAMILY OR CLAN (WILL EAT)

長
LONG, CHIEF (OF THE FAMILY, CLAN)

SHIN; MŌSU, TO SAY.

TO SAY 申 IS A FUSED COMPOSITE OF THE MOUTH 口 SPEAKING 曰 IN A "STREAM" OF WORDS OR LIKE AN ARROW | ON TARGET DEAD CENTER AS AT THE CROSSHAIRS + . REVIEW MIDDLE, INSIDE 中 JME 23 EXPLAINED AS AN ARROW | STRIKING THE TARGET 口 . TO SAY 曰 IS USED IN COMPOUNDS SUCH AS REPORT, APPLICATION, ETC. SINCE THE ARROW SYMBOLIZES A FLIGHT, STREAM OR SERIES OF WORDS.

| RAD 72 | STROKE 5 | JME 254 |

矢
ARROW

口
MOUTH
MIDDLE, INSIDE JME 23

曰
MOUTH IS SPEAKING

申
TO SAY

|
ARROW

引
PULLING, DRAWING, TO PULL, TO DRAW JME 156

知
TO KNOW, TO INFORM, TO TELL JME 112

JME 255	Stroke 7	Rad 158

SHIN; MI, BODY.

BODY 身 WAS ORIGINALLY A PREGNANT BODY FORMED BY A FUSION OF THE EARLY CHARACTER FOR NOSE 自 (LIKE A PREGNANT BELLY IN PROFILE) AND A BAND FOR SUPPORT ノ. THE KANJI FOR NOSE 自 NOW MEANS SELF, ONESELF, IN PERSON 自 JME 229 AS IS SUGGESTED BY OUR EXPRESSION "TO COUNT NOSES." THE PREGNANT BODY IS THE BODY. THE SNUB NOSE IN PROFILE AND THE PREGNANT BODY PROFILE ARE SOMEWHAT ALIKE.

THE BODY

BAND FOR ABDOMINAL SUPPORT

BODY (FETUS IS IN THE HOLLOW OR THE APERTURE

SELF, ONESELF, IN PERSON JME 229 (FORMERLY MEANT NOSE)

EAR JME 26

JME 256	Stroke 13	Rad 69

SHIN; ATARASHII, NEW; ARATANI, NEWLY, ANEW, AFRESH.

NEW, NEWLY, ANEW, AFRESH 新 IS A COMPOSITE OF AN AXE 斤 (AS IN PLACE 所 JME 246) CUTTING A STANDING 立 JME 149 TREE 木 JME 15, WHOSE WOOD 木 JME 15 IS NEW 新 OR NEWLY CUT.

TO STAND JME 149

TREE, WOOD JME 15

NEW, NEWLY, AFRESH, ANEW

KIN, 1.3 LBS. (AXE)

NEAR JME 195

PLACE JME 246

AXE (PICTURE)

SHIN, JIN; KAMI, (GAMI), GOD, DEITY, SPIRIT.

RAD	STROKE	JME
113	9	257

DIETY, GOD, SPIRIT 神 IS A COMPOSITE OF
TO SHOW, POINT OUT, INDICATE 示 IN ITS
COMPONENT FORM ネ AND TO SAY 申 JME 254.
TO SHOW, POINT OUT, INDICATE 示 JME 622
IS A COMPOSITE OF WHAT IS ABOVE 二 (AS IN
THE LAYERS 二 OF CLOUD 雲 JME 47) AND THREE
RAYS SPREADING RADIANCE 小 AS FROM THE SUN,
MOON, AND STARS WHICH SHOW, POINT OUT, AND
INDICATE 示 IN ASTROLOGY AND NAVIGATION.
THE COMPONENT FORM DEVELOPED FOR CONVENIENCE IN WRITING ネ.

COMPANY, FIRM,
CORPORATION,
SHINTO SHRINE
JME 234

TO SHOW,
POINT OUT,
INDICATE
JME 622

TO SHOW,
POINT OUT,
INDICATE
(COMPONENT)

GOD,
DEITY,
SPIRIT

TO SAY,
IS CALLED
JME 254

SHIN; FUKAI, DEEP, PROFOUND, DENSE;
FUKASA, DEPTH, PROFUNDITY.

RAD	STROKE	JME
85	11	258

DEEP, PROFOUND, DENSE, DEPTH, PROFUNDITY
IS A COMPOSITE OF A STICK 木 (AS IN TREE
JME 15) IN THE WATERY シ JME 14 DEEP,
PROFOUND DEPTHS 深 OF A HOLE 冗 (AS IN
SKY 空 JME 65). 深 NOTE THAT THE SKY HAS
DEPTHS AND A HOLE.

De blind horse stick'n in a big mud hole,
    Doodah! doodah!
Can't touch de bottom wid a ten-foot pole,
    Oh! doodah day! (Foster, Camptown Races).

PROFOUND
DEPTHS
ABOVE &
BELOW

WATER
COMPONENT

DEEP,
PROFOUND,
DENSE

TREE
JME 15

HOLE
AS
COMPONENT

SKY
JME 65

JME 259	STROKE 11	RAD 162

SHIN; SUSUMU, TO ADVANCE, TO PROGRESS, TO PROCEED.

TO ADVANCE, TO PROGRESS, TO PROCEED 進 IS A COMPOSITE OF A SHORT-TAILED BIRD 隹 (AS IN TO GATHER, TO COLLECT 集 JME 243) AND TO GO FAST AND STOP SUDDENLY 辶 (AS IN ROAD, PATH 道 JME 122). THE SHORT-TAILED BIRDS 隹 GO FAST AND STOP SUDDENLY AS THEY ADVANCE, PROGRESS, PROCEED 進. THE SHORT-TAILED BIRDS 隹 SUGGEST THE MILITARY SINCE THEY HAVE LEADERS, POST SENTINELS, ADVANCE IN FLOCKS, AND DESPOIL THE COUNTRYSIDE OF CROPS LIKE A MARAUDING ARMY.

STOP & GO, MOVEMENT

OLD SYMBOL FOR SHORT-TAILED BIRD

TO ADVANCE, TO PROGRESS, TO PROCEED

SHORT-TAILED BIRD

TO GATHER, TO COLLECT JME 243

JME 260	STROKE 16	RAD 147

SHIN; OYA, PARENT; SHITASHIMU, MAKE FRIENDS WITH, BECOME INTIMATE WITH; SHITASHII, INTIMATE, FRIENDLY.

PARENT, MAKE FRIENDS WITH, BECOME INTIMATE WITH, INTIMATE, FRIENDLY 親 SEES OR LOOKS AFTER 見 JME 67 (THE CHILD OR FRIEND) AS THO FROM A STANDING 立 JME 149 TREE 木 JME 15. OBSERVATION POSTS WERE IN TREES FOR A SUPERIOR VIEW. TO THE SMALL CHILD, ADULTS ARE SOMEWHAT LIKE WALKING TREES WHICH OVER-SEE AND OVER VIEW HIM.

NEW, NEWLY, AFRESH JME 256

OBSER-VATION POST

STAND-ING TREE

PARENT, MAKE FRIENDS WITH, INTIMATE

TO LOOK, SEE JME 67

WALKING EYE OF PARENT

ZU, DRAWING, PLAN; TO; HAKARU, TO PLAN, TO DEVISE.

RAD	STROKE	JME
31	7	261

DRAWING, PLAN, TO PLAN, TO DEVISE 図 SHOWS THE BIG DIPPER CONSTELLATION 斗 OF SEVEN STARS (AS IN COURSE, BRANCH 科斗 JME 164) ENCLOSED ⬜ BY BEING DEVISED 図 AS A PLAN, DRAWING 図.

7 STARS

PLAN OF 7 STARS

科 斗 図 口 園

DRAWING, PLAN (OF THE GREAT DIPPER)

COURSE, BRANCH JME 164

TO, (UNIT OF MEASUREMENT, 19.04 QT.) DIPPER OR GREAT DIPPER

DRAWING, PLAN, TO PLAN, TO DEVISE

ENCLOSURE

GARDEN, JME 159

SŪ, (ZŪ); KAZU, NUMBER; KAZOERU, TO COUNT.

RAD	STROKE	JME
66	13	262

NUMBER, TO COUNT 数 IS A COMPOSITE OF A WOMAN 女 JME 32 COUNTING 数 THE NUMBER 数 OF RICE 米 JME 135 GRAINS WITH A HAND 又 HOLDING A STICK ノ TO THE RIGHT TO ENSURE CONTROL AND ACCURACY.

女 米 数 攵

WOMAN, GIRL, FEMALE JME 32

RICE JME 135

NUMBER, TO COUNT

HAND HOLDING STICK CONTROLS THE COUNT

STICK IN HAND

JME 263	Stroke 5	Rad 1

SE, SEI, (GENERATION); YO, WORLD, ERA, AGE, REIGN.

WORLD, ERA, REIGN 世 DERIVES FROM THREE TEN'S OR THIRTY 卅 WRITTEN AS LINKED TEN'S FOR CONVENIENCE WITH THE LEFT TEN'S BENT TO CARRY THE OTHERS 世. THIRTY YEARS IS REGARDED AS THE SPAN OF A GENERATION OR REIGN. WHEN THAT GENERATION PASSES, A NEW WORLD OR ERA BEGINS. NOTE THE SPECIAL FORM OF THIRTY AS EXPLAINED WITH TEN 十 JME 10.

SHELLEY: "THE WORLD'S GREAT AGE BEGINS ANEW, THE GOLDEN YEARS RETURN, THE EARTH DOTH LIKE A SNAKE RENEW HER WINTER WEEDS OUTWORN."

POND, POOL JME 110 (WATER & SNAKE COMPONENTS)

SNAKE COMPONENT

(GENERATION), WORLD, ERA, REIGN, AGE

THIRTY (LINKED TENS)

TEN JME 10

ROMAN TEN

JME 264	Stroke 9	Rad 72

SEI, JŌ; HOSHI, (BOSHI), STAR.

STAR 星 IS A COMPOSITE OF SUN 日 JME 11 AND BIRTH, TO BE BORN 生 JME 34. A STAR IS THE BIRTH 生 OF A SUN 日 SINCE ALL STARS 星 ARE SUNS 日.

EXISTENCE, LIFE, TO BE BORN, TO GIVE BIRTH JME 34

STAR

SUN JME 11

DARK JME 154

SEI; HARE, FINE WEATHER.
HARERU, TO CLEAR, BECOME CLEAR (WEATHER),
TO BE DISPELLED.

CLEAR WEATHER, FINE WEATHER, TO CLEAR,
TO BECOME CLEAR, TO BE DISPELLED 晴 IS A
COMPOSITE OF BLUE 青 JME 36 (OR GREEN) FOR
THE SKY, AND THE SUN 日 JME 11 TO EMPHASIZE
THE FINE CLEAR WEATHER 晴. THE FINE CLEAR
WEATHER 日晴 IS SUCH AS WHEN THE MOON IS ABLE
TO PENETRATE THE THICK FOLIAGE 三 CASTING
BLUE SHADOWS LIKE THE BLUE 青 OF A SUNNY 日 CLEAR WEATHER 晴

RAD	STROKE	JME
72	12	265

日 晴 青 明

SUN,
DAY
JME 11

FINE WEATHER,
TO CLEAR,
BECOME CLEAR,
BE DISPELLED

BLUE
JME 36

LIGHT, CLEAR,
BRIGHT,
TO DAWN
JME 141

SEN; FUNA, FUNE, (BUNE), SHIP, BOAT, LINER.

SHIP, BOAT, LINER 船 IS A COMPOSITE OF A
PICTOGRAPH OF A BOAT 舟 AND EIGHT 八 JME 8
MOUTHS 口 JME 27 FOR THE FAMILY OR CREW
ON BOARD. THE IDEAL FAMILY CONSISTS OF
EIGHT MEMBERS. THE CATHOLIC FATHERS
SUGGESTED THAT THE EIGHT MEMBERS WERE NOAH
AND HIS FAMILY ON THE ARK. THE PICTOGRAPH
OF A BOAT SHOWS THE RUDDER, SAIL, TWO
OCCUPANTS, AND A HULL OPEN-ENDED TOWARDS THE
BOW ABOVE THE WATER LINE AS ORIENTAL SKIFFS OFTEN ARE.

RAD	STROKE	JME
137	11	266

RUDDER----
SAILOR----
SAIL----
SAILOR----
OPEN BOW--

TOP
VIEW
OF BOAT

BOAT

SHIP, BOAT,
LINER

EIGHT
JME 8

MOUTH
JME 27
(PERSON)

JME 267	Stroke 6	Rad 11

ZEN, (WHOLE, ENTIRE); MATTAKU, ENTIRELY, COMPLETELY.

WHOLE, ENTIRE, ENTIRELY, COMPLETELY 全 IS A COMPOSITE OF KING 王 JME 49 (SYMBOLIC OF COMPLETENESS IN JOINING HEAVEN, EARTH, AND MAN) AND A LARGE ROOF 人 (AS IN MEETING, TO MEET 会 JME 54) FOR THE UNITY OR HARMONY EMPHASIZING THE COMPLETENESS 全.

会
MEETING, TO MEET JME 54

人
LARGE ROOF

全
WHOLE, ENTIRE, ENTIRELY, COMPLETELY

王
KING JME 49 (JOINING HEAVEN, MAN, & EARTH)

三
THREE JME 3 (TRIAD OF HEAVEN, MAN, AND EARTH)

JME 268	Stroke 9	Rad 162

SŌ; OKURU, TO SEND.

TO SEND 送 IS A COMPOSITE OF TO GO RAPIDLY AND PAUSE SUDDENLY 辶 (AS IN ROAD, PATH 道 JME 122) AND A FUSION OF ARROW 矢 (AS IN TO KNOW, TO INFORM, TO TELL 知 JME 112) AND THE GOAT COMPONENT 䒑 (AS IN BEFORE, PREVIOUS, IN FRONT OF 前 JME 102). BOTH THE ARROW 矢 AND THE GOAT 羊 GO RAPIDLY AND PAUSE SUDDENLY 辶 AS THO SENT 送.

道
ROAD, PATH JME 122

送
TO SEND

关
(FUSION OF GOAT & ARROW)

知
TO KNOW, TO INFORM, TO TELL JME 112

前
BEFORE, PREVIOUS, IN FRONT OF JME 102

RAD	STROKE	JME
37	4	269

TA, TAI; FUTOI, BIG, THICK (IN CIRCUM-
FERENCE), DEEP (VOICE), BOLD, SHAMELESS;
FUTORU, TO BECOME FAT.

BIG, THICK, BOLD, DEEP, SHAMELESS, TO BECOME
FAT 太 IS BIG, GREAT 大 JME 22 WITH THE
DOT 丶 FOR EXTENSION OF THE BIGNESS
IN VARIOUS WAYS SUCH AS CIRCUMFERENCE,
VOICE, ATTITUDE, AND SIZE, OFTEN WITH SEXUAL
ALLUSIONS. (NOTE THE POSITION OF THE DOT 丶
BETWEEN THE LEGS 太).

BIG, GREAT
JME 22

DOG
JME 66

DOT
(INCREASE
OF SCOPE
OR RANGE
BELOW AS
IN A PHY-
SICAL WAY)

BIG, THICK,
DEEP, BOLD,
SHAMELESS,
BECOME FAT

BIG, GREAT
JME 22

RAD	STROKE	JME
188	7	270

TAI, TEI, (BODY).

THE BODY 体 IS THE ROOT, SOURCE 本 JME 45
OF A MAN, PERSON イ JME 30 (SINCE THE BODY
IS VITAL TO OTHER ACTIVITIES).

PICTURE

COMPONENT
FOR MAN,
PERSON

(BODY)

ROOT,
SOURCE,
BOOK
JME 45

TREE,
WOOD
JME 15

JME 271	Stroke 9	Rad 60

TAI; MATSU, TO WAIT FOR, TO EXPECT.

TO WAIT FOR, TO EXPECT 待 IS A COMPOSITE OF MEN 彳 (AS IN BEHIND, AFTER 後 JME 208), THE PLURAL OF THE MAN, PERSON COMPONENT 亻 AND TEMPLE 寺 JME 228. IN THE TEMPLE 寺 MEN 彳 WAIT FOR, EXPECT 待 FESTIVALS, FEASTS, OR RELIGIOUS RITES. TEMPLES 寺 WERE ALSO USED FOR PRIVATE FESTIVITIES BY MEN 彳 WHO WAITED FOR, EXPECTED 待 MEN 彳 (THEIR FRIENDS). A TEMPLE WAS A CONVENIENT MEETING PLACE.

BEHIND, AFTER JME 208

MEN, PERSONS IN THE COMPONENT FORM (FOLLOWING EACH OTHER)

TO WAIT FOR, TO EXPECT JME 271

TEMPLE JME 228

TIME JME 87

SUN SHINES ON TEMPLE

JME 272	Stroke 5	Rad 30

TAI; DAI, A STAND.

MOUTH 口 JME 27 AS A ROCK, STONE 石 (NOTE ROCK, STONE 石 JME 44) REPRESENTS USE AS AN ALTAR, STAND. IN GUEST 客 JME 184 MOUTH 口 HAS THE SAME SIGNIFICANCE AS A SEAT, STOOL 口. THE COMPONENT 厶 REPRESENTS A CONTAINER 厶 ON THE STAND. THE KANJI FOR A STAND 台 IS FAIRLY PICTOGRAPHIC. WHAT IS ON THE SEAT OR ROCK IS READY TO EXPAND BY BEING PASSED ABOUT OR USED.

TO BEGIN JME 225

PICTURE

(BASKET, COCOON, CONTAINER, ETC.)

A STAND

GUEST JME 184

MOUTH JME 27 (ROCK, SEAT, STONE, STAND)

DAI, (GRADE); PREFIX FOR NUMERALS AS DAI NI, NUMBER TWO, ETC.

GRADE, NUMBER PREFIX 第 IS A COMPOSITE OF YOUNGER BROTHER 弟 JME 282 (MINUS THE HORNS) AND BAMBOO 竹 JME 113 SLIPS USED AS TALLIES. AFTER THE FIRST SON WHO IS BIG OR GREAT 大 , THE YOUNGER BROTHERS 第 WERE NUMBERED IN ORDER OF BIRTH, AND THE NUMBER BECAME PART OF THEIR NAMES AS TWO WONG AND THREE WONG IN CHINESE. THE FIRST NAME IN JAPANESE MAY INDICATE THE BIRTH ORDER AS TARŌ, ICHIRŌ: ONE MAN, MALE; JIRŌ: TWO MAN, MALE; ETC.

| RAD | STROKE | JME |
| 118 | 11 | 273 |

YOUNGER BROTHER (WITH HORNS) JME 282

PERSON JME 235 (CARRYING EARTH)

BAMBOO

CARRYING (BOW & ARROW AS IN YOUNGER BROTHER)

(GRADE), PREFIX FOR NUMERALS

FUNERAL (BOW & ARROW HUNG UP OR PUT AWAY) TO MOURN

PULLING, DRAWING, TO PULL JME 156

TAN; SUMI, CHARCOAL.

CHARCOAL 炭 IS USUALLY MADE BY FIRING 火 WOOD (WITH LIMITED AIR) FROM THE HIGHER CLIFF 厂 PARTS OF THE MOUNTAIN 山 WHERE THE WOOD IS NOT VALUABLE FOR LUMBER.

| RAD | STROKE | JME |
| 46 | 9 | 274 |

MOUNTAIN

MOUNTAIN

CLIFF

CLIFF

FIRE

ROCK,CLIFF, CRAG JME 178 (MT.,CLIFF, & ROCK)

BANK,SHORE, COAST JME 177 (MT.,CLIFF, & SHIELD)

MT. AND CLIFF ARE USED AS A COMBINATION IN VARIOUS KANJI

CHARCOAL (MT. JME 38, CLIFF, & FIRE JME 13)

JME 275	Stroke 9	Rad 140

CHA, TEA, TEA PLANT, TEA LEAVES.

TEA 茶 IS A COMPOSITE OF THE LARGE ROOF 𠆢 (OF THE TEA HOUSE), THE TREE 木 OR BUSH ON WHICH THE TEA LEAVES GROW, AND GRASS ⺾ THE TOP COMPONENT OF LEAF 葉 JME 327 FOR THE LEAVES 葉 FROM WHICH THE TEA IS BREWED.

会	𠆢	木	茶	⺾	草
MEETING, TO MEET JME 54	LARGE ROOF (AS OF TEAHOUSE)	TREE	TEA, TEA PLANT, TEA LEAVES	GRASS COMPONENT	GRASS JME 106

JME 276	Stroke 12	Rad 123

CHAKU; KIRU, TO WEAR; TSUKU, TO ARRIVE AT, TO REACH.

TO ARRIVE AT, TO REACH 着 IS A COMPOSITE OF THE GOAT 羊 CARRIED BY OR DEPENDENT ON ノ HIS EYE 目 WHO ARRIVES AT, REACHES 着 (HIS DESTINATION AS HE ASCENDS OR DESCENDS THE PRECIPITOUS HEIGHTS). THE GOAT'S HIDE AND WOOL ARE WORN 着 .

目	ノ	着	羊	道	送
EYE, A LOOK JME 25	CARRIED BY, DEPENDENT ON	TO WEAR, ARRIVE AT, TO REACH	GOAT	ROAD, WAY, PATH JME 122	TO SEND JME 268

CHŪ; SOSOGU, TO POUR, CONCENTRATE ON.

Rad 85	Stroke 8	JME 277

TO POUR, TO CONCENTRATE ON 注 IS WHAT THE MASTER, OWNER 主 JME 237 DOES WITH THE LIQUID 氵 JME 14 (TEA OR WINE) FOR GUESTS. THE MASTER, OWNER 主 CONCENTRATES ON 注 THE LIQUID 氵 HE POURS 注.

注 主 住 王

WATER COMPO-NENT

TO POUR, CONCENTRATE ON

MASTER, OWNER JME 237

DWELLING, TO LIVE, TO DWELL, TO RESIDE JME 244

KING JME 49

CHŪ; HASHIRA, (BASHIRA), PILLAR, POST.

Rad 75	Stroke 9	JME 278

THE PILLAR, POST 柱 IS THE MASTER, OWNER 主 JME 237 AMONG THE TREES 木 JME 15 SINCE IT MUST BE SUPERIOR TIMBER FOR CONSTRUCTION PURPOSES ANALOGOUS TO THE MASTER AMONG THE HOUSEHOLD. IN OUR CARPENTRY, THERE IS THE KING POST WHICH VERTICALLY JOINS THE APEX OF A TRUSS TO THE BASE. QUEEN POSTS ALSO EXIST.

木 柱 主 王

TREE, WOOD JME 15

PILLAR, POST

MASTER, OWNER JME 237

KING JME 49

VERTICAL KING POST SHOWN IN BLACK

JME 279	STROKE 9	RAD 1

CHŪ; HIRU, NOON, DAYTIME.

NOON, DAYTIME 昼 IS A COMPOSITE OF LENGTH (THE BODY'S 尸 FOOT 尺 AS IN STATION 駅 JME 158) FOR THE LENGTH 尺 OF THE SUN'S 日 SHADOW — AT NOON 昼 OR IN THE DAYTIME 昼 .

BODY IN COFFIN

尸

BODY REVIEW SHOP JME 161

SUN OVER HORIZON AT NOON OR IN THE DAYTIME

NOON, DAYTIME

SHAKU (.995 FT.) (BODY STEPS 尺)

STATION JME 158

JME 280	STROKE 9	RAD 162

TSUI; OU, TO DRIVE AWAY, TO PURSUE, TO RUN AFTER.

TO DRIVE AWAY, TO PURSUE, TO RUN AFTER IS A COMPOSITE OF TO GO FAR AND PAUSE SUDDENLY 辶 (AS IN ADVANCE 進 JME 259) AND THE LEFT COMPONENT 𠂤 OF TEACHER, ARMY 師 JME 624. THE ARMY 師 GOES FAR AND PAUSES SUDDENLY 辶 AS IT DRIVES AWAY, PURSUES, RUNS AFTER 追 (THE ENEMY). THE TWO STORIES 𠂤 SUGGESTS A GOVERNMENT BUILDING AS IN DEPARTMENT, OFFICE, BUREAU 局 JME 194. THE HORN ノ OVER THE BUILDING 𠂤 IS FOR THE MILITARY.

運 辶 追 師 官 局

LUCK, TO CARRY, TO TRANS- PORT JME 157.

MOVEMENT, STOP & GO

DRIVE AWAY, PURSUE, RUN AFTER

TEACHER, ARMY JME 624

GOV'T., GOV'T. SERVICE OR POSITION (NOTE ROOF) JME 364

DEPT., OFFICE, BUREAU JME 194

TSŪ; TŌRU, TO PASS, PASS THROUGH, GO ALONG;
KAYOU, TO GO TO AND FROM, TO GO TO AND BACK.

RAD	STROKE	JME
162	10	281

TO PASS, PASS THROUGH, GO ALONG, TO GO TO
AND FROM, TO GO TO AND BACK 通 IS A
COMPOSITE OF WHAT IS SECRET, PRIVATE, IN A
BASKET OR A COCOON ム BEING TURNED OVER マ
AND LET OUT, AND THE INTESTINES ‡ TURNING
AND CHURNING LIKE AXLE AND WHEELS ‡ WITHIN
THE CONTAINING BODY ⊓ PASSING 通 THEIR
CONTENTS IN A GOING AND PAUSING ⻌ ACTION.
THE BODY'S ⊓ INTESTINAL ‡ CONTENTS ARE RELEASED AS FROM
AN INVERTED BASKET マ IN A GOING AND PAUSING ⻌ PASSING 通.

MOVE-
MENT,
TO STOP
& GO

TO PASS,
PASS THRU,
GO ALONG,
TO GO TO &
FROM

WHAT IS
SECRET,
PRIVATE
IN THE
BASKET,
COCOON
ム
TURNED
OVER &
DROPPED マ

BUSINESS,
TO USE
JME 146

TO PASS,
PASS THROUGH
(EMPTY THE
BREAD-BASKET)

WEEK
JME 242

TEI, DAI; OTŌTO, YOUNGER BROTHER.

RAD	STROKE	JME
57	7	282

YOUNGER BROTHER 弟 IS A RAM-BUNCTIOUS OR
GOATISH 羊 (GOAT 羊 COMPONENT ⅄) CREATURE
WITH BOW 弓 (AS IN TO PULL, TO DRAW 引
JME 156) AND ARROWS | (AS IN MIDDLE,
INSIDE 中 JME 23) SLUNG ACROSS ノ HIS
SHOULDER.

MIDDLE,
INSIDE
JME 23

TO PULL,
TO DRAW
JME 156

GOAT
COMPONENT

CARRIED OR
SLUNG OVER
(SHOULDER)

YOUNGER
BROTHER

FUNERAL
(BOW &
ARROWS
HUNG UP)

(GRADE),
PREFIX
FOR
NUMERALS
JME 273

JME	Stroke	Rad
283	13	167

TETSU, IRON, STEEL.

IRON, STEEL 鉄 IS THE METAL 金 JME 16 THAT IS LOST 失 JME 418 IN THAT THE GOVERNMENT TAKES IT FOR WEAPONS AND WAR. LOST 失 IS A FUSION OF THE HUSBAND 夫 JME 501 (MAN 人 WITH A PIN ─ IN HIS HAIR) WHO LOST THE COW 牛 JME 62 OR ARROW 矢 (AS IN TO KNOW 知 JME 112).

先 — IN PREVIOUS, ETC., "TWO LEGS" STRIDES OUT. SEE JME 33.

大 BIG, GREAT
人 MAN, PERSON

DISTINGUISH PREVIOUS, IN ADVANCE, AHEAD FROM TO LOSE

金 (GOLD), MONEY, (METAL AS COMPONENT)

鉄 IRON, STEEL

失 TO LOSE JME 418 (HUSBAND 夫 OR MAN 人 LOSES 失 COW 牛)

牛 CATTLE, BULL, OX, COW JME 62

矢 ARROW

夫 HUSBAND JME 501 (HAIRPIN ─ OF MAJORITY ON MAN 人)

JME	Stroke	Rad
284	8	53

TEN; MISE, STORE.

STORE 店 IS A COMPOSITE OF SHED 广 (AS IN WAREHOUSE 庫 JME 206) AND PROGNOSTICATE 占 (TELLING JME 27 THE MEANING OF THE FIRE PRODUCED CRACKS 卜 ON THE TORTOISE BACK OR ANIMAL BONES. REVIEW OUTSIDE, OTHER, FOREIGN 外 JME 56. THE PROFESSION OF THE DIVINER 占 WAS OF GREAT IMPORTANCE AND HIS "STORE" 店 OR PLACE OF BUSINESS ONE OF THE EARLIEST.

室 ROOM, STOREROOM, CAVE, GREENHOUSE JME 232

庫 (WAREHOUSE) JME 206

店 STORE

占 JME 295 MARKS (PROGNOSTICATE) 口 MOUTH JME 27 (SHELL THAT TELLS)

卜 (DIVINATION) SHOWS THE CRACKS ON TORTOISE SHELL OR A SCAPULA

外 (FOREIGN) OUTSIDE, OTHER JME 56

TEN, MARKS, POINT, SPOT.

MARKS, POINT, SPOT 点 IS A COMPOSITE OF
EXPLAINING 占 OR DIVINING BY THE CRACKS ⼘
(AS IN OUTSIDE, OTHER, FOREIGN 外 JME 56)
ON THE TORTOISE SHELL OR ANIMAL BONE WHEN
HEATED BY FIRE ⺬ WHICH PRODUCES THE MARKS,
POINTS, SPOTS 点.

RAD	STROKE	JME
203	9	285

FIRE MAKES
PATTERN OF
CRACKS ON
SHELL ⬡
OF TORTOISE

占

MOUTH ⬜
OF THE
DIVINER
INTERPRETS
CRACKS ⼘

点

MARKS,
POINT,
SPOT

店

STORE
JME 284

外

(FOREIGN),
OUTSIDE,
OTHER
JME 56

DEN, (LIGHTNING, ELECTRICITY).

LIGHTNING, ELECTRICITY 電 IS A COMPOSITE OF
RAIN 雨 JME 42 (THE SIGNIFIER FOR KANJI
MEANING SNOW, CLOUD, THUNDER, DEW, ETC.)
AND THE FIELD 田 JME 40 THROUGH WHICH THE
LIGHTNING BOLT ⌐ PASSES.

RAD	STROKE	JME
173	13	286

RAIN
JME 42

CLOUD
JME 47

(LIGHTNING,
ELECTRICITY)

RICE FIELD,
PADDY
JME 40

LIGHTNING
BOLT

(STRIKES
LIKE SNAKE'S
TAIL).

JME 287	Stroke 11	Rad 163

TO, TSU; MIYAKO, CAPITAL, METROPOLIS.

CAPITAL, METROPOLIS 都 IS A COMPOSITE OF PERSONS 者 JME 235 AND TOWN, CITY 阝 (AN ABBREVIATION OF 邑) WHICH IS A COMPOSITE OF MOUTH 口 JME 27 FOR THE WAY THE CITY CONTAINS ITS PEOPLE 者 AND SNAKE 巴 FOR THE SINUOUS APPEARANCE OF THE CITY WALL WHICH COILS ABOUT THE CAPITAL OR METROPOLIS 都.

PERSONS JME 235 — CAPITAL, METROPOLIS — ABBREVIATION OF OLD FORM TO RT. — MOUTH OVER SNAKE COMPONENT IN COLOR — TOWN, CITY

JME 288	Stroke 9	Rad 53

DO, DEGREE, EXTENT, TIME, TIMES.

DEGREE, EXTENT, TIME, TIMES 度 IS A COMPOSITE OF A HAND 又 UNDER A SHED-TYPE ROOF 广 (AS IN STORE 店 JME 284) WITH NUMBERS OR LAYERS 廿 FOR THE DEGREE, EXTENT, TIME, TIMES 度. THE IMPLICATION IS THAT THE LAYERS ARE SEPARATED OR DIVIDED TO A CERTAIN DEGREE, EXTENT, OR NUMBER OF TIMES 度. THIS SAME COMPONENT 廿 IS USED TO REPRESENT AN INDEFINITE NUMBER OF "THINGS" IN THE BACKGROUND AND EVOLVED FROM HANDS IN COOPERATION.

STORE JME 284 — SHED-TYPE ROOF — DEGREE, EXTENT, TIME, TIMES — NUMBERS, LAYERS — TWENTY — TEN — HAND — HAND — TO TAKE JME 238

TŌ; KATANA, (GATANA), SWORD, BLADE.

SWORD, BLADE 刀 IS A REPRESENTATION OF THE SWEEP OF THE ARM ノ WITH THE SWORD OR BLADE MOVING ㇆ IN THE HAND. NOTE SWORD, BLADE'S 刀 CORRESPONDENCE TO A QUADRANT 卐 OF THE SWASTIKA 卐 AND SIMILARITY TO SUCH KANJI AS STRENGTH 力 JME 148. THE COMPONENT FORM OF SWORD, BLADE ⺉ IS MORE PICTOGRAPHIC.

Rad	Stroke	JME
18	2	289

STRENGTH, POWER JME 148

SUPER-IMPOSITION

SWASTIKA

SWEEP OR STROKE OF ARM

SWORD, BLADE

ARC OR MOVEMENT OF BLADE

TŌ; ATARU, TO HIT, TO STRIKE, TO SUCCEED, TO WIN, (I.V.); ATERU, TO HIT, TO SUCCEED, TO GUESS, (T.V.).

TO HIT, TO STRIKE, TO SUCCEED, TO WIN, TO GUESS 当 IS A COMPOSITE OF THE GLEAMING (AS IN LIGHT, BRILLIANCE, TO SHINE 光 JME 72) TUSKS ON THE SNOUTED HEAD 彐 OF THE WILD BOAR. THE WILD BOAR IS FAMOUS FOR THE FEROCITY OF HIS CHARGE WHICH HITS, STRIKES, SUCCEEDS, WINS 当. HIS VERY FEROCITY MAY RESULT IN A MISS, THUS SUGGESTING TO GUESS 当. NOTE HOW THE BOAR'S HEAD OR SNOUT 彐 IS LIKE A HAND 彐 (AS IN TO HURRY 急 JME 186). THE SNOUT IS MARVELOUSLY ADAPTED FOR USE AS A HAND (AS IN DIGGING TRUFFLES). THE SNOUT CAN DIG, PUSH, PROBE, AND ACT AS A LEVER.

Rad	Stroke	JME
42	6	290

BABYLONIAN SYMBOL FOR BOAR

TYPE OF AUSTRAL-ASIAN BOAR

(GLEAMING) TUSKS

SUPERIMPOSITION ON FUSION OF HAND WITH BOAR'S HEAD

JME	Stroke	Rad
291	7	64

TŌ; NAGERU, TO THROW, TO GIVE UP.

TO THROW, TO GIVE UP 投 IS A COMPOSITE OF HAND, ARM 手 JME 28 AND TO STRIKE 殳 (A COMPOSITE OF HAND 又 AND A BIRD'S WING 几 WHICH STRIKES 殳 LIKE A HAND 又 . THE HAND, ARM 手 THROWS 投 TO STRIKE. TO GIVE UP 投 IS A DERIVED MEANING JUST AS WE SAY "TO THROW THE FIGHT, TO THROW THE GAME."

HAND, ARM JME 28   TO THROW, TO GIVE UP   TO STRIKE   ULNA RADIUS DIGITS HUMERUS WING BONES   TO STRIKE   HAND

JME	Stroke	Rad
292	10	46

TŌ; SHIMA, (JIMA), ISLAND.

ISLAND 島 IS A COMPOSITE OF A LONG-TAILED BIRD 鳥 JME 117 WITH THE FEET 灬 REPLACED BY A MOUNTAIN 山 JME 38. AN ISLAND 島 IS A MOUNTAIN 山 (IN THE WATER) WITH LONG-TAILED BIRDS 鳥.

LONG-TAILED BIRD ON MT. PEAK IN WATER: ISLAND   MOUNTAIN JME 38   ISLAND   LONG-TAILED BIRD JME 117

146   146

TŌ, (DŌ); KOTAE, ANSWER; KOTAERU, TO ANSWER.

RAD	STROKE	JME
118	12	293

ANSWER, TO ANSWER 答 IS A COMPOSITE OF THE BAMBOO 竹 (LEAVES RUSTLING FOR THE SOUND OF THE ANSWER 答), THE LARGE ROOF 𠆢 (FOR A SCHOOL SETTING, ETC.), AND ONE 一 MOUTH 口 (FOR THE ANSWER'S 答 CONFORMITY OR AUTHORITY.

RUSTLE OF BAMBOO LEAVES ANSWERS

BAMBOO JME 113

ANSWER, TO ANSWER

TO FIT, TO SUIT, TO AGREE, TO BE TO- GETHER JME 77

ANSWER AS FROM ONE MOUTH UNDER THE ROOF

TŌ, (DŌ), ZU; ATAMA, HEAD, BRAIN, TOP, LEADER.

RAD	STROKE	JME
181	16	294

HEAD, BRAIN, TOP, LEADER 頭 IS A COMPOSITE OF 豆 PEA, BEAN, MINIATURE (DOLL, ETC.) AND HEAD 頁 AS IN FACE 顔 JME 179. THE IMPLICATION OF PEA, BEAN, MINIATURE 豆 SOMETHING IS DIMINUTIVE RESEMBLANCE TO THE HEAD 頁 AS WE SAY "PEA-BRAINED." ORIGINALLY PEA, BEAN, ETC. WAS A VASE 豆 ALSO HEAD-SHAPED. HEAD 頁 SHOWS A COVERED EYE OR HEAD 目 WALKING AS IT SUPERVISES.

CREST OR COVERING

VASE (RESEMBLES AND/OR HOLDS PEAS, BEANS, ETC.)

PEA, BEAN, MINIATURE SOMETHING

HEAD, BRAIN, TOP, LEADER

COMPO- NENT HEAD

FACE JME 179

SUPER- IMPOSITION OF EYES & MOUTH ON THE HEAD COMPONENT

JME	STROKE	RAD
295	6	30

DŌ; ONAJI, SAME.

SAME 同 IS ONE — MOUTH 口 IN A SPACE 冂 FOR SAMENESS 同 OF OPINION, OF ECONOMIC BASE, OF POLITICAL STRUCTURE, ETC.

FLESH, MEAT
JME 297
(HANGS IN
SPACE OR
ENCLOSURE)

(SPACE,
ENCLOSURE)

SAME

ONE
MOUTH:
SAMENESS
OF OPINION,
ECONOMIC
BASE, OF
POLITICAL
STRUCTURE,
ETC.

TO FIT,
TO SUIT,
TO AGREE, TO
BE TOGETHER
JME 77

JME	STROKE	RAD
296	11	19

DŌ; UGOKU, TO MOVE.

TO MOVE 動 IS THE STRENGTH 力 JME 148 TO MOVE 動 A HEAVY, WEIGHTY 重 JME 245 (DOUBLE-WHEELED) VEHICLE OR CHARIOT 車 JME 88.

CART   HEAVY CART   TURNED 90°

(CHARIOT),
WHEEL,
VEHICLE
JME 88

HEAVY,
WEIGHTY
JME 245

TO MOVE

STRENGTH,
POWER
JME 148

NIKU, FLESH, MEAT.

FLESH, MEAT 肉 IS A PICTOGRAPH OF FLESH, MEAT 仌 (HANGING TO CURE OR DRY) IN A PARTLY ENCLOSED SPACE 冂.

RAD	STROKE	JME
130	6	297

(SPACE OR ENCLOSURE)   FLESH, MEAT   TWO FLITCHES OF MEAT ARE HANGING TO DRY OR CURE   MEAT HANGING TO AGE OR CURE OR DRY

HA; NAMI, WAVE.

WAVE 波 IS A COMPOSITE OF SKIN 皮 JME 307 AND WATER 氵 JME 14. THE WAVE 波 IS THE SKIN 皮 OF THE WATER 氵.

SKIN 皮 JME 307 SHOWS THE HAND 又 HOLDING A KNIFE OR SHELL l SCRAPING THE SKIN OF THE BODY 尸 (AS IN SHOP 屋 JME 161).

RAD	STROKE	JME
85	8	298

 屋 波 皮 又

SHOP JME 161   WAVE (SKIN OF WATER OR WATER HAND SCRAPES & STRIKES THE CLIFF)   SKIN JME 307   HAND & SCRAPER   PICTURE OF HAND AND SCRAPER   BODY, CORPSE

尺

MEASURE OF LENGTH

JME 299	STROKE 10	RAD 164

HAI, (PAI); KUBARU, TO DISTRIBUTE,
TO DELIVER, TO ALLOCATE.

TO DISTRIBUTE, TO DELIVER, TO ALLOCATE 配
IS A COMPOSITE OF A WINE JUG 酉 AND WHAT
IS PRIVATE 己 TURNING OR CIRCLING 己 LIKE
A SNAKE 巴.
THE WINE JUG 酉 IS A PICTOGRAPH COMBINING
THE STOPPER 丆 , JUG 口 , AND LIQUOR LEVEL —.

WEST
JME 96

(BIRD
COVERS
NEST
AS AN
ANALOGY)

WINE
JUG
PICTO-
GRAPH
NOTE
STOPPER
& WINE
LEVEL

DISTRIBUTE,
DELIVER,
ALLOCATE

(I, MY-
SELF,
ONESELF)
REFLEXIVE,
AS SNAKE
TURNING &
SWALLOWING
ITS OWN TAIL

COMPONENT
SNAKE

COLOR
JME 94
(COLOR
OF SNAKE)

JME 300	STROKE 12	RAD 154

BAI; KAU, TO BUY.

TO BUY 買 IS A COMPOSITE OF THE COWRIE
SHELL 貝 JME 169 (USED AS A MEDIUM OF
EXCHANGE) AND THE NET 罒 IN WHICH THE
COWRIES 貝 ARE CARRIED (AS IN A SHOPPING
BAG) IN ORDER TO BUY 買.

NET SHOPPING BAG
WITH COWRIE SHELLS

SEA
SHELL
JME 169

TO BUY

NET
(HOLDING
COWRIE
SHELLS)

EYES
(AS OF A
NET)

VOLUME FOUR: KANJI 301-338; INDEXES

CATTLE, COW, BULL, OX

in the Japanese <u>kanji</u> and
in the Chinese characters

BAI; URI, SALE; URU, TO SELL.

SALE, TO SELL 売 IS A COMPOSITE OF A GENTLEMAN, FIGURE 士 JME 410 AT A DESK OR STAND 冗 (AS IN TO READ 読 JME 123) SELLING, TO SELL 売. 読

| | | | | | RAD 33 | STROKE 7 | JME 301 |

仕
WORK, TO SERVE JME 221

士
PERSON, MAN, FIGURE, GENTLEMAN JME 410

-|-
PICTURE OF MAN'S FEATURES

売
TO SELL

冗
DESK

売
TO SELL, SALE (MAN IS AT DESK SELLING)

読
TO READ JME 123

HATA, HATAKE, (BATAKE), FARM, FIELD, CULTIVATED FIELD, PLANTATION.

FARM, FIELD, CULTIVATED FIELD, PLANTATION IS A COMPOSITE OF FIRE 火 JME 13 AND RICE FIELD 田 JME 40. A FARM, FIELD, CULTIVATED FIELD, PLANTATION 田 IS PREPARED FOR CULTIVATION BY FIRING 火 OR BURNING THE WILD GROWTH OR STUBBLE FROM THE PREVIOUS HARVEST.

| | | | | RAD 86 | STROKE 9 | JME 302 |

火
FIRE JME 13

畑
FARM, FIELD, CULTIVATED FIELD, PLANTATION

田
PADDY, RICE FIELD

FIRE (PICTURE)

FORTY ACRES & NO MULE

MAYAN FIELDS WERE CULTIVATED BY THE "SLASH AND BURN" (MILPA) TECHNIQUE; SWIDDEN ARE CLEARINGS BY SHIFTING CULTIVATORS.

JME	STROKE	RAD
303	9	105

HATSU, (PATSU), (DEPARTURE, TO LEAVE, TO SHOOT).

DEPARTURE, TO LEAVE, TO SHOOT 発 IS A COMPOSITE OF THE LEGS 癶 STRETCHED OUT WITH TWO SHORT LINES ``` ON EACH SIDE FOR THE HIP AND KNEE JOINTS (LIKE THE KNEE JOINT IN FOOT, LEG 足 JME 29) AND 无 A COMPOSITE OF THE FEET HOLDING A BOW, THE HANDS DRAWING THE ARROW, AND THE ARROW LASHING OUT L LIKE A BOLT OF LIGHTNING L (AS IN LIGHTNING 電 JME 286 WHERE THE BOLT L IS BELOW AND TO THE RIGHT).

MOVEMENT OF LEG JOINTS IN SHOOTING THE ARROW	LEGS SHOWING HIP & KNEE JOINTS	発 DEPARTURE, TO LEAVE, TO SHOOT	无 HANDS ON THE BOWSTRING	BOW-STRING	電 LIGHTNING JME 286

JME	STROKE	RAD
304	7	32

HAN; SAKA, (ZAKA), A SLOPE, HILL.

A SLOPE, HILL 坂 IS THE ANTITHESIS, OPPOSITE 反 JME 492 OF EARTH, SOIL 土 JME 17 (WHICH IS LEVEL). ANTI-, ANTITHESIS, OPPOSITE 反 IS REPRESENTED BY THE HAND 又 FROM THE CLIFF 厂 (AS IN ROCK, CLIFF, CRAG 岩 JME 178) WHICH IS THAT OF THE MOUNTAINEER WHO IS AGAINST, ANTI-, OPPOSED 反 TO ANY INCURSION BY TRADITION AND INCLINATION.

土 EARTH, SOIL, JME 17	坂 A SLOPE, HILL	反 ANTI-, ANTI-THESIS, OPPO-SITE JME 492	THE SLOPE, HILL (BY THE HAND THAT THROWS FROM THE CLIFF)	岩 ROCK, CLIFF, CRAG JME 178

HAN, (BAN); ITA, BOARD.

A BOARD 板 (OF FINISHED WOOD) IS THE ANTITHESIS, OPPOSITE 反 JME 492 OF A (LIVING GROWING) TREE 木 JME 15. ANTITHESIS, OPPOSITE 反 IS A COMPOSITE OF THE HAND 又 FROM THE CLIFF 厂 (AS IN ROCK, CLIFF, CRAG 岩 JME 178) OF THE MOUNTAINEER WHO IS OPPOSED BY TRADITION AND INCLINATION TO ANY ALIEN INCURSION.

RAD	STROKE	JME
75	8	305

TREE
JME 15

BOARD
(OPPOSITE
OF TREE)

ANTI-,
ANTI-
THESIS,
OPPO-
SITE
JME 492

A SLOPE,
HILL
JME 304

ROCK,
CLIFF,
CRAG
JME 178

TREE AND
OPPOSING
HAND BY THE
CLIFF

BAN, WATCH, GUARD, NUMBER, ORDER, TURN.

WATCH, GUARD, NUMBER, ORDER, TURN 番 IS THE WATCHING, GUARDING 番 BY NUMBER, ORDER, TURN 番 OF THE RICE FIELD 田 JME 40 AGAINST ANIMALS (REPRESENTED BY THE HORN ノ AND THE TRACK OR PAW PRINT 米 .) THERE IS ALSO THE SUGGESTION THAT THE RICE 米 IS RIPE 米 AND MUST BE GUARDED 番 .

RAD	STROKE	JME
165	12	306

HORN
(FOR ANI-
MALS OR
RIPENESS
OF RICE OR
DEFENSE)

WATCH, GUARD,
NUMBER, TURN

ANIMAL PAW
PRINT,
(RICE
JME 135)

RICE FIELD,
PADDY,
JME 40

"the mound builders"
any time they build a mound,
a watching star lies on the ground;
some day by counting stars you'll know
how many mounds stand guard below.

ed
asich

eta
draco-
nis

(the thumb)
thuban

ursa
minor
bowl

dsiban

PAW OR HAND PRINT FROM
URSA MINOR, DRACO, &
DSIBAN. NUMBER OF CLAWS,
ETC. MAY VARY.

JME 307	Stroke 5	Rad 107

HI; KAWA, (GAWA), SKIN, HIDE, LEATHER.

SKIN, HIDE, LEATHER 皮 IS A COMPOSITE OF A HAND 又 HOLDING A KNIFE | TO SKIN 皮 THE BODY 尸 (AS IN SHOP 屋 JME 161).

SHOP
JME 161

BODY, CORPSE

SKIN, HIDE, LEATHER

SCRAPER

HAND

HAND & SCRAPER

WAVE
JME 298
(THE SKIN OF THE WATER)

JME 308	Stroke 9	Rad 123

BI, BEAUTY; UTSUKUSHII, BEAUTIFUL.

BEAUTY, BEAUTIFUL 美 IS A GREAT 大 JME 22 RAM 羊. THERE IS BEAUTY TO THE HUNTER IN THE MASSIVE CURVING HORNS OF THE RAM, BEAUTY TO THE MOUNTAINEER IN THE RAM'S ABILITY TO ASCEND AND DECEND PRECIPITOUS CLIFFS, AND AN ETHICAL BEAUTY IN THE RAM'S NON-PREDATORY LIFE AMONG THE CLOUDS, IN HIS PROTECTION OF THE YOUNG AND FEMALES, ETC. SEE JME 102.

FORE LEGS
HIND LEGS
BODY

GREAT, BIG
JME 22

BEAUTIFUL, BEAUTY

RAM, GOAT

TO WEAR, ARRIVE AT, REACH
JME 276

NECK
JME 239

ROAD, WAY, PATH
JME 122

SOUTH
JME 124

TO SEND
JME 268

HYŌ, (PYŌ), LIST, SCHEDULE, TABLE;
OMOTE, THE EXTERIOR, FRONT, SURFACE;
ARAWASU, TO SHOW, INDICATE, DISPLAY, EXPOSE,
EXPRESS.

RAD	STROKE	JME
145	8	309

THE EXTERIOR, FRONT, SURFACE 表 OF THE
LAYERS 主 OF CLOTHING, ROBES 衣 JME 341
IS SHOWN, DISPLAYED, EXPOSED 表. OTHER
MEANINGS SUCH AS LIST, SCHEDULE, TABLE 表
RESULT SINCE LISTS, SCHEDULES, TABLES 表 表
ARE NECESSARILY SHOWN, DISPLAYED, EXPOSED 表.
THE COMPONENT FOR LAYERS 主 WAS IN BLUE, GREEN, INEXPER-
IENCED 青 JME36 AND IN SPRING 春 JME 91. CLOTHING, ROBES
表 WAS A COMPONENT IN GARDEN 園 JME 159 AND IN DISTANT,
FAR 遠 JME 160.

BLUE, GREEN JME 36

LAYERS (OF CLOTHING, FOLIAGE, ETC.) THAT FORM THE VISIBLE SURFACE

表 LIST, SCHEDULE, TABLE, EXTERIOR

衣 MULTI-BRANCHED AS FOLDS OF CLOTHES

GARDEN JME 159

FAR, DISTANT JME 160

BYŌ; YAMAI, SICKNESS, DISEASE;
YAMU, TO BECOME SICK.

RAD	STROKE	JME
104	10	310

SICKNESS, DISEASE, TO BECOME SICK 病 HAS A
LOWER RIGHT COMPONENT 丙 REPRESENTING A
FIRE 丙 (MODIFIED FROM 火 JME 13) FLAMING UP
FROM WITHIN A SPACE 冂. THE FIRE 丙 IS THE
RISING FEVER OF THE SHUT-IN 冂. THE UPPER
LEFT COMPONENT 疒 IS NOW A FUSION OF A
BED 爿 TURNED VERTICALLY 丬 AND A SHED-TYPE
SHELTER 广 FOR THE FEVERISH 丙 SHUT-IN 冂.
THIS UPPER LEFT COMPONENT 疒 IS A SIGNIFIC IN MANY KANJI
RELATING TO SICKNESS 病.

BED TURNED 90° TO FORM PART OF SICKNESS KANJI ORIENTAL BED IS. BOARDS ON "HORSES".

BED & ROOF (COMPONENT FOR KANJI RELATING TO ILLNESS)

病 SICKNESS, DISEASE, TO BECOME SICK

冂 SPACE OR ENCLOSURE FOR SICK PERSON

一 天 人 FLAT (SICK) MAN

MOD. FIRE

火 FIRE, (FEVER)

JME	STROKE	RAD
311	9	30

HIN, ELEGANCE, REFINEMENT, DIGNITY, GOODS;
SHINA, GOODS, WARES.

ELEGANCE, REFINEMENT, DIGNITY, GOODS, WARES
品 ARE REPRESENTED BY THREE BOWLS OR VASES.
MOUTH 口 JME 27 WHICH HAS VARIED APPLICA-
TIONS SUCH AS STONE 口 IN STONE, ROCK 石
JME 44 IS PARTICULARLY SUITABLE SINCE THE
MOUTH 口 IS A CONTAINER LIKE THE TRIPLICATED
BOWLS OR VASES 品 .

ELEGANCE,
REFINEMENT,
DIGNITY, GOODS,
WARES

THREE VASES
INDICATIVE
OF ELEGANCE,
REFINEMENT,
DIGNITY, &
WHICH ARE
GOODS, WARES

MOUTH
JME 27
(ROCK, STONE,
SEAT, BOWL,
VASE, ETC.)
MOUTH HOLDS
OR CONTAINS
LIKE A BOWL
OR VASE, ETC.;
MOUTH SHAPED
AS ROUND STONE

JME	STROKE	RAD
312	9	154

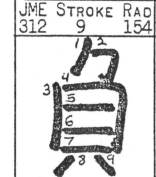

FU, (BU); OU, TO BEAR, TO OWE;
MAKE, A DEFEAT, A LOSS;
MAKERU, TO BE DEFEATED, TO BE OVERCOME,
TO BE INFERIOR, TO REDUCE IN PRICE.

TO BEAR, TO OWE, A DEFEAT, A LOSS, TO BE
DEFEATED, TO BE OVERCOME, TO BE INFERIOR,
TO REDUCE IN PRICE 負 DERIVE FROM THE
COMPOSITE OF A MAN BENDING OVER 勹 A COWRIE
SHELL 貝 JME 169 WHICH HE WILL BEAR 負 (CARRY
ON HIS BACK) AS OWED 負 AFTER BECOMING
INFERIOR 負 BY HIS DEFEAT, LOSS 負 AFTER BEING DEFEATED,
OVERCOME 負 . TO REDUCE IN PRICE 負 IS TO BE DEFEATED 負
IN BUSINESS. THE DEFEATED ONE OWES AND BEARS THE DEBT.

MAN BENDS
TO PICK UP
SHELLS FOR
RANSOM, TRI-
BUTE, DEBT

TO BEAR,
TO OWE,
A DEFEAT,
A LOSS

SEA SHELL
JME 169

EYE,
A LOOK
JME 25

EAR
JME 26

EAR
(PICTURE)

BUTSU, MOTSU; MONO, THING, ARTICLE, OBJECT, GOODS.

RAD	STROKE	JME
93	8	313

THING, ARTICLE, OBJECT, GOODS 物 IS REPRE-
SENTED BY A COMPOSITE OF COW, OX, CATTLE,
BULL 牛 (THE LARGEST ANIMAL COMMON ON THE
FARM) AND THE LEGS AND TAIL 勿 OF THE LIZARD
OR CHAMELEON 易 (WHICH IS THE SMALLEST).
THUS THINGS, ARTICLES, OBJECTS, GOODS RANGE
AS FROM THE COW TO THE CHAMELEON.

牛　牛　物　勿　易

| COMPONENT FOR COW,OX, CATTLE | COW,OX, CATTLE, BULL JME 62 | THING, ARTICLE, OBJECT, GOODS | LEGS & TAIL OF LIZARD OR CHAMELEON (SUGGESTS ALSO RAYS OF SUN IN WHICH HE BASKS) | (EASY), DIVINATION JME 545 CHAMELEON OR LIZARD PICTOGRAPH (SEE JME 252) | PICTURE OF CHAMELEON OR LIZARD (FOURTH LEG IS BEHIND BODY) |

BUN; KIKU, TO HEAR, TO LISTEN TO, TO ASK,
TO OBEY, TO HEAR OF; KIKOERU, TO BE HEARD.

RAD	STROKE	JME
128	14	314

TO HEAR, TO LISTEN TO, TO ASK, TO OBEY,
TO HEAR OF, TO BE HEARD 聞 IS A COMPOSITE OF
THE EAR 耳 JME 26 (OF THE PERSON) WITHIN THE
(OUTER, DOUBLE) GATES 門 JME 143 (AS OF THE
ESTATE) WHO HEARS, LISTENS TO, ASKS, HEARS
OF, AND BY WHOM THINGS ARE HEARD 聞. THE
MEANING TO OBEY 聞 PROBABLY DERIVES FROM THE
PERSON OFTEN BEING THE WATCHMAN OR GATEMAN
WHO IS A SERVANT OBEYING 聞.

耳　聞　門　　開　間

| EAR JME 26 | TO HEAR, TO LISTEN, TO ASK, TO OBEY, TO HEAR OF, TO BE HEARD | GATE JME 143 | (EAR IN THE GATE-WAY) HEARS, LISTENS | TO OPEN JME 171 | INTERVAL, SPACE, DISTANCE, ROOM, TIME JME 58 |

To hear is to obey, my lord.

JME 315	Stroke 5	Rad 51

HEI, BYŌ; TAIRA, FLATNESS, EVENNESS; HIRATAI, EVEN, LEVEL, SIMPLE.

FLATNESS, EVENNESS, EVEN, LEVEL, SIMPLE 平 IS REPRESENTED BY THE SHINING, GLEAMING (SURFACE) OF A SHIELD 干 (AS IN NOON 午 JME 207). ALSO REVIEW GOLD, MONEY 金 JME 16 FOR THE SHIELD 干 AND SHINING NUGGETS 丷 AS COMPONENTS. LIGHT, BRILLIANCE, TO SHINE 光 JME 72 ALSO HAS RAYS OF LIGHT 丷 AS A COMPONENT.

SHINING, GLEAMING

FLATNESS, EVENNESS, EVEN, LEVEL, SIMPLE

SHIELD

SHIELD SUPERIMPOSED

(NOON) JME 207 (CALENDAR ZODIAC HORSE)

LIGHT, BRILLIANCE, TO SHINE JME 72

(GOLD), MONEY JME 16

NUGGETS

JME 316	Stroke 7	Rad 162

HEN; KAESU, TO RETURN, TO GIVE BACK, REPAY; KAESHI, (GAESHI), A RETURN PRESENT.

TO RETURN, TO GIVE BACK, TO REPAY, A RETURN PRESENT 返 IS A COMPOSITE OF TO GO AND PAUSE 辶 (IN THE SENSE OF TO TRAVEL OR ROAD) AND OPPOSITE 反 (THE HAND 又 AND THE CLIFF 厂 MEANING THE OPPOSING 反 HAND 又 OF THE MOUNTAINEER). TO RETURN 返 IS TO GO 辶 IN THE OPPOSITE 反 DIRECTION. TO GIVE BACK, REPAY 返 IS FOR SOMETHING TO GO 辶 IN THE OPPOSITE 反 DIRECTION. THE SAME IS TRUE OF A RETURN PRESENT.

MOVEMENT, STOP & GO

TO RETURN, GIVE BACK, REPAY, A RETURN PRESENT

ANTI-, ANTI- THESIS, OPPO- SITE JME 492

HAND

A SLOPE, HILL JME 304 (OPPOSITE OF LEVEL EARTH)

BOARD JME 305 (OPPOSITE OF TREE)

BEN, (TO EXERT ONESELF, BE DILIGENT, BE INDUSTRIOUS).

Rad 19	Stroke 10	JME 317

TO EXERT ONESELF, BE DILIGENT, BE INDUSTRIOUS 勉 IS A COMPOSITE OF OGRE, FIEND, GHOST, DEMON 免 (AS A COMPONENT) AND STRENGTH 力 JME 148. OGRE, FIEND, GHOST, DEMON 免 IS A PICTOGRAPH. THERE IS A SUGGESTION HERE AS OF DEMONIAC STRENGTH, BUT IT IS MILDER AND INVOLVES STUDY, WORK, PHYSICAL EXERTION, ETC.

OGRE, FIEND GHOST, DEMON	TO EXERT ONESELF, BE DILIGENT BE INDUSTRIOUS	STRENGTH JME 148	PICTURE OF LEGS REPRESENTING STRENGTH OR POWER

MAI, EVERY (USED AS A PREFIX).

Rad 80	Stroke 6	JME 318

EVERY 毎 IS A COMPOSITE OF MAN 𠂉 JME 30 (AS A TOP COMPONENT) AND MOTHER 母 JME 137.
EVERY 毎 MAN 𠂉 HAS A MOTHER 母.

MILK CAN BE POISON BECAUSE OF CONTAMINATION OR BECAUSE CATTLE OR SHEEP EAT POISONOUS AND SOMETIMES MILKY WEEDS. SO THE KANJI FOR POISON AND FOR MOTHER ARE RELATED.

MOTHER JME 137

POISON JME 686

MAN, PERSON (AS THE TOP COMPONENT)	EVERY	MOTHER (DOTS OF BREASTS OR NIPPLES DONE AS A LINE)

JME 319	Stroke 8	Rad 38

MAI; IMŌTO, YOUNGER SISTER.

YOUNGER SISTER 妹 IS A COMPOSITE OF WOMAN, GIRL, FEMALE 女 JME 32 AND A TREE 木 JME 15 WITH SHORT, UPPER BRANCHES — ADDED TO SHOW THAT, LIKE THE YOUNGER SISTER 妹, IT IS DEVELOPING AS WITH BUDDING BREASTS.

YOUNGER SISTER (PICTURE) BREASTS ARE PROMINENTLY DISPLAYED

WOMAN, GIRL, FEMALE JME 32

YOUNGER SISTER

(YET, NEVER, TILL NOW, UN-) JME 872

TREE JME 15

You stand straight like a palm;
Your breasts are like clusters of fruit.
Song of Solomon

JME 320	Stroke 3	Rad 140

BAN, (ALL); MAN, TEN THOUSAND.

TEN THOUSAND 万 IS RELATED TO DIRECTION 方 JME 138. HOWEVER, THE DOT ` WHICH IS THE TOP STROKE OF DIRECTION 方 IS REMOVED FOR TEN THOUSAND 万. THE ABSENCE OF THE DOT ` MEANS A LACK OF CONTROL OR AUTHORITY GIVING DIRECTION 方. AS A RESULT, THE MEANING IS TEN THOUSANDS OR (ALL) 万 (PROBABLY IN THE SENSE OF POSSIBLE DIRECTIONS). TEN THOUSAND HAS THE SUPPLEMENTARY MEANING OF ALL BECAUSE OF ITS SIZE AND COMPLETENESS. UNDER HEAVEN — THE SWASTIKA 卍 OR SAILLESS UNMANNED BOAT 卍 TURNS OR DRIFTS IN ALL OR TEN THOUSAND 万 DIRECTIONS 方 LIKE A FLAG.

SWASTIKA QUADRANT OR OPEN-ENDED BOAT

10,000 (ALL)

ONE, HEAVEN (AS A COMPONENT)

DRIFTING BOAT

DIRECTION JME 138

MEI; NAKU, TO SING, TWITTER (BIRDS),
TO HUM, BUZZ (INSECTS), TO GRUNT, GROWL,
ROAR (ANIMALS).

TO SING, TWITTER, HUM, BUZZ, GRUNT, GROWL,
ROAR 鳴 IS A COMPOSITE OF A MOUTH 口 JME 27
AND A LONG-TAILED BIRD 鳥 JME 117. THE
SINGING OR TWITTERING 鳴 FROM THE MOUTH 口
OF LONG-TAILED BIRDS 鳥 WAS EXTENDED TO
BIRD, INSECT, AND ANIMAL SOUNDS GENERALLY.

RAD	STROKE	JME
30	14	321

MOUTH
JME 27

TO SING,
TWITTER,
HUM, BUZZ,
GRUNT,
GROWL, ROAR

LONG-
TAILED
BIRD
JME 117

BEAK

HEAD

WINGS

TAIL

LEGS

ANCIENT
BIRD
SYMBOL

ISLAND
JME 292

MEN, FACE, FEATURES, MASK; OMO, SURFACE;
OMOTE, FACE, EXTERIOR, FRONT, SURFACE.

FACE, FEATURES, MASK, SURFACE, EXTERIOR,
FRONT 面 IS A PICTOGRAPH OF A MASK 面 AND
A FUSED CONGLOMERATE OF THE ARCHAIC KANJIS
FOR HEAD 百, FOR NOSE 自, FOR BEARD 而;
AND THE CURRENT KANJIS FOR EYE 目 JME 25,
AND FOR EAR 耳 JME 26 AS PART OF THE FUSED
CONGLOMERATE.

RAD	STROKE	JME
176	9	322

EAR
JME 26

EYE
JME 25

ARCHAIC
NOSE
KANJI

HEAD
COMPONENT

ARCHAIC
BEARD
KANJI

FACE,
FEATURES,
MASK,
SURFACE,
EXTERIOR,
FRONT

MASK

MASK

MASK

JME	Stroke	Rad
323	11	166

YA; <u>NO</u>, FIELD, PLAIN.

FIELD, PLAIN 野 IS A COMPOSITE OF VILLAGE, NATIVE PLACE, LINEAR UNIT 里 JME 332, AND PREVIOUS 予 JME 525. VILLAGE, NATIVE PLACE 里 IS A COMPOSITE OF RICE FIELD 田 JME 40 AND EARTH 土 JME 17 (SUGGESTING ONE'S RURAL OR COUNTRYSIDE ORIGIN). THE LINEAR UNIT <u>RI</u> (2.44 MI.) WAS USUALLY A MEASUREMENT USED TOWARDS A VILLAGE 里. PREVIOUS 予 MAY BE ANALYZED AS NAILS 丁 (AS IN TOWN 町 JME 115) TAKEN FROM THE BASKET マ (INVERTED AS IN TO PASS 通 JME 281) PREVIOUSLY OR PREVIOUSLY USED. THE CONCEPTION IS THAT A FIELD, PLAIN 野 EXISTS PREVIOUS 予 TO A VILLAGE 里 (BEFORE THE CONSTRUCTION OF THE VILLAGE).

PADDY

EARTH | VILLAGE, NATIVE PLACE, <u>RI</u> (2.44 MI.) | FIELD, PLAIN | PREVIOUS JME 525 | NAILS, SPIKES | INVERTED BASKET OR CONTAINER WHOSE CONTENTS SPREAD OR EXPAND

JME	Stroke	Rad
324	7	60

YAKU, OFFICE, POST, POSITION, DUTY, ROLE, SERVICE; EKI, WAR, CAMPAIGN.

OFFICE, POST, POSITION, DUTY, ROLE, SERVICE, WAR, CAMPAIGN 役 IS A COMPOSITE OF MEN 彳 (AS IN TO WAIT FOR 待 JME 271) AND TO STRIKE 殳 (AS IN TO THROW 投 JME 291). MEN 彳 IS A DOUBLING OF THE COMPONENT MAN 亻 JME 30. STRIKE 殳 IS A COMPOSITE OF HAND 又 (WHICH STRIKES 几 LIKE THE WING OF A BIRD) AND A STRIKING OR FLAPPING 几 WING. THE STRIKING MEN 役 DEALT OUT PUNISHMENT IN THE COURTS WITH BAMBOO RODS. THEIR OFFICE, POST, POSITION, DUTY, ROLE, SERVICE, ETC. WAS EXTENDED TO WAR OR CAMPAIGNS IN WHICH THEY COULD ACCOMPANY THE MAGISTRATE.

WING BONES

MEN: DOUBLED COMPONENT | OFFICE, POST | HAND | STRIKING WING | TO THROW JME 291

YŪ, YU; YOSHI, REASON, SIGNIFICANCE.

REASON, SIGNIFICANCE 由 IS A PICTOGRAPH OF
A TORTOISE 甲 (WITH BODY 田 AND PROJECTING
HEAD ｜) INVERTED 由 FOR HIS DEATH SO THAT
THE TORTOISE SHELL CAN BE USED IN DIVINATION
TO DIVINE REASONS, SIGNIFICANCE 由 . THE
TORTOISE SHELL WAS HEATED AND THE RESULTING
CRACKS USED IN DIVINATION AS MENTIONED IN
OUTSIDE, FOREIGN, OTHER 外 JME 56, STORE 店
JME 284, AND MARKS, POINT, SPOT 点 JME 285.

RAD	STROKE	JME
102	5	325

TORTOISE
VIEWED FROM
UNDERNEATH
(PLASTRON)

TORTOISE
SHELL:
CARAPACE,
GRADE A,
BACK OF
HAND

REASON,
SIGNI-
FICANCE

(FOREIGN),
OUTSIDE,
OTHER
JME 56

STORE
JME 284

MARKS,
POINT,
SPOT
JME 285

YŪ; ASOBU, TO PLAY, TO AMUSE ONESELF,
                              TO BE IDLE.

TO PLAY, TO AMUSE ONESELF, TO BE IDLE 遊
IS A MAN 𠆢 JME 30 (WHO IS) LIKE A CHILD 子
JME 31 GOING AND PAUSING 辶 (AS IN ROAD,
WAY, PATH 道 JME 122) IN SOME DIRECTION 方
JME 138 AS HE PLAYS, AMUSES HIMSELF.

RAD	STROKE	JME
162	12	326

MOVEMENT,
STOP & GO

TO PLAY,
AMUSE ONE-
SELF,TO BE
IDLE

DIRECTION
JME 138

CHILD
JME 31

MAN,
PERSON,
MANKIND
AS A TOP
COMPONENT

PICTURE

JME 327	Stroke 12	Rad 140

YŌ; HA, (BA), LEAF, FOLIAGE.

LEAF, FOLIAGE 葉 IS THE GRASS ⼐ (GRASS ⼐ COMPONENT AS IN GRASS, VEGETATION 草 JME 106) OF THE WORLD 世 JME 263 OF TREES 木 JME 15.

GRASS COMPONENT

PICTURE OF GRASS

TREE
JME 15

LEAF, FOLIAGE

WORLD, ERA, REIGN
JME 263

JME 328	Stroke 14	Rad 75

YŌ, WAY, STYLE, MODE, MANNER, APPEARANCE; SAMA, SAN, MR., MRS., MISS, PERSONAL NAME SUFFIX (I.E. TERI-SAN), ETC.; SAMA, STATE, CONDITION.

WAY, STYLE, MODE, MANNER, APPEARANCE, STATE, CONDITION 様 IS A COMPOSITE AND FUSION OF TREE 木 JME 15, OF A GOAT COMPONENT ⺶ (AS IN BEAUTY, BEAUTIFUL 美 JME 308), AND OF A WATER COMPONENT 氺 (AS IN GLOBE, SPHERE 球 JME 188). THESE THREE COMPONENTS ARE OUTSTANDING IN THEIR DIFFERENCES REPRESENTING ANIMAL ⺶, PLANT 木, AND NON-LIVING SUBJECT MATTER, WATER, WHICH 氺 ASSUMES SUCH FORMS AS ICE, STEAM, AND WAVES. ALL THREE HAVE HIGHLY VARIANT WAYS, STYLES, MODES, CONDITIONS 様. THIS CONCEPT IS ALSO APPLIED TO APPEARANCES 様, ETC. OF PEOPLE. PROVERBS 30:19 SAYS, "THE WAY OF AN EAGLE IN THE AIR; THE WAY OF A SERPENT UPON A ROCK; THE WAY OF A SHIP IN THE MIDST OF THE SEA; AND THE WAY OF A MAN WITH A MAID."

GLOBE, SPHERE
JME 188

TREE

WAY, STYLE

WATER

WATER

GOAT, RAM

YŌ, (USED IN THE NAMES OF THE DAYS OF THE WEEK).

YŌ IS A COMPOSITE OF SUN, DAY 日 JME 11, OF CLAWS ヨヨ , AND OF THE SHORT-TAILED BIRD 隹 (AS IN TO ADVANCE 進 JME 259). THE SHORT-TAILED BIRDS 隹 WINGING 羽 OR PERCHED ヨヨ (GREET) THE DAY, SUN 日 EACH DAY OF THE WEEK.

RAD 72	STROKE 18	JME 329

DAY, SUN JME 11

YŌ: USED IN DAYS OF THE WEEK

CLAWS (HANDS) OF BIRDS

羽

WINGS (AT TIMES WINGS MAY BE PRINTED INSTEAD OF CLAWS (OR HANDS)

SHORT-TAILED BIRD

OLD SYMBOL FOR SHORT-TAILED BIRD

RAKU; OCHIRU, TO FALL, TO DROP, (I.V.); TO BE INFERIOR TO, TO BE OMITTED; OTOSU, TO DROP, TO LET FALL, TO LOSE, (T.V.); TO DEBASE, TO MAKE WORSE.

TO FALL, TO DROP, TO BE INFERIOR TO, TO BE OMITTED, TO LET FALL, TO LOSE, TO DEBASE, TO MAKE WORSE 落 IS A COMPOSITE OF GRASS ⧾ , OF WATER ⺡ , AND OF THE SEATED GUEST 各 (AS IN GUEST 客 JME 184, BUT LACKING THE ROOF ⼧). OBJECTS OFTEN FALL, DROP, OR ARE DROPPED 落 INTO GRASS ⧾ OR WATER ⺡ AND ARE LOST 落 . FOR A GUEST 客 TO LET SOMETHING FALL 落 OR DROP 落 IS A BREACH OF ETIQUETTE INVOLVING INFERIORITY 落, OMISSION 落, DEBASEMENT 落 , OR MAKING MATTERS WORSE 落 . THE SAME IS TRUE IF SUCH A THING HAPPENS IN THE PRESENCE OF A GUEST ON THE PART OF THE HOST.

RAD 140	STROKE 12	JME 330

WATER COMPO-NENT   落 TO FALL, TO DROP, TO LOSE

GRASS COMPONENT

EACH, EVERY JME 568

PICTURE OF GUEST DROPPING CUP

GUEST JME 184

JME Stroke Rad
331   13   75

GAKU, MUSIC; RAKU, COMFORT, EASE;
TANOSHII, PLEASANT.

MUSIC, COMFORT, EASE, PLEASANT 楽 SHOWS A
STAND 木 (TREE 木 JME 15) HOLDING A DRUM 白
AND DRUMSTICK ✓ WITH SOUND VIBRATIONS ⠂⟨
FROM THE DRUM 白 ON BOTH SIDES.

TREE, WOOD
JME 15
WOODEN
(STAND FOR
DRUM)

MUSIC, EASE,
COMFORT,
PLEASANT

WHITE
JME 37
(DRUM &
HORN FOR
DRUMSTICK)

VIBRATORY
SOUNDS OF
DRUM

DRUMSTICK,
DRUM,
VIBRATIONS,
AND STAND

JME Stroke Rad
332   7   166

RI, A 2.44 MILE LINEAR UNIT; SATO, (ZATO),
VILLAGE, COUNTRY, ONE'S NATIVE HOME.

THE 2.44 MILE LINEAR UNIT, VILLAGE, COUNTRY,
ONE'S NATIVE HOME 里 IS A COMPOSITE OF RICE
FIELD 田 JME 40 ON EARTH, SOIL, 土 JME 17.

THE FERTILE EARTH, SOIL 土 OF THE RICE
FIELDS 田 CONTAINS VILLAGES 里. DISTANCE
IN LINEAR UNITS OF 2.44 MILES 里 CALLED RI
IS MEASURED TO AND FROM THE VILLAGES 里.

RICE FIELD,
PADDY
JME 40

RI:
2.44 MI.,
VILLAGE,
COUNTRY,
NATIVE HOME

EARTH,
SOIL
JME 17

1 RI
2.44 MI.

RI, REASON, LOGIC.

REASON, LOGIC 理 IS FOR THE VILLAGES, COUNTRYSIDE, NATIVE HOMES 里 TO HAVE A KING 王 JME 49 (SYMBOLIC OF GOVERNMENT). REASON, LOGIC 理 IS TO HAVE A KING'S 王 JME 49 (STANDARD) UNIT OF LINEAR MEASURE 里, THE RI OF 2.44 MILES. (IT IS ANALOGOUS TO THE KING'S FOOT, ETC. AS STANDARD MEASURE).

RAD	STROKE	JME
96	11	333

KING
JME 49

REASON,
LOGIC

RI:
2.44 MI.,
VILLAGE,
COUNTRY-
SIDE,
NATIVE
HOME

RICE FIELD,
PADDY
JME 40

EARTH,
SOIL
JME 17

RYŪ, RU; NAGARE, STREAM, CURRENT; NAGARERU, TO FLOW, TO RUN, TO STREAM, (I.V.); NAGASU, TO POUR, TO SET ADRIFT, TO WASH AWAY, (T.V.).

STREAM, CURRENT, TO FLOW, TO RUN, TO STREAM, TO POUR, TO SET ADRIFT, TO WASH AWAY 流 IS A COMPOSITE OF WATER 氵, DIRECTIONAL 亠 (AS IN THE CAP OF AUTHORITY OR THE TERMS HEADSTREAM, HEAD WATERS, FOUNTAINHEAD), A SECRET, CLOUDY, SELFISH, BASKET-LIKE 厶 (PLACE ABOVE, WHICH TEMPORARILY HOLDS THE WATERS), AND THE STREAM 川 (AS OF THREE CHANNELS LIKE RIVER 川 JME 39 AND WATER 水 JME 14).

RAD	STROKE	JME
85	10	334

WATER
COM-
PONENT

STREAM,
CURRENT,
TO FLOW,
TO RUN,
TO STREAM

DIRECTIONAL
HEADWATERS
RELEASE A
3-CHANNELED
STREAM

WATER FROM
ABOVE FLOWS
AWAY

RIVER,
JME 39

WATER
JME 14

JME	STROKE	RAD
335	10	70

RYO; TABI, TRAVEL, JOURNEY, TOUR, TRIP.

TRAVEL, JOURNEY, TOUR, TRIP 旅 IS A COMPOSITE OF DIRECTION, WAY 方 JME 138 AND A GOWNED FAMILY 𧘇 DRESSED FOR TRAVEL OF PERSONS, MEN 亻 (COMPONENT FORM) JME 30. REVIEW THE GOWNED PERSON 𧘇 IN GARDEN 園 JME 159 AND IN FAR, DISTANT 遠 JME 160.

| DIRECTION, WAY JME 138 | TRAVEL, JOURNEY, TOUR,TRIP | MAN, PERSON COMPONENT JME 30 | GOWN, CLOTHING COMPONENT (SEE JME 341) | FAR,DISTANT JME 160 | GARDEN JME 159 |

(THE TWO KANJI ABOVE ARE LENGTHENED SO THE GOWN,CLOTHING COMPONENT MATCHES)

JME	STROKE	RAD
336	6	1

RYŌ, OLD MONETARY UNIT; RYŌ, (TWO, BOTH).

THE FORM OF THIS KANJI HAS THE SAME SHAPE AS ANCIENT COINS. THE KANJI ALSO GIVES THE IMPRESSION OF A BALANCE HAVING TWO, BOTH SCALES AND AN INDICATOR BETWEEN FOR PRECISE MEASURING. ALTHOUGH COINS WERE IN USE, COPPER AND SILVER SO PURE AND SOFT THAT THEY COULD BE CUT WITH A SHEARS WERE ALSO USED AS CURRENCY AND WERE WEIGHED ON SCALES AFTER BEING CUT.

NOTE THE HOLE IN THE HAN CASH FOR STRING- ING OR BALANCING.

BALANCE WITH TWO SCALES

RYŌ, TWO, BOTH

HOLE->

HAN ERA CASH CIRCA 9 A.D.

REI, SALUTATION, BOW, COURTESY, THANKS.

SALUTATION, BOW, COURTESY, THANKS 礼 IS TO THE GOD ネ (COMPONENT FORM) WHO SHOWS, POINTS OUT 示 JME 622. SALUTATION, BOW, COURTESY, THANKS 礼 IS ALSO FOR MILK L (COMPONENT FORM) CUSTOMARILY GIVEN AS A COURTESY 礼 IN A PASTORAL HERDSMAN CULTURE.

神 GOD JME 257   社 SHINTO SHRINE, COMPANY JME 234

RAD	STROKE	JME
113	5	337

TO SHOW, POINT OUT JME 622 (HEAVEN'S RAYS SHOW & POINT OUT)	GOD IN COMPONENT FORM (HE SHOWS POINTS OUT) SUPER-IMPOSITION	GOD, DIVINE AS COMPO-NENT	SALUTATION, BOW, COURTESY, THANKS (MILK OF HUMAN KINDNESS)	SUPER-IMPOSITION OF MILK COMPONENT ON BREAST (SIDE VIEW)	BREAST

WA, HARMONY, PEACE, JAPAN; TO SOFTEN, PACIFY, CALM DOWN.

HARMONY, PEACE, JAPAN, TO PACIFY, CALM DOWN, SOFTEN 和 IS HAVING RICE OR GRAIN 禾 (SEE JME 164) in ONE'S MOUTH 口 OR BEING FED. THE RICE OR GRAIN IS SOFTENED IN THE MOUTH AND PACIFIES OR CALMS DOWN BRINGING PEACE AND HARMONY AS IN JAPAN.

RAD	STROKE	JME
115	8	338

RICE OR GRAIN AS A PLANT	RICE, GRAIN (SEE JME 164)	RICE OR GRAIN FED OR EATEN BY MOUTH OF MAN OR BEAST	HARMONY, PEACE, JAPAN, SOFTEN, PACIFY, CALM DOWN	MOUTH JME 27	PICTURE OF MOUTH

Katakana and hiragana are used in Japanese writing to supplement the kanji. Katakana are used to represent sounds in foreign languages. Hiragana are used with the kanji for easier writing to conclude verbs, when the meaning is clear, or when no kanji exists for the purpose.

KATAKANA						HIRAGANA				
ア	サ	ナ	マ	ル		あ	さ	な	ま	る
a	sa	na	ma	ru		a	sa	na	ma	ru
イ	シ	ニ	ミ	レ		い	し	に	み	れ
i	shi	ni	mi	re		i	shi	ni	mi	re
ウ	ス	ヌ	ム	ロ		う	す	ぬ	む	ろ
u	su	nu	mu	ro		u	su	nu	mu	ro
エ	セ	ネ	メ	ワ		え	せ	ね	め	わ
e	se	ne	me	wa		e	se	ne	me	wa
オ	ン	ノ	モ	ヲ		お	そ	の	も	を
o	so	no	mo	o		o	so	no	mo	o
カ	タ	ハ	ヤ	ン		か	た	は	や	ん
ka	ta	ha	ya	n		ka	ta	ha	ya	n
キ	チ	ヒ	ユ			き	ち	ひ	ゆ	
ki	chi	hi	yu			ki	chi	hi	yu	
ク	ツ	フ	ヨ			く	つ	ふ	よ	
ku	tsu	fu	yo			ku	tsu	fu	yo	
ケ	テ	ヘ	ラ			け	て	へ	ら	
ke	te	he	ra			ke	te	he	ra	
コ	ト	ホ	リ			こ	と	ほ	り	
ko	to	ho	ri			ko	to	ho	ri	

			3 STROKES		
THE 214 RADICALS	10 儿 man, legs.	20 勹 wrap.	30 口 mouth.	40 宀 roof.	50 巾 cloth, kerchief.
1 STROKE 1 一 one, unity.	11 入 to enter.	21 匕 spoon, pointer, corpse.	31 囗 enclosure, boundaries.	41 寸 "inch," unit of length.	51 干 shield, weapon.
2 丨 (up or down movement).	12 八 eight, to divide.	22 匚 basket, chest, vessel, enclosure.	32 土 earth, soil, ground.	42 小 small, little.	52 幺 small.
3 丶 point, dot. (extended power).	13 冂 borders, empty space.	23 匸 cover, conceal, squareness, capacity.	33 士 samurai, scholar.	43 尢 feeble, weak, lame.	53 广 lean-to, shed, shelter.
4 丿 support, horn, scyth.	14 冖 cover.	24 十 ten, perfect, complete.	34 夂 follow, march, end.	44 尸 corpse.	54 廴 walk.
5 乙 (tail of snake or dragon).	15 冫 ice.	25 卜 to divine (scapula & plastron cracks).	35 夊 walk.	45 屮 sprout, sprouting plant.	55 廾 joined hands raised or folded.
6 亅 (barbed hook, nail body).	16 几 table, stool.	26 卩 seal.	36 夕 evening, end, moon.	46 山 mountain.	56 弋 a dart.
2 STROKES 7 二 two, duality, (heaven & earth).	17 凵 open vessel.	27 厂 cliff.	37 大 big, great.	47 川 巛 river, stream.	57 弓 a bow.
8 亠 head, cover, authority of heaven.	18 刀 sword, knife.	28 厶 private, selfish, basket, cocoon.	38 女 woman, girl, female.	48 工 work(man), square or plumb line.	58 彐 boar's or pig's head.
9 亻 人 man, human, person.	19 力 strength, power, energy.	29 又 rt. hand, again, also.	39 子 child, son.	49 己 personal, self.	59 彡 hair, shape.

60 彳 step, walk.	70 方 square, direction, way.	80 毋 do not.	90 爿 slice, bed. wood, tree's left half	100 生 birth, life, grow.	110 矛 spear, lance.
4 STROKES 61 心 忄 heart, mind.	71 旡 无 not, no, have not.	81 比 compare, sort, kind.	91 片 side, strip, tree's rt. half.	101 用 use, business.	111 矢 arrow.
62 戈 spear.	72 日 sun, day.	82 毛 hair, wool, fur, feathers.	92 牙 tooth, tusk.	102 田 field, paddy.	112 石 stone.
63 戶 door, house.	73 曰 say, speak.	83 氏 clan, family.	93 牛 cow, ox, bull.	103 疋 足 cloth, foot in motion.	113 礻 示 to show, inform.
64 扌 手 hand, arm.	74 月 moon, month.	84 气 air.	94 犭 犬 dog.	104 疒 disease, sickness.	114 禸 pawprint, track.
65 支 branch, obstinate.	75 木 tree, wood.	85 氵 水 water.	5 STROKES 95 玄 dark, black, mysterious	105 癶 leg joints	115 禾 grain or rice (as plants).
66 攴 to rap.	76 欠 exhale, owe, yawn.	86 灬 火 fire.	96 王 玉 gem, jade.	106 白 white, clear.	116 穴 hole, cave, pit.
67 文 literary, pattern.	77 止 stop.	87 爫 爪 claw, hoof.	97 瓜 melon, cucumber.	107 皮 skin, leather, fur, bark.	117 立 to stand.
68 斗 unit of capacity, Great Dipper.	78 歹 歺 bad, evil.	88 父 father.	98 瓦 tile, pottery.	108 皿 dish, saucer, vessel.	6 STROKES 118 竹 ⺮ bamboo.
69 斤 unit of weight, axe.	79 殳 lance, to kill, to strike.	89 爻 mix, interwind.	99 甘 sweet.	109 罒 目 eye.	119 米 rice (polished but uncooked).

	120	130	140	150	160	170
0	120 糸 silk, thread, string.	130 朋朋肉月 flesh, meat.	140 艹艸 grass, plants.	150 谷 valley, ravine.	160 辛 bitter, painful, metallic taste.	170 阝 mound, hill.
1	121 缶 clay pot, vessel.	131 臣 minister.	141 虍 tiger.	151 豆 bean, pea, vessel.	161 辰 dragon, hour.	171 隶 reach.
2	122 网罒罓网 net, trap.	132 自 self.	142 虫 insect, bug, worm.	152 豕 pig, hog.	162 辶辶辶 go fast and stop suddenly.	172 隹 short-tailed bird.
3	123 羊 sheep.	133 至 reach, arrive.	143 血 blood.	153 豸 beast, reptile, worm.	163 阝邑 village, city.	173 雨 rain.
4	124 羽羽 wings, feathers.	134 臼 mortar.	144 行 go, walk, conduct, a row.	154 貝 shell, cowrie.	164 酉 bird, wine vessel.	174 青 blue, green, unripe, inexperienced.
5	125 耂老 old.	135 舌 tongue.	145 衤衣 clothes, garment.	155 赤 red.	165 采 distinguish, divide.	175 非 not, is not.
6	126 而 and, but.	136 舛 confuse, oppose.	146 西 a cover.	156 走 run, walk fast.	166 里 village, unit of distance.	9 STROKES 176 面 face, front, surface, mask.
7	127 耒 plow handle, till, cultivate.	137 舟 boat, ship.	7 STROKES 147 見 see, show.	157 足 foot, leg.	8 STROKES 167 金 gold, money, metal.	177 革 leather, hide, skin.
8	128 耳 ear.	138 艮 hard, perverse, obstinate.	148 角 horn, corner.	158 身 body.	168 镸長 chief, senior, grow, long.	178 韋 leather, to rebel.
9	129 聿 pen, pencil.	139 色 color.	149 言 word, expression.	159 車 vehicle, chariot, carriage, cart.	169 門 gate, door.	179 韭 leeks, onions.

THE 214 RADICALS

The 214 radicals are used to construct kanji or characters much as words are formed from letters of the alphabet. Some of the radicals are complicated; some have more than one form. Learn their meanings and try to understand how and why they belong in the character or kanji. The radicals are the keys to the meaning of the kanji. They may have different meanings just as words in English may have different meanings. Often you can guess at the meaning of a strange or new character by examining the radical. Sometimes a radical such as "tree" is used as part of the kanji(s) for many different kinds of trees. The same thing is true of the radical for "gold" and different metals.

	180	190	200	210
0	180 音 sound, noise, voice, tone.	190 髟 hair.	200 麻 hemp.	210 齊 even, level.
1	181 頁 head, page.	191 鬥 fight.	12 STROKES 201 黃 yellow.	15 STROKES 211 齒 tooth.
2	182 風 wind, style, fashion, custom.	192 鬯 wine.	202 黍 millet.	16 STROKES 212 龍 dragon.
3	183 飛 fly, jump, leap.	193 鬲 caldron.	203 黑 black.	213 龜 tortoise.
4	184 食 eat.	194 鬼 devil, ogre, demon.	204 黹 embroidery, needlework.	17 STROKES 214 龠 flute, fife.
5	185 首 head, neck.	11 STROKES 195 魚 fish.	13 STROKES 205 黽 toad, frog.	
6	186 香 odor, fragrance, incense.	196 鳥 bird.	206 鼎 tripod.	
7	10 STROKES 187 馬 horse.	197 鹵 brine, barren, plunder.	207 鼓 drum.	
8	188 骨 bone.	198 鹿 deer.	208 鼠 rat, mouse.	
9	189 高 high, tall.	199 麥 wheat, barley.	14 STROKES 209 鼻 nose.	

KANJI LOCATOR I, STROKE INDEX FOR JME NUMBERS IN THE KANJI ABC
Look up kanji of your text by stroke number
to get their JME numbers in The Kanji ABC.

1	下 21	中 23	引 156	犬 66	外 56	皮 307	同 295	気 59	**7**	村 107	走 105
一 1	千 101	五 5	心 95	王 49	左 18	目 25	名 140	池 110	住 244	決 202	足 29
2	口 27	今 81	戸 69	**5**	市 222	石 44	向 213	当 290	何 51	汽 60	身 255
七 7	土 17	元 68	手 28	世 263	平 315	礼 337	回 169	百 130	作 82	男 109	車 88
九 9	夕 98	公 210	文 134	主 237	広 211	立 149	地 111	竹 113	体 270	町 115	近 195
二 2	大 22	六 6	方 139	仕 221	本 45	台 272	多 108	米 135	来 147	社 234	返 316
人 30	女 32	分 133	日 11	兄 199	正 46	号 215	字 86	糸 83	助 248	究 185	里 332
入 125	子 31	切 99	月 12	冬 120	母 137	**6**	安 153	考 74	君 198	声 97	麦 128
八 8	小 24	化 163	木 15	出 90	玉 64	交 212	寺 228	耳 26	図 261	花 43	**8**
刀 289	山 38	午 207	止 220	北 139	生 34	休 61	年 126	肉 297	坂 304	見 67	事 230
力 148	川 39	友 145	毛 142	半 129	用 146	先 33	早 104	自 229	局 194	角 173	京 63
十 10	工 71	円 48	水 14	去 189	田 40	光 72	会 54	色 94	弟 282	谷 78	使 224
3	才 217	天 119	火 13	古 70	由 325	全 267	次 227	虫 114	形 200	貝 169	取 238
三 3	万 320	太 269	父 131	右 19	申 254	両 336	死 223	行 73	役 324	売 301	愛 240
上 20	**4**	少 93	牛 62	四 4	白 37	合 77	毎 318	西 96	投 291	赤 35	和 338

KANJI LOCATOR I, STROKE INDEX FOR JME NUMBERS IN THE KANJI ABC
Look up kanji of your text by stroke number
to get their JME numbers in The Kanji ABC.

国 79	波 298	乗 251	春 91	級 187	**10**	病 310	球 188	黒 80	落 330	新 256	駅 158
夜 144	注 277	前 102	昭 249	美 308	勉 317	紙 85	理 333	**12**	葉 327	暗 154	鳴 321
妹 319	物 313	南 124	昼 279	茶 275	原 205	荷 165	第 273	勝 250	買 300	楽 320	**15**
始 225	画 167	品 311	柱 279	草 106	夏 52	記 180	細 218	場 252	遊 326	話 151	**16**
学 57	知 112	客 184	活 174	計 201	家 53	起 181	終 241	寒 175	運 157	遠 160	橋 193
実 233	空 65	室 232	海 55	負 312	島 292	通 281	組 103	晴 265	道 122	鉄 283	親 260
岩 178	者 235	屋 161	炭 274	追 280	庫 206	配 299	船 266	暑 247	開 171	電 286	頭 294
岸 177	苦 197	度 288	界 170	送 268	弱 236	馬 127	週 242	朝 118	間 58	**14**	**17**
店 284	表 309	待 271	畑 302	重 245	旅 335	高 76	進 259	期 183	集 243	様 328	**18**
所 246	金 16	後 208	発 303	面 322	時 87	**11**	都 287	森 41	雲 47	歌 166	曜 329
明 141	長 116	思 84	県 203	音 50	書 92	動 296	野 323	温 162	**13**	算 219	顔 179
東 121	門 143	急 186	研 204	風 132	校 75	強 192	雪 100	番 306	園 159	聞 314	
板 305	雨 42	持 231	神 257	食 253	根 216	悪 152	魚 190	答 293	意 155	語 209	
林 150	青 36	指 226	秋 89	首 239	帰 182	教 191	鳥 117	絵 172	感 176	読 123	
歩 136	**9**	星 264	科 164	点 285	流 334	深 258	黄 214	着 276	数 262	銀 196	

ALPHABETICAL JAPANESE WORD INDEX FOR JME NUMBERS
(On readings are in capitals; kun readings in small letters).

A
agaru 上 20
ageru 上 20
aida 間 58
aka 赤 35
akai 赤 35
akarui 明 141
akeru 明 141
aki 秋 89
akiraka 明 141
AKU 悪 152
ame 雨 42
ame 天 119
AN 行 73
AN 安 153
AN 暗 154
ani 兄 199
ao 青 136
aoi 青 136
aratani 新 256
arawasu 表 309
aruku 歩 136
asa 朝 118
ashi 足 29
asobu 遊 326
atama 頭 294
atarashii 新 256
ataru 当 290
ateru 当 290
atsui 暑 247
atsumaru 集 243
atsumeru 集 243
au 会 54
au 合 77
ayumu 歩 136
aza 字 86

B
BA 馬 127
ba 場 252
BAI 買 300
bakasu 化 163
bakeru 化 163
BAKU 麦 128
BAN 番 306
BAN 万 320
BEI 米 135
BEN 勉 317
BI 美 308
BO 母 137
BOKU 木 15
BU 分 133
BU 歩 136
BUN 分 133
BUN 文 134
BUN 聞 314
BUTSU 物 313
BYAKU 白 37
BYŌ 病 310
BYŌ 平 315

C
CHA 茶 275
CHAKU 着 276
CHI 池 110
CHI 地 111
CHI 知 112
chi 千 101
chichi 父 131
chiisai 小 24
chikai 近 195
chikara 力 148
CHIKU 竹 113
CHŌ 町 115

(continued)
CHŌ 長 116
CHŌ 鳥 117
CHŌ 朝 118
CHŌ 重 245
CHŪ 中 23
CHŪ 虫 114
CHŪ 注 277
CHŪ 柱 278
CHŪ 昼 279

D
DAI 大 22
DAI 台 272
DAI 第 273
DAI 弟 282
DAN 男 109
dasu 出 90
DEN 田 40
DEN 電 286
deru 出 90
DO 土 17
DO 度 288
DŌ 道 122
DŌ 同 295
DŌ 動 296
DOKU 読 123

E
E 会 54
E 絵 172
EI 泳 352
EI 英 353
EKI 駅 158
EKI 役 324
EN 円 48
EN 園 159
EN 遠 160

F
FU 父 131
FU 負 312
FŪ 風 132
fukai 深 258
fukasa 深 258
FUN 分 133
funa 船 266
fune 船 266
furui 古 70
futa 二 2
futatsu 二 2
futoi 太 269
futoru 太 269
fuyu 冬 120

G
GA 画 167
GAI 外 56
GAKU 学 57
GAKU 楽 331
GAN 元 68
GAN 岸 177
GAN 岩 178
GAN 顔 179
-gata 形 200
GATSU 月 12
GE 下 21
GE 外 56
GEN 元 68
GEN 原 205
GETSU 月 12
GIN 銀 196
GO 五 5
GO 期 183
GO 午 207
GO 後 208

GO 語 209	haya 早 104	**I**	JO 女 32
GŌ 合 77	hayai 早 104	I 意 155	JO 助 248
GŌ 強 192	hayashi 林 150	ICHI 一 1	JŌ 上 20
GŌ 号 215	HEI 平 315	ichi 市 222	JŌ 乗 251
GYO 魚 190	HEN 返 316	ie 家 53	JŌ 場 252
GYŌ 行 73	HI 皮 307	ike 池 110	
GYŌ 形 200	hi 日 11	ikiru 生 34	JU 受 240
GYOKU 玉 64	hi 火 13	iku 行 73	JŪ 十 10
GYŪ 牛 62	hidari 左 18	ima 今 81	JŪ 住 244
H	higashi 東 121	imōto 妹 319	JŪ 重 245
HA 波 298	hikari 光 72	IN 音 50	**K**
ha 葉 327	hikaru 光 72	IN 引 156	KA 火 13
HACHI 八 8	hiki 引 156	inu 犬 66	KA 下 21
haha 母 137	hiku 引 156	ireru 入 125	KA 花 43
HAI 配 299	HIN 品 311	iri 入 125	KA 何 51
hajimaru 始 225	hiraku 開 171	iro 色 94	KA 夏 52
hajimeru 始 225	hiratai 平 315	ishi 石 44	KA 家 53
hakaru 計 201	hirogaru 広 211	isogu 急 186	KA 化 163
hakaru 図 261	hirogeru 広 211	ita 板 305	KA 科 164
hakobu 運 157	hiroi 広 211	ito 糸 83	KA 荷 165
HAKU 白 37	hiromaru 広 211	itsu 五 5	KA 歌 166
HAN 半 129	hiru 昼 279	itsutsu 五 5	kado 門 143
HAN 坂 304	hito 人 30	iwa 岩 178	kaeru 帰 182
HAN 板 305	hitotsu 一 1	**J**	kaeshi 返 316
hana 花 43	HO 歩 136	JAKU 弱 236	kaesu 返 316
hanashi 話 151	HŌ 方 138	JI 耳 26	KAI 会 54
hanasu 話 151	hoka 外 56	JI 字 86	KAI 海 55
hara 原 205	HOKU 北 139	JI 時 87	KAI 回 168
hare 晴 265	HON 本 45	JI 地 111	KAI 界 170
hareru 晴 265	hoshi 星 264	JI 次 227	KAI 開 171
haru 春 91	hosoi 細 218	JI 寺 228	KAI 絵 172
hashi 橋 193	HYAKU 百 130	JI 自 229	kai 貝 169
hashira 柱 278	HYŌ 表 309	JI 事 230	KAKU 画 167
hashiru 走 105		JI 持 231	KAKU 角 173
hata 畑 302		JIN 人 30	KAKU 客 184
hatake 畑 302		JIN 神 257	kaku 書 92
HATSU 発 303		JITSU 日 11	
		JITSU 実 233	

kami 上 20
kami 紙 85
kami 神 257
KAN 間 58
KAN 寒 175
KAN 感 176
kane 金 16
kangae 考 74
kangaeru 考 74
kao 顔 179
kasanaru 重 245
kasaneru 重 245
kata 方 138
katachi 形 200
katana 刀 289
katari 語 209
kataru 語 209
KATSU 活 174
katsu 勝 250
kau 買 300
kawa 川 39
kawa 皮 307
kayou 通 281
kaze 風 132
kazoeru 数 262
kazu 数 262
KE 家 53
KE 気 59
KE 化 163
ke 毛 142
KEI 京 63
KEI 兄 199
KEI 形 200
KEI 計 201
KEN 間 58
KEN 犬 66
KEN 見 67
KEN 県 203
KEN 研 204

KETSU 決 202
KI 気 59
KI 汽 60
KI 記 180
KI 起 181
KI 帰 182
KI 期 183
ki 木 15
ki 生 34
ki 黄 214
kikoeru 聞 314
kiku 聞 314
kimaru 決 202
kimeru 決 202
kimasu 来 147
kimi 君 198
KIN 金 16
KIN 今 81
KIN 近 195
kiru 切 99
kiru 着 276
kishi 岸 177
kita 北 139
KO 戸 69
KO 古 70
KO 去 189
KO 庫 206
ko 小 24
ko 子 31
KŌ 口 27
KŌ 工 71
KŌ 光 72
KŌ 行 73
KŌ 考 74
KŌ 校 75
KŌ 高 76
KŌ 後 208
KŌ 公 210
KŌ 広 211

KŌ 交 212
KŌ 向 213
KŌ 黄 214
koe 声 97
koi 来 147
kokono 九 9
kokonotsu 九 9
kokoro 心 95
KOKU 石 44
KOKU 谷 78
KOKU 国 79
KOKU 黒 80
komakai 細 218
kome 米 135
KON 金 16
KON 今 81
KON 根 216
kotae 答 293
kotaeru 答 293
koto 事 230
九
KU 九 9
KU 口 27
KU 工 71
KU 苦 197
KŪ 空 65
kubaru 配 299
kubi 首 239
kuchi 口 27
kudaru 下 21
kumi 組 103
kumu 組 103
kumo 雲 47
KUN 君 198
kuni 国 79
kurai 暗 154
kuro 黒 80
kuroi 黒 80
kuru 来 147
kuruma 車 88

kurushii 苦 197
kusa 草 106
kuu 食 253
KYAKU 客 184
KYO 去 189
KYŌ 京 63
KYŌ 教 191
KYŌ 強 192
KYŌ 橋 193
KYŌ 兄 199
KYOKU 局 194
KYŪ 九 9
KYŪ 休 61
KYŪ 究 185
KYŪ 急 186
KYŪ 級 187
KYŪ 球 188

M
ma 間 58
machi 町 115
mae 前 102
MAI 米 135
MAI 毎 318
MAI 妹 319
majiru 交 212
majiwaru 交 212
make 負 312
makeru 負 312
MAN 万 320
manabu 学 57
matsu 待 271
mattaku 全 267
mawaru 回 168
mawasu 回 168
me 目 25
MEI 名 140
MEI 明 141
MEI 鳴 321
MEN 面 322

Column 1 (mi-SE)

mi 三 3
mi 実 233
mi 身 255
michi 道 122
migi 右 19
mimi 耳 26
minami 南 124
minoru 実 233
miru 見 67
mise 店 284
mittsu 三 3
miyako 都 287
mizu 水 14
mizukara 自 229
MŌ 毛 142
mochi 持 231
motsu 持 231
mochiiru 用 146
MOKU 木 15
MOKU 目 25
MON 文 134
MON 門 143
mono 者 235
mono 物 313
mori 森 41
mōsu 申 254
moto 下 21
moto 元 68
MOTSU 物 313
mugi 麦 128
mukau 向 213
muku 向 213
mura 村 107
muro 室 232
mushi 虫 114
muttsu 六 6
MYŌ 名 140
MYŌ 明 141

Column 2 (N)

N

na 名 140
nagai 長 116
nagare 流 334
nagareru 流 334
nagasu 流 334
nageru 投 291
naka 中 23
nakaba 半 129
naku 鳴 321
nama 生 34
nami 波 298
NAN 男 109
NAN 南 124
nana 七 7
nanatsu 七 7
nan 何 51
nani 何 51
natsu 夏 52
ne 音 50
ne 根 216
NEN 年 126
NI 二 2
ni 荷 165
NICHI 日 11
nigai 苦 197
NIKU 肉 297
NIN 人 30
nishi 西 96
no 野 323
noboru 上 20
nochi 後 208
noru 乗 251
noseru 乗 251
nushi 主 237
NYO 女 32
NYŪ 入 125

Column 3 (O)

O

o 小 24
o 王 49
o 黄 214
ochiru 落 330
oeru 終 241
ōi 多 108
ōkii 大 22
okiru 起 181
okonau 行 73
okosu 起 181
CKU 屋 161
okuru 送 268
omo 面 322
omoi 重 245
omote 面 322
omote 表 309
omou 思 84
ON 音 50
ON 遠 160
ON 温 162
onaji 同 295
onna 女 32
oshieru 教 191
oto 音 50
otoko 男 109
otosu 落 330
otōto 弟 282
ou 追 280
ou 負 312
owari 終 241
owaru 終 241
oya 新 260
ōyake 公 210

Column 4 (R, S)

R

RAI 来 147
RAKU 落 330
RAKU 楽 331
REI 礼 337
RI 里 332
RI 理 333
RIKI 力 148
RIN 林 150
RITSU 立 149
ROKU 六 6
RU 流 334
RYO 旅 335
RYŌ 両 336
RYOKU 力 148
RYŪ 流 334

S

SA 左 18
SA 作 82
sagaru 下 21
sageru 下 21
SAI 西 96
SAI 切 99
SAI 才 217
SAI 細 218
saka 坂 304
sakana 魚 190
saki 先 33
SAKU 作 82
sama 様 328
samui 寒 175
SAN 三 3
SAN 山 38
SAN 算 219
saru 去 189
sato 里 332
SE 世 263

SEI 生 34	shimo 下 21	SHŪ 集 243	takai 高 76
SEI 青 36	SHIN 森 41	SHUN 春 91	take 竹 113
SEI 正 46	SHIN 心 95	SHUTSU 出 90	tama 玉 64
SEI 西 96	SHIN 申 254	SO 組 103	TAN 炭 274
SEI 声 97	SHIN 身 255	SŌ 早 104	tani 谷 78
SEI 世 263	SHIN 新 256	SŌ 走 105	tanoshii 楽 331
SEI 星 264	SHIN 神 257	SŌ 草 106	tariru 足 29
SEI 晴 265	SHIN 深 258	SŌ 送 268	tasukaru 助 248
SEKI 赤 35	SHIN 進 259	SOKU 足 29	tasukeru 助 248
SEKI 石 44	SHIN 親 260	SON 村 107	tatsu 立 149
SEKI 夕 98	shina 品 311	sono 園 159	te 手 28
SEN 先 33	shinu 死 223	sora 空 65	TEI 体 270
SEN 川 39	shiraseru 知 112	sosogu 注 277	TEI 弟 282
SEN 千 101	shiru 知 112	soto 外 56	TEN 天 119
SEN 船 266	shiro 白 37	SU 子 31	TEN 店 284
SETSU 切 99	shiroi 白 37	SU 主 237	TEN 点 285
SETSU 雪 100	shita 下 21	SŪ 数 262	tera 寺 228
SHA 車 88	shitashii 親 260	SUI 水 14	TETSU 鉄 283
SHA 社 234	shitashimu 親 260	SUI 出 90	TO 土 17
SHA 者 235	SHITSU 室 232	-suke 助 248	TO 図 261
SHAKU 赤 35	SHO 書 92	sukoshi 少 93	TO 都 287
SHAKU 石 44	SHO 所 246	sukunai 少 93	to 戸 69
SHI 四 4	SHO 暑 247	sumi 炭 274	TŌ 冬 120
SHI 子 31	SHŌ 小 24	sumu 住 244	TŌ 東 121
SHI 糸 83	SHŌ 生 34	susumu 進 259	TŌ 刀 289
SHI 思 84	SHŌ 青 36		TŌ 当 290
SHI 紙 85	SHŌ 正 46	**T**	TŌ 投 291
SHI 止 220	SHŌ 少 93	TA 多 108	TŌ 島 292
SHI 仕 221	SHŌ 昭 249	TA 太 269	TŌ 答 293
SHI 市 222	SHŌ 勝 250	ta 田 40	TŌ 頭 294
SHI 死 223	SHOKU 色 94	taberu 食 253	tō 十 10
SHI 使 224	SHOKU 食 253	tabi 旅 335	tōi 遠 160
SHI 始 225	SHU 手 28	tachi 立 149	toki 時 87
SHI 指 226	SHU 主 237	tadashii 正 46	tokoro 所 246
SHI 次 227	SHU 取 238	TAI 大 22	TOKU 読 123
SHI 自 229	SHU 首 239	TAI 太 269	tomaru 止 220
SHICHI 七 7	SHŪ 秋 89	TAI 体 270	tome 止 220
SHIKI 色 94	SHŪ 終 241	TAI 待 271	tomeru 止 220
shima 島 292	SHŪ 週 242	TAI 台 272	tomo 友 145
		taira 平 315	

tori 鳥 117
toru 取 238
tōru 通 281
toshi 年 126
TSU 都 287
TSŪ 通 281
tsuchi 土 17
tsugi 次 227
tsugu 次 227
TSUI 追 280
tsukaeru 仕 221
tsukau 使 224
tsuki 月 12
tsuku 着 276
tsukuru 作 82
tsuno 角 173
tsuyoi 強 192

U

U 右 19
U 雨 42
ue 上 20
ugoku 動 296
uke 受 240
ukeru 受 240
uma 馬 127
umareru 生 34
umi 海 55
umu 生 34
UN 雲 47
UN 運 157
uo 魚 190
uri 賣 301
uru 賣 301
ushi 牛 62
ushiro 後 208
uta 歌 166
utau 歌 166
utsukushii 美 308

W

WA 話 151
WA 和 338
wakareru 分 133
wakeru 分 133
warui 悪 152

Y

YA 夜 144
YA 野 323
ya 家 53
ya 屋 161
YAKU 役 324
yama 山 38
yamai 病 310
yamu 病 310
yashiro 社 234
yasui 安 153
yasumi 休 61
yasumu 休 61
yattsu 八 8
yawaragu 和 338
yo 四 4
yo 夜 144
yo 世 263
YŌ 用 146
YŌ 葉 327
YŌ 様 328
YŌ 曜 329
yoko 横 355
yomu 読 123
yon 四 4
yoru 夜 144
yoshi 由 325
yottsu 四 4
yowai 弱 236
yowaru 弱 236
YU 由 325
yū 夕 98

yubi 指 226
yuki 雪 100
yuku 行 73

Z

ZEN 前 102
ZEN 全 267

1 i², yi² 一	31 tzǔ³ 子	61 hsiu¹ 休	91 ch'un¹ 春
2 êrh⁴ 二	32 nü³ 女	62 niu² 牛	92 shu¹ 書
3 san¹ 三	33 hsien¹ 先	63 ching¹ 京	93 shao³ 少
4 szǔ⁴ 四	34 sheng¹ 生	64 yü⁴ 玉	94 se⁴ 色
5 wu³ 五	35 ch'ih⁴ 赤	65 k'ung¹ 空	95 hsin¹ 心
6 liu⁴ 六	36 ch'ing¹ 青	66 ch'üan³ 犬	96 hsi¹ 西
7 ch'i 七	37 pai² 白	67 chien⁴ 見	97 shêng¹ 聲 声 *
8 pa¹ 八	38 shan¹ 山	68 yüan² 元	98 hsi⁴,¹ 夕
9 chiu³ 九	39 ch'uan¹ 川	69 hu⁴ 戶	99 ch'ieh⁴ 切
10 shih² 十	40 t'ien² 田	70 ku³ 古	100 hsüeh³ 雪 *
11 jih⁴ 日	41 sên¹, shên¹ 森	71 kung¹ 工	101 ch'ien¹ 千
12 yüeh⁴ 月	42 yü³ 雨	72 kuang¹ 光	102 ch'ien² 前
13 huo³ 火	43 hua¹ 花	73 hsing² 行	103 tsu³ 組
14 shui³ 水	44 shih² 石	74 k'ao³ 考	104 tsao³ 早
15 mu⁴ 木	45 pen³ 本	75 hsiao⁴ 校	105 tsou³ 走
16 chin¹ 金	46 chêng⁴ 正	76 kao¹ 高	106 ts'ao³ 草
17 t'u³ 土	47 yün² 雲	77 ho² 合	107 ts'un¹ 村
18 tso³ 左	48 yüan² 圓 *	78 ku³ 谷	108 to¹ 多
19 yu⁴ 右	49 wang² 王	79 kuo² 國 * 国 *	109 nan² 男
20 shang⁴ 上	50 yin¹ 音	80 hei¹ 黑 *	110 ch'ih² 池
21 hsia⁴ 下	51 ho² 何	81 chin¹ 今	111 ti⁴ 地
22 ta⁴ 大	52 hsia⁴ 夏	82 tso⁴ 作	112 chih¹ 知
23 chung¹ 中	53 chia¹ 家	83 mi⁴ 糸	113 chu² 竹
24 hsiao³ 小	54 hui⁴ 會 * 会 *	84 szǔ¹ 思	114 ch'ung² 虫
25 mu⁴ 目	55 hai³ 海 *	85 chih³ 紙	115 t'ing³ 町
26 êrh³ 耳	56 wai⁴ 外	86 tzǔ⁴ 字	116 chang² 長
27 k'ou³ 口	57 hsüeh² 學 * 学 *	87 shih² 時	117 niao³ 鳥
28 shou³ 手	58 chien¹ 間	88 ch'e¹ 車	118 chao¹ 朝
29 tsu² 足	59 ch'i⁴ 氣 *	89 ch'iu¹ 秋	119 t'ien¹ 天
30 jen² 人	60 ch'i⁴ 汽	90 ch'u¹ 出	120 tung¹ 冬

121	tung¹ 東	151	hua⁴ 話	181	ch'i³ 起	211	kuang³ 廣 *
122	tao⁴ 道 *	152	o⁴ 惡 *	182	kuei¹ 歸 * 归	212	chiao¹ 交
123	tu² 讀 *	153	an¹ 安	183	ch'i¹'² 期	213	hsiang⁴ 向
124	nan² 南	154	an⁴ 暗	184	k'o⁴,k'e⁴ 客	214	huang² 黃 *
125	ju⁴ 人	155	i⁴ 意	185	chiu¹'⁴ 究	215	hao² 號 *
126	nien² 年	156	yin³ 引	186	chi² 急 *	216	ken¹ 根
127	ma³ 馬	157	yün⁴ 運	187	chi² 級	217	ts'ai² 才
128	mai⁴ 麥 *	158	i⁴,yi⁴ 驛 *	188	ch'iu² 球 *	218	hsi⁴ 細
129	pan⁴ 半	159	yüan² 園	189	ch'ü⁴ 去	219	suan⁴ 算
130	pai³ 百	160	yüan³ 遠	190	yü² 魚	220	chih³ 止
131	fu⁴ 父	161	wu¹ 屋	191	chiao⁴ 教 *	221	shih⁴ 仕
132	feng¹ 風 風 *	162	wen¹ 溫	192	ch'iang³ 強	222	shih⁴ 市
133	fên¹ 分	163	hua⁴ 化	193	ch'iao² 橋	223	szu³ 死
134	wên² 文	164	k'o¹,k'e¹ 科	194	chü² 局	224	shih³ 使
135	mi³ 米	165	ho² 荷	195	chin⁴ 近 *	225	shih³ 始
136	pu⁴ 步	166	ko¹,ke¹ 歌	196	yin² 銀	226	chih³ 指
137	mu³ 母	167	hua⁴ 畫 画 *	197	k'u³ 苦	227	tz'u⁴ 次
138	fang¹ 方	168	hui² 回	198	chun¹ 君	228	szu⁴ 寺
139	pei³ 北	169	pei⁴ 貝	199	hsiung¹ 兄	229	tzu⁴ 自
140	ming² 名	170	chieh⁴ 界	200	hsing² 形	230	shih⁴ 事
141	ming² 明	171	k'ai¹ 開	201	chi⁴ 計	231	ch'ih² 持
142	mao² 毛	172	hui⁴ 繪 *	202	chüeh² 決	232	shih⁴ 室
143	mên² 門	173	chüeh² 角	203	hsien⁴ 縣 *	233	shih² 實
144	yeh⁴ 夜	174	huo² 活	204	yen² 研	234	she⁴ 社
145	yu³ 友	175	han² 寒	205	yüan² 原	235	che³ 者
146	yung⁴ 用	176	kan³ 感	206	k'u⁴ 庫	236	jo⁴,je⁴ 弱
147	lai² 來 来	177	an⁴ 岸	207	wu³ 午	237	chu³ 主
148	li⁴ 力	178	yen² 岩	208	hou⁴ 後	238	ch'ü³ 取
149	li⁴ 立	179	yen² 顏	209	yü³ 語	239	shou³ 首
150	lin² 林	180	chi⁴ 記	210	kung¹ 公	240	shou 受

241 chung¹ 終	271 tai⁴ 待	301 mai⁴ 賣	331 le⁴ 樂*
242 chou¹ 週*	272 t'ai² 台	302 — 一	332 li³ 里
243 chi² 集	273 ti⁴ 第	303 fa¹ 發	333 li³ 理
244 chu⁴ 住	274 t'an⁴ 炭	304 fan³ 坂	334 liu² 流
245 chung⁴ 重	275 ch'a² 茶	305 pan³ 板	335 lü³ 旅
246 so³ 所	276 cho²,⁵ 着	306 fan¹ 番	336 liang¹ 兩雨*
247 shu³ 暑*	277 chu⁴ 注	307 p'i² 皮	337 li³ 礼
248 chu⁴ 助	278 chu⁴ 柱	308 mei³ 美	338 ho² 和
249 chao¹ 昭	279 chou⁴ 晝*	309 piao³ 表	
250 sheng⁴ 勝	280 chui¹ 追*	310 ping⁴ 病	
251 ch'eng² 乘*	281 t'ung¹ 通*	311 p'in³ 品	
252 ch'ang² 場	282 ti⁴ 弟	312 fu⁴ 負	
253 shih² 食	283 t'ieh³ 鉄	313 wu⁴ 物	
254 shen¹ 申	284 tien⁴ 店	314 wen² 聞	
255 shen¹ 身	285 tien³ 點*	315 p'ing² 平	
256 hsin¹ 新	286 tien⁴ 電	316 fan³ 返	
257 shen² 神	287 tou¹ 都	317 mien³ 勉*	
258 shen¹ 深	288 tu⁴ 度	318 mei³ 每*	
259 chin⁴ 進*	289 tao¹ 刀	319 mei⁴ 妹	
260 ch'in¹ 親	290 tang¹ 當当*	320 wan⁴ 万	
261 t'u² 圖*	291 t'ou² 投	321 ming² 鳴	
262 shu⁴ 數*	292 tao³ 島	322 mien⁴ 面	
263 shih⁴ 世	293 ta² 答	323 yeh³ 野	
264 hsing¹ 星	294 t'ou² 頭	324 i⁴,yi⁴ 役	
265 ch'ing² 晴	295 t'ung² 同	325 yu² 由	
266 ch'uan² 船*	296 tung⁴ 動	326 yu² 遊*	
267 ch'üan² 全	297 jou⁴ 肉	327 yeh⁴ 葉	
268 sung⁴ 送*	298 po¹ 波	328 yang⁴ 様*	
269 t'ai⁴ 太	299 p'ei⁴ 配	329 yao⁴ 曜	
270 t'i³ 体體*	300 mai³ 買	330 lao⁴ 落	

*Chinese characters which may be variants are marked with an asterisk. The much-abbreviated recent characters are not given since explanations often do not apply. You need to learn the alternate forms because printed and written forms may differ and you may read older books as well as contemporary material. The numbers are for the tones. The meanings can be found in a Chinese-English dictionary such as Fenn's, but are usually much the same in Chinese and Japanese.